THE UNDERGROUND FOOTBALL

FOOTBALL

ENCYCLOPEDIA

THE UNDERGROUND FOOTBALL ENCYCLOPEDIA

Football Stuff You Never Needed to Know
and Can Certainly Live Without

ROBERT SCHNAKENBERG

TRIUMPH
BOOKS

Copyright © 2011 by Robert Schnakenberg

No part of this publication may be reproduced, stored in a retrieval system, or transmitted in any form by any means, electronic, mechanical, photocopying, or otherwise, without the prior written permission of the publisher, Triumph Books, 542 South Dearborn Street, Suite 750, Chicago, Illinois 60605.

Triumph Books and colophon are registered trademarks of Random House, Inc.

Library of Congress Cataloging-in-Publication Data

Schnakenberg, Robert.
    The underground football encyclopedia : football stuff you never needed to know and can certainly live without / Robert Schnakenberg.
        p. cm.
    ISBN 978-1-60078-516-0
    1. Football—Miscellanea. I. Title.
    GV950.5.S36 2011
    796.332—dc22

                              2011010693

This book is available in quantity at special discounts for your group or organization. For further information, contact:

Triumph Books
542 South Dearborn Street
Suite 750
Chicago, Illinois 60605
(312) 939–3330
Fax (312) 663–3557
www.triumphbooks.com

Printed in U.S.A.
ISBN: 978-1-60078-516-0
Design by Paul Petrowsky
Page production by Patricia Frey
Title page photo courtesy of AP Images
Cover photos courtesy of Getty Images, AP Images, and Charles Angell

Introduction

Football is America's most popular spectator sport by a wide margin, yet baseball titles occupy more real estate in those antiquated purveyors of paper known as bookstores. Why is this? In part, it merely reflects the longevity of the respective sports. While professional football has been played in this country almost as long as professional baseball has—the earliest games date back to the late 19th century—it wasn't until the 1950s that the pro game started to exert its grip on the popular imagination. And only with the advent of the Super Bowl in the late 1960s did football truly become a mass pop cultural phenomenon. (You could also argue that baseball's pastoral elegance attracts the kind of literary types who appeal to the major U.S. publishers, but since this is anything but a literary book, that's of no concern to us.)

More than 40 years have passed since *Monday Night Football* premiered and ushered in an era of unprecedented television dominance for the NFL. That's 40 years of end zone dances, team rap videos, Super Bowl halftime shows, and advances in cheerleader technology. Clearly, the history of pro football can no longer be confined to stat books and the occasional windy retelling of the story of the 1958 NFL Championship Game or the 1967 Ice Bowl. We need a football encyclopedia for the rest of us—a ready resource covering all those aspects of the game that aren't covered in all those other football reference books. That's what this book aspires to be.

Some notes on the selection of entries: to keep things manageable, I have confined myself almost entirely to the world of American professional football and to aspects of pop culture that reflect or depict it. That means no entry for Adam Sandler's college football comedy *The Waterboy*, alas, but more coverage for *Gus*—a 1976 Disney movie about a fictional pro team and its placekicking mule—than any of that film's devotees could hope to find anywhere else. The choice of topics is somewhat subjective, of course, but as with my companion book, *The Underground Baseball Encyclopedia*, I hope the idiosyncratic selection spurs debate, discussion, and argument. There are dozens of other sports reference books where you can read about the life and career of Red Grange. Why shouldn't there be one where "Fireman Ed" Anzalone takes center stage instead?

Finally, every attempt has been made to make this encyclopedia as comprehensive as possible. However, there will always be oversights, unintentional omissions, or aspects and artifacts of the game that I didn't know about or get around to researching. I encourage readers to contact me via the usual online channels with corrections and suggestions for additions.

A note on cross-references: items in bold are cross-references to other entries in this book.

A-Team, The

Popular action/adventure television series about a group of misfit ex-commandos who travel the country finding work as soldiers of fortune, the premiere episode of which aired directly following NBC's telecast of Super Bowl XVII on January 30, 1983. The debut installment attracted nearly 22 million viewers and began a tradition of networks using the post–Super Bowl time slot to showcase new programming. *The A-Team* went on to become one of the iconic series of the 1980s. **Joe Namath** was one of many celebrity guest stars to appear on the program during its five-year run.

AFL

Acronym most commonly associated with the American Football League, the professional football league that competed with the NFL from 1960 to 1969 before finally merging with its competitor before the 1970 season. A breeding ground for strategic innovation and coaching talent, the AFL has come to be associated in the public mind with a freewheeling, pass-happy style of play, garish uniforms, and the counterculture élan of many of its marquee players, several of whom were tacitly encouraged to adopt nicknames and defy the rigid sartorial and grooming conventions of the era. Iconic figures of the AFL include coaches Sid Gillman, **Al Davis**, and **Hank Stram** and players **Joe Namath**, Lance "**Bambi**" Alworth, and Cookie Gilchrist. Among the innovations the AFL introduced to the professional ranks are revenue sharing among franchises, two-point conversions, names on the backs of player uniforms, and on-field game clocks. AFL teams were also pioneers in the recruitment of African American college players. See also: **USFL**; **WFL**; **XFL**

'Aints

Derisive nickname bestowed on the New Orleans Saints beginning in 1980 and not fully exorcised from franchise lore until the team's Super Bowl season in 2009. Most historians credit the 'Aints coinage to New Orleans TV sports anchor Bernard "Buddy D" Diliberto, the man who first encouraged fans to don paper bags of shame during the Saints' 1–15 1980 campaign. Diliberto's original bag—festooned with holiday lights and cut-out holes for eyes—had the now-famous moniker scribbled across the front. Fans by the hundreds soon began showing up at Saints games with their own variations, typically decorated in the team's black-and-gold colors. Diliberto died in 2005, five years before the Saints expiated decades of futility with a victory in Super Bowl XLIV. After that triumph, a jazz funeral was held in which New Orleans fans ritually buried their 'Aints paper bags in a giant coffin.

Air Coryell

Nickname used to describe the innovative pass-first offenses of longtime NFL head coach Don Coryell. Air Coryell is most closely associated with Coryell's tenure as coach of the San Diego Chargers from 1978 to 1986, when the Hall of Fame trio of quarterback Dan Fouts, wide receiver Charlie Joiner, and tight end Kellen Winslow formed the core of one of the most productive passing attacks in NFL history.

Allen, George

Hall of Fame head coach known for his infectious sideline enthusiasm, his intense approach to the game, and his preference for cagey veterans over younger players. Allen achieved his greatest success during a memorable mid-1970s tenure with the aging, overachieving Washington Redskins—nicknamed the **Over-the-Hill Gang**—whom he guided to the NFC title in 1972. As a young man, Allen once challenged **Albert Einstein** to a game of checkers. His death may have been caused by an ill-timed **Gatorade**

Shower. Political junkies know him as the father of Republican politician George Felix Allen, the former U.S. senator and governor of Virginia.

"All My Rowdy Friends Are Here for Monday Night"

Customized version of the 1984 **Hank Williams Jr.** song "All My Rowdy Friends Are Coming Over Tonight" that has been the opening theme of **Monday Night Football** since 1989. The rousing country-rock number was a sequel of sorts to Williams' 1981 hit "All My Rowdy Friends (Have Settled Down)." It first attracted the attention of ABC Sports executive George Greenberg when he was searching for a theme song to accompany the network telecast of the 1985 **USFL** championship game. The lyrics, including the opening howl "Are you ready for some football?" have become something of a national catchphrase. They were written via fax in a three-way collaboration between Williams, Greenberg, and ABC Sports vice president for production Bob Toms. Rolled out as the main theme in time for *MNF*'s 20th anniversary season, the high-decibel party starter irritated many traditionalists. "What's with this Hank Williams Jr. opening each and every show with a bunch of apparently semi-soused yahoos yelping in the background?" groused columnist Roger Fischer in the *St. Petersburg Times*. Most of the telecast's young, male fans seemed to disagree with that assessment. In fact, when Williams' tune was briefly dropped during the 1993 season in favor of a rotating repertoire of rockers by the likes of Kiss, Bon Jovi, and Def Leppard, an avalanche of complaint mail prompted ABC to bring Hank back in time for the playoffs.

Alzado, Lyle

Burly, bearded defensive lineman of the 1970s and '80s known for his savage on-field demeanor and early death from brain cancer. One of the linchpins of the Denver Broncos' **Orange Crush** defense of the late 1970s,

DEFENSIVE END
LYLE ALZADO

Alzado leveraged his reputation as a brawling wild man into a successful entertainment career. In 1979, he partook in an exhibition boxing match against heavyweight champion Muhammad Ali at Denver's Mile High Stadium. The clash lasted eight rounds in 100-degree heat and featured more air-punching, dancing, and clutching than actual fisticuffs. After retiring from the NFL in 1985, Alzado concentrated on acting. He did bit parts on several short-lived television series and appeared as a villain opposite hayseed comedian Jim Varney in the 1987 stinker *Ernest Goes to Camp*. In 1988, he played a demented killing machine in the low-budget horror movie *Destroyer*. That same year, he headlined his own sitcom, *Learning the Ropes*, playing a mild-mannered schoolteacher who moonlights as a professional wrestler. The series lasted only two seasons on Canadian television. In 1991, Alzado announced to the world that he had an inoperable brain tumor, crediting the disease to 22 years of anabolic steroid use. He died in May of 1992.

America's Team

Nickname bestowed upon the Dallas Cowboys in 1979 by **NFL Films**, largely in recognition of the franchise's nationwide fan base. The phrase "America's Team" was the brainchild of NFL Films editor in chief Bob Ryan, who was looking for a catchy title for the Cowboys' 1978 season highlight film and was struck by the presence of so many Dallas rooters at away games during the team's glory years of the 1970s.

"I think people appreciated announcers a little more."

–NBC Sports executive **Don Ohlmeyer**, summing
up the lessons learned from the **announcerless game**

Announcerless Game

Curious broadcasting experiment, also known as the announcerless telecast
or the Silent Game, that aired December 20, 1980, on NBC. A meaningless
late-season contest between the New York Jets and the Miami Dolphins at
the Orange Bowl in Miami, the game was broadcast entirely without
commentary by announcers. Viewers were forced to rely upon on-screen
graphics to follow the action. The announcerless gimmick was the brainchild
of NBC Sports executive **Don Ohlmeyer**—best known for his longtime
patronage of accused murderer **O.J. Simpson**—who believed that
conventional football telecasts were too noisy and freighted with
sportscaster clichés. But the barrage of statistics and bone-crunching
enhanced audio made for a dizzying and nausea-inducing sensory overload
that belied Ohlmeyer's rationale for the experiment. The Jets won the game
24–17, but ratings were actually below average despite considerable
pregame media hype. While some critics championed the telecast—
sportswriter Red Smith lauded it for containing "no banalities, no pseudo-
expert profundities phrased in coachly patois, no giggles, no inside jokes, no
second-guessing, no numbing prattle"—most were happy to see
announcerless games consigned to the dustbin of broadcasting history.

"Another One Bites the Dust"

Bass-driven Queen mega-hit that became the unofficial **fight song** of the
1980 Detroit Lions after defensive back Jimmy "Spiderman" Allen recorded
his own lyrics over the song's instrumental track. The Lions had won all of

two games in 1979, but their drafting of Heisman Trophy winner Billy Sims foretold a turn in fortunes—at least in the mind of mush-mouthed rapper Allen. "Last year's team was 2–14, but this is the year for New Orleans," Allen threatens at one point on the track. "Come and watch the Detroit Lions that no one seems to beat." Sadly, six different teams found a way to beat the Lions as the team compiled a 9–7 record and missed out on the playoffs entirely.

Any Given Sunday

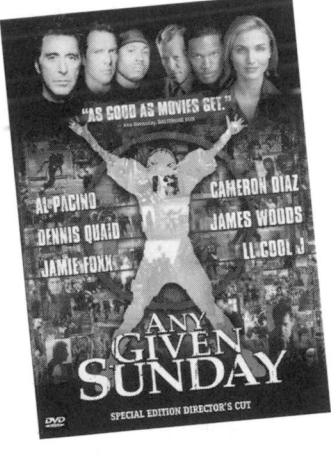

Polarizing 1999 film lauded by some as one of the most honest portrayals of life in professional football, and derided by others as an unfocused, hyperkinetic video game of a movie. Director Oliver Stone's sprawling 162-minute opus follows the intertwined stories of three members of the fictional Miami Sharks: Tony D'Amato, the team's over-the-hill head coach, played by Al Pacino; Cap Rooney, an aging, injury-riddled white quarterback, played by Dennis Quaid; and "Steamin'" Willie Beamen, the hotshot young African American QB who replaces Rooney as the starter, played by Jamie Foxx. Also in the mix are Cameron Diaz as the cold-blooded heiress who owns the team; James Woods as an unscrupulous, painkiller-dispensing trainer; and John C. McGinley as an obnoxious sports journalist loosely based on radio host **Jim Rome**. Numerous ex-NFL greats appear in cameo and supporting roles, including legends Y.A. Tittle, Dick Butkus, and Johnny Unitas as opposing coaches. Capping the orgy of self-indulgent stunt casting, Stone himself appears as a football announcer. Based in part on a tell-all memoir by Robert Huizenga, the onetime team physician for the Los

Angeles Raiders, *Any Given Sunday* is brutal in its depiction of the morally compromised, eat-or-be-eaten ethos of the pro football locker room. Stone manages to coax credible performances out of rapper turned actor LL Cool J, as well as Hall of Famers **Lawrence Taylor** and Jim Brown. He has less luck with Diaz, whose appalling lack of talent is all-too-evident during scenes in which she's blown off the screen by Pacino and longtime Pathmark spokesman James Karen.

Anzalone, Ed
See **Fireman Ed**

Arena Football
Indoor version of American football that has proved an intermittently popular alternative to the NFL since 1986. Arena Football is played on a hockey-rink-sized field under rules that facilitate an explosive offensive pace and high-scoring games, not to mention a heightened risk of injury. The basic blueprint for Arena Football was literally scrawled on the back of a Manila envelope by onetime NFL promotions executive James E. Foster as he watched a Major Indoor Soccer League all-star game at Madison Square Garden in 1981. After several years of delays due in part to the advent of the **USFL**, Foster—with cooperation from the NFL—succeeded in launching the Arena Football League in 1986. A test game was staged that year, followed by full-season play starting in June of 1987. While the indoor game's popularity has waxed and waned since then—the AFL briefly went out of business in 2009—it has produced respectable television ratings and at least one bona fide NFL superstar in quarterback Kurt Warner, who took snaps for the Iowa Barnstormers from 1995 to 1997. **Mike Ditka**, John Elway, country superstar Tim McGraw, and rocker Jon Bon Jovi are a few of the AFL's more notable celebrity owners. The league's annual championship game is called the Arena Bowl.

Arli$$

Inexplicably long-running HBO sitcom of the late 1990s, starring comic actor Robert Wuhl as titular sports agent Arliss Michaels. Though widely reviled by critics, *Arli$$* somehow managed to remain on the air for seven years. The show featured numerous cameo appearances by NFL stars of the period, including Marshall Faulk, Dan Marino, and Emmitt Smith.

Artificial Turf

Synthetic grass that emerged as the dominant surface used in major professional sports stadiums in the 1970s. Originally developed by the agrochemical giant Monsanto at the behest of Houston Astros owner Judge Roy Hofheinz for use in his new Astrodome, artificial turf migrated quite easily from baseball to football. In 1969, Franklin Field, home of the Philadelphia Eagles, became the first NFL stadium to switch from grass to artificial turf. (According to legend, the synthetic sod was so convincing that before the first game groundskeepers had to clear the field of thousands of dead grasshoppers that had mistaken it for the real thing.) Use of artificial turf, which required much less care and expense to maintain than natural grass, proliferated throughout the lean economic years of the 1970s. In the 1980s, players and media members grew more vocal in pointing out its defects—in particular the increased risk of injury. Because the turf rested on a protective pad that sat atop a slab of asphalt, the surface was rock hard and incapable of absorbing shock. The seams often came apart. The turf did not yield easily to planted cleats, and there was the problem of friction burns during tackles. In response to these concerns, NFL stadium operators began to turn to a new artificial surface called **FieldTurf** in the 1990s, which was both more forgiving and economical to maintain.

AstroTurf

Trade name for the brand of **artificial turf** used in the Houston Astrodome. See also: **FieldTurf**

Autry, Gene

Legendary country crooner, known as "the Singing Cowboy," who became a sports mogul in his dotage and helped entice the Los Angeles Rams to move to Anaheim in the 1980s. Autry was the founder and owner of baseball's Los Angeles Angels and held a minority stake in the Rams for many years. His refurbishment of Anaheim Stadium in 1980 paved the way for the Rams to decamp south to Orange County. Autry's songs are also prominently featured on the soundtrack of the football-themed comedy *Semi-Tough*.

B

Bachelor, The

Popular reality TV program of the 2000s centered around a single man attempting to cull marital prospects from a pool of 25 unattached female beauties. In 2004, the featured bachelor was quarterback Jesse Palmer of the **New York Football Giants**. After weeks of searching, the journeyman backup eventually found bliss in the arms of Jessica Bowlin, a 22-year-old law student from

Huntington Beach, California. Hopes for a lifelong love match were dashed, however, as the pair ended up severing their relationship shortly after the season ended.

Bachelors III

Mobbed-up New York City watering hole co-owned by New York Jets legend **Joe Namath**, the controversial clientele of which nearly drove him from pro football in 1969. Scandal erupted that spring after Namath was seen cavorting in his new bar with various unsavory underworld figures including gamblers, con men, bookmakers, and made men in the New York Mafia. Mortified NFL commissioner Pete Rozelle ordered Namath to divest himself of all holdings in the Upper East Side establishment. Namath refused and, in a dramatic press conference, quit professional football. After a summerlong media firestorm, the quarterback and the league reached a compromise whereby Namath would sell his interest in the Bachleors III's New York flagship but reserve the right to franchise it elsewhere. The name Bachelors III refers to the bar's three swinging bachelor proprietors— Namath, restaurateur Bobby Van, and ex-Jets defensive back Ray Abruzzese.

AP Images

Bad Newz Kennels

Official name of the infamous interstate dogfighting ring operated by Atlanta Falcons quarterback **Michael Vick** and three of his friends from 2002 to 2007 on the grounds of Vick's 15-acre Virginia estate. "Bad Newz" is a play on Newport News, the name of Vick's hometown.

Holly Olsson

Bad Weather Game

Game played in inclement weather or poor field conditions which fans often cherish as embodying the drama and epic grandeur of professional football. See also: **Fog Bowl**; **Freezer Bowl**; **Ice Bowl**; **Mud Bowl**; **Snowplow Game**

Bambi

Nickname bestowed upon Hall of Fame wide receiver and **AFL** icon Lance Alworth, a reference to his graceful movements and lithe, deer-like frame.

Barberie, Jillian

See **Reynolds, Jillian**

Barrel Man

Persona adopted by Denver Broncos **superfan** Tim McKernan, who wore an orange aluminum barrel—and little else—to the team's home games for more than 30 years. A retired United Airlines aircraft mechanic from Gunnison, Colorado, McKernan first donned his barrel in 1977 after betting his brother $10 that doing so would get him on television. That first barrel

Audibles

"Outside the barrel, my father was very quiet, an introverted calm person."

–Todd McKernan, son of Barrel Man

was actually a cask of industrial solvent painted to resemble an Orange Crush soda can. Over the decades, McKernan acquired some 21 different barrels in all—including one that he wore to Super Bowl XXXII, which he had autographed by 49 members of the Broncos' first world championship team and later sold on eBay for $30,000 to a casino. After suffering an abdominal aneurysm in 2002 that severely curtailed his ability to withstand the often frigid game-day weather in Denver, McKernan hung up his barrel for good in 2007. He died of lung failure in 2009.

Bayless, Skip

Sports columnist and ESPN personality who disseminated rumors about the supposed homosexuality of Dallas Cowboys quarterback Troy Aikman in the 1990s. Bayless' 1996 bestseller *Hell-Bent: The Crazy Truth About the "Win or Else" Dallas Cowboys* liberally reprints unsubstantiated speculation from teammates and Dallas-area residents, strongly insinuating that the unmarried Aikman was a closeted gay racist. Aikman steadfastly denied the claim, leading to Bayless' ostracism at the hands of some members of the journalistic fraternity. Bayless' younger brother is *Top Chef Masters* champion Rick Bayless.

Willie Stark ONE/MILLION

"Bear Down, Chicago Bears"

Official **fight song** of the Chicago Bears, played every time the team scores at home games since 1941. "We'll never forget the way you thrilled the nation/With your T formation" go the lyrics to the ditty, a direct reference to the innovative offensive formation the Bears employed in their 73–0 drubbing of the Washington Redskins in the 1940 NFL Championship Game. The composer of "Bear Down, Chicago Bears" was Russian-born songwriter Al Hoffman (using the pseudonym Jerry Downs), the lyricist behind such popular favorites as "Mairzy Doats," "Hot Diggity," and "If I Knew You Were Coming I'd a Baked a Cake."

Beautymist

Line of pantyhose endorsed by New York Jets quarterback **Joe Namath** in a celebrated 1974 television commercial. The spot begins with a slow pan up Namath's shaved, well-manicured legs while a female voice-over coos, "This commercial is going to prove to the women of America that Beautymist Pantyhose can make anybody's legs look like a million dollars." A leering Namath, wearing his Jets jersey, is then shown addressing the camera directly. "If Beautymist can make my legs look this good," he says, "think what they can do for yours." The ad concludes with Namath being kissed by an attractive young woman—a tag that was added at the last minute to assuage Namath's fears that the commercial made him look too much like a

Audibles

"I hated how I looked. I hated how I sounded. I almost got sick."

–Joe Namath, on his initial response
to his Beautymist Pantyhose commercial

gay transvestite. Broadway Joe was sold on doing the unusual spot by the Long, Haymes & Carr ad agency, reportedly after Burt Reynolds asked for too much money.

Bednarik, Chuck

Hard-hitting Philadelphia Eagles linebacker of the 1950s best known for leveling New York Giant **Frank Gifford** with an epically ferocious tackle during a game at Yankee Stadium on November 20, 1960. The Eagles won the game 17–10, but it was the hit that earned a place in NFL history. A classic photo of the play's aftermath shows Bednarik exulting over Gifford's unconscious body. The Giants flanker suffered a concussion that kept him off the field for the entire 1961 season. Bednarik, whose off-season job as a concrete salesman won him the nickname "Concrete Charlie," was inducted into the Pro Football Hall of Fame in 1967.

Getty Images

Belichick, Bill

Notoriously prickly head coaching legend of the 2000s. See also: **HC of NYJ**; **Spygate**

Berman, Chris

Burly ESPN personality, widely despised by sports media columnists and many fans, who has nevertheless carved out an outsized role for himself on the cable sports network's NFL coverage. One of ESPN's first on-air hires in 1979, Berman has served as host of its flagship NFL highlight show, *NFL Primetime*, since 1987. There he became known for his forced, hacky, schtick-laden calls—often appropriated from other announcers. In an homage to **Howard Cosell**, Berman will often bellow "He could…go…all…the…way!" over highlights of someone running to daylight for a touchdown. Repeated shouts of "Whoop!" in the manner of Curly from the Three Stooges, invocations of "frozen Lambeau Field" à la **John Facenda**, and references to the "NFC Norris Division" are all staples of his repertoire as well. Berman is also notorious for his relentless and irritating Buffalo Bills boosterism, as exemplified in his mantra-like repetition of the catchphrase "No one circles the wagons like the Buffalo Bills." In tandem with *NFL Primetime* co-host Tom Jackson, he will occasionally sing the chorus from the team's disco era **fight song "San Diego Super Chargers"** whenever Chargers highlights are shown. Loathed by many, Berman is considered a treasured eminence by ESPN executives, one of whom famously dubbed him "the face of ESPN." See also: **Swami, The**

A² Images

Big Fan

Critically acclaimed 2009 indie film about a fanatical New York Giants fan who has an unfortunate run-in with the team's star linebacker. Po-faced comic Patton Oswalt plays the titular rooter, Paul Aufiero, an opinionated yutz who makes ranting late-night calls to the local sports radio station under the name "Paul from Staten Island." Life descends into a living hell for Paul after he is viciously beaten by his favorite player in a New York City strip club. Real-life radio gabber Scott Ferrall plays a sports talk host, and Michael Rapaport portrays Paul's Eagles-obsessed opposite number, Philadelphia Phil. Reviewers praised the low-budget film for its unnervingly accurate portrayal of the fringes of football fandom.

Big Red

Anthropomorphized passerine bird who has been the official mascot of the Phoenix/Arizona Cardinals since 1998. While he usually confines himself to revving up crowds at Cardinals home games or making personal appearances at Phoenix-area schools, hospitals, parades, and charitable events, the 6'4" Big Red does occasionally stoop to the kind of puerile taunting associated with the Jacksonville Jaguars' **Jaxson de Ville**. At a pep rally in Phoenix days before Super Bowl XLIII, the costumed character infuriated Pittsburgh Steelers fans everywhere by wiping his armpit with a **Terrible Towel**.

Big Sombrero, The

Commonly used nickname for Tampa Stadium, the home field of the Tampa Bay Buccaneers from 1976 to 1997. The nickname was a reference to the stadium's unique shape, which resembled the brim of a Mexican hat. The Big Sombrero was demolished by controlled implosion in April of 1999. The Buccaneers' new home, Raymond James Stadium, is occasionally referred to as the New Sombrero.

Billy Buffalo

Eight-foot-tall costumed bison who has served as the official mascot of the Buffalo Bills since 2000. The blue-furred monstrosity, whose aspect is vaguely reminiscent of one of Jim Henson's lesser Muppets, was designed by an old Disney hand, Ralph Kent. The so-called Keeper of the Mouse also designed Billy the Marlin, the fish-costumed mascot of the Florida Marlins baseball team. Billy Buffalo often tools around the Bills' home field at Ralph Wilson Stadium on a pimped-out orange chopper.

Black Hole

Name attached to the seating sections behind the south end zone at McAfee Coliseum in Oakland—and by extension to the especially fanatical group of Oakland Raiders fans who populate them. Black Hole denizens are known for donning black apocalyptic attire and occasionally pelting opposing players with beer, batteries, and other debris.

Black Sunday

Big-screen blockbuster from 1979 about a terrorist plot to detonate the **Goodyear Blimp** at the Super Bowl. Based on the novel of the same name by Thomas "*Silence of the Lambs*" Harris, *Black Sunday* stars twitchy 1970s icon Bruce Dern as Michael Lander, a deranged Vietnam vet who falls under the sway of a Palestinian terrorist, played by Marthe Keller. Together they hatch a plot to load up the blimp's gondola with plastic explosives and fly it into the jam-packed Orange Bowl. Robert Shaw plays the Israeli secret agent sent to stop them. Director John Frankenheimer filmed the crowd scenes and game action (including a performance by **Up with People**) at Super Bowl X, which featured the Pittsburgh Steelers and the Dallas Cowboys. Miami Dolphins owner Joe Robbie and announcers Pat Summerall and Tom Brookshier all play themselves in the film, which is noteworthy for its use of authentic NFL and corporate logos. Clearly, no one in the league office vetted the screenplay before giving their imprimatur to the project. *Black Sunday* caused a bit of a stir in 1979 when NBC aired the disturbing film immediately preceding its telecast of Super Bowl XIII, a game played at the Orange Bowl again between the Steelers and the Cowboys. In a sign of the film's enduring place in the popular imagination, comedian turned *Monday Night Football* analyst **Dennis Miller** once greeted the appearance of the Budweiser blimp at a game by wondering on the air whether Dern was at the controls.

Blitz

Enormous, glowering costumed bird who has been the official mascot of the Seattle Seahawks since 1998. Shortly after taking the reins as mascot, Blitz

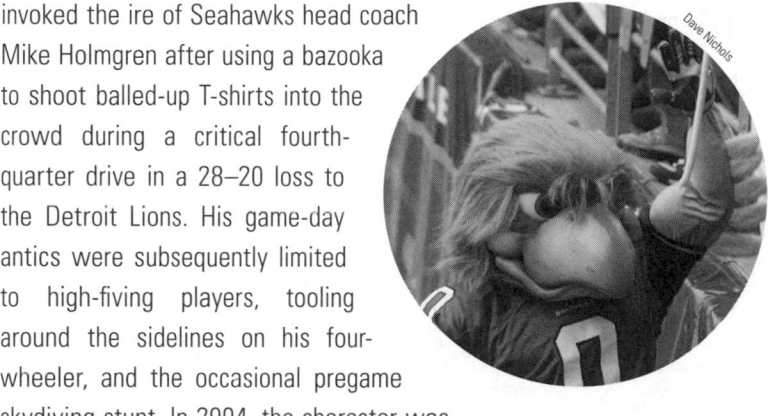

invoked the ire of Seahawks head coach Mike Holmgren after using a bazooka to shoot balled-up T-shirts into the crowd during a critical fourth-quarter drive in a 28–20 loss to the Detroit Lions. His game-day antics were subsequently limited to high-fiving players, tooling around the sidelines on his four-wheeler, and the occasional pregame skydiving stunt. In 2004, the character was given a dramatic makeover designed to render him less frightening to small children. Since 2009, Blitz has been active in raising money and awareness in the fight against multiple sclerosis. Ryan Asdourian, the Microsoft employee who plays Blitz in his spare time, was diagnosed with the disease in December of 2008.

Blue

Anthropomorphized horse who has been the official mascot of the Indianapolis Colts since 2006. Blue was the brainchild of Trey Mock, a 24-year-old marketing coordinator from Cobb County, Georgia, who won the chance to create a mascot character from the ground up. The 40-pound acrylic horse costume comes with a detachable mane and a variety of custom-colored tails. Blue is known for his trademark belly and booty shake. Shortly before making his second Super Bowl appearance in January of 2010, Blue emerged unscathed from an auto accident on I-69 in Indianapolis while on his way to a personal appearance at a Fort Wayne shopping mall.

Boltman

Lightning bolt–headed muscleman who served as the unofficial mascot of the San Diego Chargers from 1996 to 2008. Boltman was the brainchild of Dan Jauregui, a Ramona, California, realtor and rabid Chargers fan who was dismayed by the franchise's lack of an official mascot. In 1995, Jauregui built a scale model of a Boltman suit, pitched team officials on his idea, and briefly attained official mascot status. But he could never work out a long-term agreement with the Chargers and was soon relegated to attending home games on his own dime dressed in Boltman regalia. In his original incarnation, Boltman could best be described as a nude, anthropomorphized lightning bolt wearing sunglasses. Jauregui later refined the concept, adding a Chargers jersey and de-emphasizing some of the costume's more phallic design elements. Drained by the expense of maintaining his alter ego, Jauregui hung up his bolt after the 2008 season.

Bonnes Amies

Beloved New Orleans Saints cheerleading squad that revved up fans at the team's home games from 1975 to 1978. Named for the French term for "good female friends," the Bonnes Amies succeeded the team's previous dance team, the **Mam'selles**. They made their debut at a preseason game in August of 1975, dancing to a rousing rendition of the Dixieland Jazz chestnut "(Won't You Come Home) Bill Bailey." While reasonably popular—the Bonnes Amies were fixtures on the local New Orleans Muscular Dystrophy Association telethon and once appeared on CBS' pregame *Super Bowl Saturday Night* variety extravaganza alongside **Joe Namath**—the spirited dance team lasted only three seasons, whereupon it was reorganized and renamed the **New Orleans Saints Angels** in time for the 1978 preseason home opener.

Bosworth, Brian

Celebrated collegiate linebacker known for his dyed Mohawk hairstyle and outrageous behavior. He is commonly ranked alongside quarterback **Ryan Leaf** among the all-time biggest NFL draft busts. Known as "the Boz," Bosworth was a two-time All-American at the University of Oklahoma with a carefully cultivated "outsider" image. A first-round pick of the Seattle Seahawks in the 1987 supplemental draft, he arrived at his contract signing in a chartered helicopter and almost immediately embarked upon a media tour. He appeared on MTV, *The Tonight Show*, and *Good Morning America*—all in the course of one week—and published an autobiography, *The Boz*, after just one professional season. But Bosworth's lackluster play never quite lived up to the off-field hype. He retired after just two injury-plagued seasons and half-heartedly pursued an acting career, appearing in the 1991 action bomb *Stone Cold* and the 2005 remake of ***The Longest Yard***, among other questionable projects.

Bounty Bowl

Informal designation for a heated divisional game played by the Dallas Cowboys and the Philadelphia Eagles on **Thanksgiving Day**, 1989, during which Eagles head coach **Buddy Ryan** reportedly placed a bounty on the head of Cowboys placekicker **Luis Zendejas**. Ryan, who bore an unspecified grudge against the 5'6" 160-pound former Eagle, allegedly offered a $200 cash reward to any Eagle who knocked Zendejas out of the game. Sure enough, after kicking off to start the second half, Zendejas was dealt a vicious blow by Eagles rookie linebacker Jessie Small. The tackle, which occurred a full 20 yards away from the play, concussed Zendejas and sent him staggering over to the opposing bench in a daze. In a vituperative postgame press conference, Cowboys coach Jimmy Johnson derided Ryan's tactics. But his demands for a full-scale investigation by the NFL fell on deaf ears. Bounty Bowl II came two weeks later in Philadelphia. Although no bounties were offered this time, Eagles fans lustily booed Zendejas when he took the field and pelted Johnson and his coaching staff with snowballs.

Bradshaw, Terry

Hall of Fame quarterback, two-time Super Bowl MVP, and four-time world champion who has enjoyed a sustained post-retirement career as a network NFL analyst, actor, and commercial pitchman. A genial good ol' boy from Shreveport, Louisiana, Bradshaw was widely dismissed as a talented but erratic, mush-brained hayseed until he led the Pittsburgh Steelers to the first of four Super Bowl titles in 1974. By the end of the decade, he had solidified his reputation as one of the greatest clutch quarterbacks of the modern era. With enhanced public stature came endorsement deals and media opportunities. Bradshaw's burgeoning friendship with actor Burt Reynolds led to his being cast in the feature films *Hooper, Smokey and the Bandit II*, and *The Cannonball Run*. Apparently under the impression he could sing, he recorded a cover version of Hank Williams' "I'm So Lonesome I Could Cry" and a country gospel album, *Until You*. In 1976, he married ice skating champion **Jo Jo Starbuck**. The couple became a fixture on the television variety show circuit of the late 1970s. Their troubled marriage ended in divorce in 1983. That same year, Bradshaw retired from the NFL and devoted himself full-time to an entertainment and broadcasting career. He has served as a color commentator and studio analyst for both CBS and Fox and leveraged his good-natured redneck persona into memorable supporting roles on TV's *The Jeff Foxworthy Show* and in the motion picture

Failure to Launch, where he appeared nude. To date, Bradshaw is the only NFL player to receive a star on the Hollywood Walk of Fame.

Brady Bunch, The

Beloved family sitcom of the early 1970s and a regular landing spot for aging sports stars looking to make the transition to their post-retirement acting careers. Notable NFL players who appeared as themselves on *The Brady Bunch* include defensive end **Deacon Jones**, who guest starred in the 1971 episode "The Drummer Boy" as a football coach who encourages Peter Brady to sing in his school's glee club; and quarterback **Joe Namath**, who visits the Brady household after Bobby Brady bamboozles him into believing he has a terminal illness in the 1973 episode "Mail Order Hero."

Brian's Song

Maudlin 1971 made-for-TV movie, later released theatrically, that dramatizes the friendship between legendary Chicago Bears running back Gale Sayers and his cancer-stricken teammate Brian Piccolo. Suave African American icon Billy Dee Williams plays Sayers, with a pre-*Godfather* James Caan as Piccolo. An early example of "guy cry" football cinema, the film won numerous

Emmy Awards, including one for veteran character actor Jack Warden for his portrayal of head coach George **"Papa Bear"** Halas. Hall of Fame linebacker Dick Butkus and several other Bears of the period play themselves. The set used for the home of Sayers and his wife was the same one shared by Darrin and Samantha Stephens on the long-running ABC sitcom *Bewitched*. A markedly less memorable remake, starring Mekhi Phifer and Sean Maher as Sayers and Piccolo, aired in December of 2001. See also: *Something for Joey*

Bronco Belles
Original name of the Denver Broncos cheerleading squad, later rechristened the **Pony Express**.

Bronkettes
Original 1960s Denver Broncos dance team, composed entirely of underage girls. The Bronkettes were replaced by the adult cheerleading squad the **Bronco Belles** later in the decade.

Bronko
Nickname bestowed in childhood on future Hall of Fame fullback Bronislau Nagurski by a teacher who could not pronounce his first name.

Brownie the Elf
Grinning, pointy-eared hobgoblin who has been an official mascot of the Cleveland Browns since the late 1940s. It was Browns owner Arthur McBride who hit upon the idea of an elf mascot, part of an effort to raise the franchise's brand profile. (In Scottish folklore, a "brownie" is a mischievous household imp known to perform chores for food.) After making his debut in 1946, Brownie changed his appearance only slightly over the ensuing

decades. The addition of a crown to commemorate the team's 1964 NFL championship was one of the few noteworthy alterations to his standard regalia of orange blouse, belt, and pointed booties. In the late 1960s, new owner **Art Modell** phased Brownie out entirely—evidence, some said, of his distaste for the sly woodland creature. Brownie did not grace team publications and paraphernalia again until 1999, when the Browns returned to the NFL under new ownership following a four-year absence.

Bruno, Ralph

Milwaukee upholstery worker credited with inventing the **cheesehead**. Bruno was working in a foam factory as an apprentice pattern maker in 1987 when he hit upon the idea to take a leftover piece of yellow couch cushion, cut it into a triangle, and wear it on his head to a Milwaukee Brewers baseball game. In the 1990s, the wearing of cheeseheads became widely associated with the Green Bay Packers.

Bucco Bruce

Fey, winking pirate who served as the helmet mascot of the Tampa Bay Buccaneers from 1976 to 1996. The feather-capped orange swashbuckler with the cutlass clenched between his teeth was designed by longtime Tampa newspaper cartoonist Lamar Sparkman. Sparkman at first proposed a more intimidating skull-and-bones icon, but the team's front office rejected it in favor of Bruce—a much different sort of buccaneer than the one featured on the Oakland Raiders logo. With his enormous plumed hat and his immaculately

waxed moustache, Bruce came to be known derisively among fans as the "gay pirate." His image was also tarnished by association with the slapstick early years of the Tampa Bay franchise. The mocking reception irked Sparkman, who saw his creation as an homage to the old-school movie pirates played by the likes of Errol Flynn. In 1996, new Bucs owner Malcolm Glazer ditched the team's sickmaking creamsicle color scheme in favor of a more butch red-and-pewter ensemble. Bucco Bruce was replaced on the helmet by a menacing skull-and-bones logo—similar, ironically enough, to the one Sparkman had originally designed.

Bud Bowl

Animated football championship game played between teams of stop-motion beer bottles that aired as part of a multimedia ad campaign during eight Super Bowl telecasts between 1989 and 1997. The Bud Bowl pitted Anheuser-Busch's flagship lager Budweiser against rival Bud Light in a contest for gridiron supremacy. Not surprisingly, Budweiser dominated, winning six of the eight Bud Bowls—none by more than a single score. The ad wizards at the St. Louis–based agency of D'Arcy Masius Benton & Bowles came up with the

Bud Bowl Results (1989-1997)

Bud Bowl I (1989)	**Budweiser 27**	Bud Light 24
Bud Bowl II (1990)	**Budweiser 36**	Bud Light 34
Bud Bowl III (1991)	Budweiser 21	**Bud Light 23**
Bud Bowl IV (1992)	**Budweiser 27**	Bud Light 24
Bud Bowl V (1993)	**Budweiser 35**	Bud Light 31
Bud Bowl VI (1994)	Budweiser 14	**Bud Light 20**
Bud Bowl VII (1995)	**Budweiser 26**	Bud Light 24
Bud Bowl VIII (1997)	**Budweiser 27**	Bud Light 24

Note: There was no Bud Bowl played in 1996

campaign, which so captured the public imagination that fans were known to wager on the outcome. Over the years, Bud Bowl productions grew increasingly elaborate, with ex-NFL players, coaches, and announcers taking roles in the pageant. Bob Costas, **Terry Bradshaw**, Tom Landry, **Chris Berman**, **Don Meredith**, and **Mike Ditka** were among those who lent their voices to the cartoon commercials, which often featured sly references to such real-world football elements as the **end zone dance** and **John 3:16** signs.

"Buddy's Watching You"

Music video recorded by members of the 1988 Philadelphia Eagles. The "Buddy" of the title is head coach **Buddy Ryan**, whose unseen figure looms over this Bobby Brown–esque number. Eagles standouts Randall Cunningham, Keith Jackson, **Reggie White**, and others take turns spewing out the boastful verses that were the hallmarks of team rap videos of the period, as periodic shouts of "Yeaahhh boy!" indelibly watermark this as an artifact of the late 1980s. Surprisingly, most of the MCs don't totally embarrass themselves—with the notable exception of kicker **Luis**

Days of Infamy | November 23, 1997

Washington Redskins quarterback Gus Frerotte sprains his neck head-butting a padded wall in the end zone at Jack Kent Cooke Stadium after scoring a touchdown late in the first half of what would become a meaningless 7–7 tie with the New York Giants.

Zendejas, whose mush-mouthed flow brings the entire track to a screeching halt about a minute in.

Buffalo Jills

Official cheerleading squad of the Buffalo Bills since 1967. The Jills replaced the Bills' previous cheerleading squad, a group of eight young women from nearby Buffalo State College. Originally, all the Jills were required to be married and at least 22 years old. For many years, the Jills ranked among the lowest-compensated cheerleaders in the NFL. A 1977 *Newsweek* article revealed that in lieu of a salary, each Buffalo Jill received one free ticket per home game, a sandwich and a soft drink at halftime, and free parking at Rich Stadium.

John Bauld

C

Caliendo, Frank

Pudgy, talented mimic best known to football fans for his regular appearances on the *Fox NFL Sunday* pregame show in the 2000s, where he invariably performed an uncanny impression of color commentator **John Madden**. Persistent rumors claiming that Madden was incensed by the impersonation gained steam in 2008, when the legendary coach threatened legal action after the *Frank TV* star began appearing in a series of commercials for the Dish Network satellite TV service. Caliendo also does impressions of NFL pregame host James Brown, Hall of Fame quarterback **Terry Bradshaw**, and bombastic sports radio host **Jim Rome**, among others.

Todd Kravos/Kravos.com

Audibles

"It's always said that I don't like him. I've never said that. The guy's making a living. That's his job, and he's a good little comedian."

—**John Madden**, to *Time* magazine, responding to reports that he loathed impressionist **Frank Caliendo**

Candy, John

Morbidly obese film and television comedian whose conspicuous presence in the stands at Super Bowl XXIII may have contributed to the San Francisco 49ers' dramatic come-from-behind victory. According to the oft-told story,

Field Guide to Zebras

Mike Carey
Trailblazing NFL official who became the first African American referee in a Super Bowl game in 2008.

Niners quarterback Joe Montana entered the huddle with 3:20 left on the clock, his team trailing by three, and the atmosphere rife with tension. "Hey, isn't that John Candy over there?" he said to worrywart right tackle Harris Barton. The offhand comment was widely credited with loosening the mood and allowing the San Francisco offense to drive down the field for the winning touchdown.

Captain Fear

Costumed pirate who has been the official mascot of the Tampa Bay Buccaneers since 2000. Captain Fear replaced **Bucco Bruce**, the team's original pirate icon, whose fey affect made him the object of public ridicule. A menacing figure with a jagged scar, crimson do-rag, and creepy, staring eyes, the black-bearded Captain Fear lives on a giant replica pirate ship and fires a cannon every time the Buccaneers score.

Cassie Chief

Short-lived, unlamented mid-1980s mascot of the Kansas City Chiefs. A bulbous-nosed Native American caricature complete with war bonnet, fringed buckskin coat, and moccasins, Cassie Chief was widely reviled by fans, who were known to spit on him, serenade him with profane epithets, and plant "Kick Me" signs on his back.

C.B.

Costumed canine who has been one of four official **mascots** of the Cleveland Browns since the franchise's return to the NFL in 1999. C.B., a bull mastiff, is the alpha mascot of a "Dawg Pound" modeled on the team's notoriously raucous end zone fan community. His fellow pack members are **Chomps** (a Labrador retriever), **T.D.** (a German Shepherd), and **Trapper** (a Weimaraner).

C.C. and Company

Misbegotten 1970 feature film that was supposed to kick-start the fledgling acting career of New York Jets quarterback **Joe Namath**. Namath plays C.C. Ryder, a motorcycle mechanic who gets mixed up with an outlaw biker gang. Ann-Margret plays Namath's love interest, whom he must rescue from being brutally gang raped in one of many, many regrettable scenes. Onetime Marlboro Man William Smith plays Namath's biker nemesis. Critical response to *C.C. and Company* was almost uniformly negative, although the *The New York Times*' Vincent Canby charitably called it "a work of such opportunism, such vulgarity and such old-fashioned, romantic nuttiness that it's impossible not to be charmed by it." So scarred was Namath by the experience that after making just one more film (the 1971 western *The Last Rebel*) he put his thespian ambitions on hold until his retirement in 1977. See also: ***Waverly Wonders, The***

Cell Phone Incident

Infamous **end zone celebration** stunt staged by New Orleans Saints wide receiver Joe Horn during a nationally televised game against the New York Giants in 2003. After catching the second of four touchdown passes, Horn had teammate Michael Lewis pull a planted cell phone out of the goalpost padding and hand it to him. Horn then proceeded to place a call to his children to inform them that he had just scored. The prank, which came just one year after San Francisco 49ers wideout **Terrell Owens**' famous **Sharpie Incident** prompted a league-wide crackdown on choreographed celebrations, cost Horn a $30,000 fine, in addition to a 15-yard unsportsmanlike conduct penalty.

CFL

Initialism for the Canadian Football League, which has been Canada's principal professional football league since 1958. It is the second-most-popular sports league in Canada, after the National Hockey League. Notable NFL players who played in the CFL include **Jack Kemp** and **Doug Flutie**. The annual CFL championship game is called the Grey Cup.

Charger Girls

Popular cheerleading squad of the San Diego Chargers, founded in 1990, and regularly cited in national publications as one of the best in the NFL. The Charger Girls succeeded the disgraced **Chargette** troupes of the 1970s. Actress Charisma Carpenter, best known for her role as Cordelia Chase on TV's *Buffy the Vampire Slayer*, is a former Charger Girl.

John Bryant

Chargettes

San Diego Charger cheerleading squad of the 1970s, often erroneously referred to as the Chargerettes. The scantily clad pep squad was formed in the wake of the exploding popularity of the **Dallas Cowboys Cheerleaders**. Unlike most other professional cheerleading teams of the era who received $15 a game for their efforts, the Chargettes were an all-volunteer force. The lack of payment compelled several members of the troupe to start making public appearances for cash while wearing their

---

Audibles

"The only thing I can say is that this is all male chauvinism."

–San Diego **Chargettes** director Rhonda Bosworth, responding to the mass firing of the cheerleading squad in 1978

Chargettes attire. The moonlighting operation culminated in the team-ordered disbanding of the Chargettes in September of 1978, when one of the group's members, Elizabeth Caleca (also known as "Miss Nude California"), was fired after posing naked for a *Playboy* pictorial.

Cheerleaders

See **Bonnes Amies**; **Bronco Belles**; **Bronkettes**; **Buffalo Jills**; **Charger Girls**; **Chargettes**; **Chiefettes**; **Cincinnati Ben-Gals**; **CowBelles & Beaux**; **Dallas Cowboys Cheerleaders**; **Derrick Dolls**; **Dolphin Dolls**; **Dolphin Starbrites**; **Eaglettes**; **Embraceable Ewes**; **Falconettes**; **49er Nuggets**; **Golden Girls**; **Green Bay Sideliners**; **Honey Bears**; **Jacksonville ROAR**; **Liberty Belles**; **Lousiannes**; **New Orleans Saints Angels**; **Packerettes**; **Pony Express**; **Raiderettes**; **Redskinettes**; **Saintsations**; **San Francisco Gold Rush**; **Seattle Sea Gals**; **Steelerettes**; **SwashBucklers**; **TopCats**

Cheesehead

Commonly used term for a Green Bay Packers fan, many of whom show up at games wearing yellow foam triangles intended to evoke wedges of Wisconsin cheese. While now almost exclusively associated with Packers football, the first cheeseheads were worn at Milwaukee Brewers baseball games in the late 1980s. See also: **Bruno, Ralph**

Chiefettes

Popular high-stepping Kansas City Chiefs cheerleading squad of the 1970s and '80s. The all-female Chiefettes, known for their miniskirts and high-heeled go-go boots, were replaced by a less politically incorrect (and much less popular) coed cheerleading squad beginning with the 1986 season.

Chief Zee

Outlandish Native American persona adopted by Zema Williams, a retired car salesman and Washington Redskins **superfan** who has served as the team's unofficial mascot since 1978. The African American resident of Oxon Hill, Maryland, first showed up to a Redskins game in a feathered headdress on October 1, 1978, when the **_Monday Night Football_** cameras caught him pretending to bludgeon a Cowboys fan with a rubber tomahawk. Emboldened by his brush with fame, Williams dubbed himself Chief Zee and began showing up at virtually all Washington home games and select road games. In Dallas, he cultivated a friendly rivalry with **Crazy Ray**, the Cowboys' chaps-wearing, gun-toting superfan. In 2006, at the age of 65, Chief Zee was stricken with a blood clot in his leg and had one of his big toes amputated, forcing him to adopt a moped as his principal means of transportation.

Peter Law

Days of Infamy | September 11, 1983

Enraged Philadelphia Eagles fans attack visiting Washington Redskins **superfan Chief Zee** in the Veterans Stadium parking lot. They steal his war bonnet, stomp on his leg until it breaks, and shatter his orbital bone so that his eyeball pops out of its socket. The Chief, who is left unattended on the pavement clad only in his underwear, vows never to return to the City of Brotherly Love.

Chomps

Costumed Labrador Retriever who has been one of four official **mascots** of the Cleveland Browns since 1999. The other members of his "Dawg Pound" are **C.B.**, **T.D.**, and **Trapper**. According to the team's website, Chomps' favorite song is "Bad to the Bone" by George Thorogood.

Jeff Poteat

"Christmas in Dallas"

Treacly holiday song recorded by the 1986 Dallas Cowboys at the height of the team **music video** boom. The synthesizer-laden anthem extols the splendors of spending the Yuletide season in America's most dangerous big city. Herschel Walker, Bill Bates, and a bevy of other Cowboys standouts embarrass themselves on the track, which is immediately identifiable for its heinous 1980s fashions—including copious popped collars, garish sweaters, and feathered hairstyles. See also: **"Good Ol' Days"**

Chucky

Nickname bestowed on onetime NFL head coach
turned *Monday Night Football* commentator Jon
Gruden, in recognition of his strong resemblance to
the malevolent doll in the *Child's Play* horror movie
series.

Chunky Soup Curse

Supposed hex that bedevils any NFL players who appear in ads for Campbell's
Chunky Soup. The Curse dates back to the late 1990s when NFL stars like
Reggie White, Kurt Warner, and Terrell Davis were first enlisted to endorse
the popular canned stew product in television commercials. When mysterious
injuries began afflicting players who had shilled for Chunky, an urban legend/
Internet meme was born. Among those supposedly affected by the Curse:
Eagles quarterback Donovan McNabb, who suffered a broken ankle after his
first Chunky Soup commercial; Bears linebacker Brian Urlacher, whose
endorsement preceded his landing on the injured reserve list and missing
almost half of the 2004 season; and Steelers quarterback Ben
Roethlisberger, whose near-death
motorcycle accident in 2006
occurred one day before he was to
film his first Chunky spot. Sometimes
the Curse is associated with diminished performance rather than
injury, as when LaDainian Tomlinson
of the San Diego Chargers posted
the lowest yardage totals of his
career the season after he appeared
in a Chunky commercial. See also:
Madden Curse

Cincinnati Ben-Gals

Official cheerleading squad of the Cincinnati Bengals widely regarded as one of the least-wholesome-looking troupes in the NFL. Originally clad somewhat demurely in short skirts and sweaters, the Ben-Gals underwent a makeover in 1978 to reflect the trend toward sexy cheerleader attire in the wake of the worldwide fame of the **Dallas Cowboys Cheerleaders**. Bengals entertainment director Shirley Bird designed the new, more revealing uniforms, comprised of tights and clinging sarongs. The team held tryouts at which some 224 applicants competed for 24 open cheerleading positions. Local media personalities were brought in to judge the appearance and disco dancing ability of the applicants, who included a Playboy Bunny and a belly dancer. The titillating troupe was briefly disbanded for the 1987 season but returned in 1988 and has entertained the home crowds at

Craig Steinberg

Great Moments in Cheerleaders Scandal

In 2009, Sarah Jones, a Cincinnati Ben-Gal with a day job as a schoolteacher in northern Kentucky, sued the gossip website TheDirty.com for libel after the site published an article claiming she had had sex with the entire Bengals team and contracted two STDs.

Bengals games ever since. In 2005, wide receiver **Chad Johnson** famously proposed marriage to a Ben-Gal on the field after scoring a touchdown in a game against the Indianapolis Colts.

Cleatus

Bracingly irritating animated robot who has capered nonsensically during pre- and post-commercial "bumpers" on Fox football telecasts since 2005. Equipped with a helmet and shoulder pads, Cleatus is known to dance, flex his "muscles," run in place, strut, play air guitar, and/or get pummeled by other animated characters, including Iron Man, a Transformer, and the T-1000 Terminator from the Fox series *Terminator: The Sarah Connor Chronicles*. For the first two years of his existence, the character was known simply as the Fox Sports Robot. In October of 2007, Fox announced plans for a "name the robot" contest to be hosted on the social networking site MySpace. The winning moniker, Cleatus, was unveiled to a waiting world during Fox's halftime show on December 16, 2007. Around the same time, the network began teaming up with toy companies to market fully articulated action figures and electronic accessories based on what it grandly dubbed "the recognized and celebrated icon of America's favorite spectator sport."

Coleco Football

See **Electronic Quarterback**

"Commitment to Excellence"

Official motto of the Oakland Raiders, personally coined by team owner **Al Davis** and trademarked along with "Pride and Poise" and **"Just Win Baby."** The words "Commitment to Excellence" are emblazoned in various places all over the Raiders' corporate offices, home stadium, and practice facilities.

Cosell, Howard

Nasal, hairpiece-wearing know-it-all who rocketed to fame in the early 1970s as an analyst on ABC's ***Monday Night Football***. An attorney by training, Cosell parlayed 1960s stints as a "tell-it-like-it-is" radio sports commentator and a high-profile boxing announcer closely associated with Muhammad Ali into a spot on the maiden *MNF* announcing triad in 1970. The audience found much to hate in the bewigged, pseudointellectual

Cosell—who wore his contempt for jocks on his sleeve—but that was exactly the point. He was the man Joe Sixpack loved to hate, and his constant needling of boothmates **Don Meredith** and **Frank Gifford** provided some great theater-of-the-absurd exchanges. Even blowouts and mismatches drew huge audiences, as viewers tuned in to hear what "Humble Howard" had to say. Before long, Cosell was a bona fide media superstar, appearing on everything from *The Odd Couple* to *Battle of the Network Stars*. He even briefly hosted his own late-night show, *Saturday Night Live with Howard Cosell*. But as his fame mushroomed, he became increasingly disenchanted with the games he was ostensibly covering. He generated a firestorm of criticism when he called Washington Redskins wide receiver **Alvin Garrett** a "little monkey" during a telecast in September of 1983. After that season, Cosell left the *Monday Night Football* booth for good. As a result, the show lost much of its unique claim on the viewers' attention and reaped a harvest of bad press when the outspoken former analyst refused to go quietly. After taking every opportunity to gloat over *MNF*'s precipitous ratings decline following his departure, Cosell produced a scathing memoir, *I Never Played the Game*, in 1985. In it, he lambasted his former co-workers for their idiocy and incompetence. Grammatically challenged ex-jocks **O.J. Simpson** and **Joe Namath** gamely tried to fill Cosell's analyst's chair, with predictably stupefying results. Cosell never again called a professional football game and faded from public view. He died of a heart embolism in 1995 at the age of 77.

Days of Infamy | November 16, 1970

Play-by-play man **Keith Jackson**'s slacks catch on fire after analyst **Howard Cosell** accidentally drops his cigarette butt into his boothmate's pants cuff.

CowBelles & Beaux

Original coed Dallas Cowboys cheerleading squad, comprised of six male and six female high school students from the Dallas/Ft. Worth Metroplex. The wholesome troupe led the home crowd in traditional sis-boom-bah-style cheers from 1960 until 1972, at which point Cowboys general manager Tex Schramm ordered them disbanded and replaced with a sexier, more entertaining all-female squad dubbed the **Dallas Cowboys Cheerleaders**.

Cowlings, Al "A.C."

Journeyman NFL defensive tackle of the 1970s best known for his role as wingman to his good friend **O.J. Simpson** during Simpson's infamous flight from arrest in June of 1994. The two men were best friends dating back to their childhood in San Francisco. After earning All-America honors as a starting tackle on USC's celebrated "Wild Bunch" defensive line in 1969, Cowlings was picked fifth overall by the Buffalo Bills in the 1970 NFL Draft. He wound up playing nine years with five NFL teams, including two separate stints as Simpson's

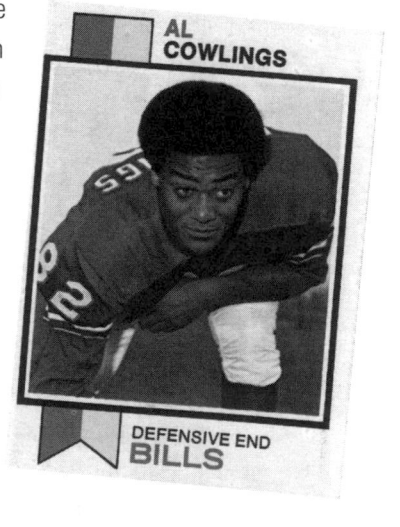

AL COWLINGS

DEFENSIVE END
BILLS

teammate with the Bills and the 49ers. But his name would probably be lost to history had he not taken the wheel of the Ford Bronco occupied by the accused double murderer—along with Simpson's passport, $8,000 in cash, a change of clothes, a loaded .357 Magnum, and a false goatee. Cowling's 911 messages to the police—"This is A.C. I have O.J. in the car" and "You know who I am, goddammit!"—briefly became national catchphrases.

Craver, Stanley

Demented, jock-sniffing ex-NFL official played by actor **Dennis Hopper** in a disquieting series of mid-1990s Nike television commercials. From 1993 to 1995, ads promoting Nike's line of turf trainer shoes featured the onetime *Easy Rider* auteur as Craver, an unhinged former referee who sneaks into NFL locker rooms to sniff players' footwear. At one point he attempts to establish telepathic communication with Troy Aikman and Michael Irvin of the Dallas Cowboys. Craver appeared in 15 commercials in all, culminating in a 90-second, $3 million monologue/manifesto that aired during ABC's telecast of Super Bowl XXIX in 1995.

Stanley Speaks!

Text of speech read by Dennis Hopper (as Stanley Craver) in a TV ad that run during Super Bowl XXIX:

"When I was a boy, I dreamed of playing football. But I was allergic to milk, and the soybean juice substitute that my mother gave me made my bones weak. But I digress. My point is: I love football. Football. The ballet of bulldozers. The moments of grace in a sea of fury. The crowd: fickle, fanatical, and faithful. Every kickoff is possibility. Every down a war. And every now and then, it doesn't come down to fancy strategy or speed or strength. It comes down to who has more heart. Yes. You see, football is in my bones, and where goes the two-point conversion, the on-side kick, and the TV timeout, so go I. I have seen the locker room, my friends. I have smelled the shoes, stormed the field, and sung the songs. And I have heard the footsteps. Yes. And they say to me, they say, 'Stanley, is football the greatest game in the world?' And I say, 'Yes, footsteps. Yes it is!'"

Audibles

"You've heard of people who zig and zag.
Well, Elroy also has a zog and a couple of zugs!"

–Norm Van Brocklin, on Elroy Hirsch

Crazylegs

Nickname bestowed on Hall of Famer Elroy Hirsch by Francis Powers of the *Chicago Daily News*. "Hirsch ran like a demented duck," Powers famously wrote of the limber-limbed, jug-eared wideout/halfback, who was one of the iconic NFL stars of the 1950s. "His crazy legs were gyrating in six different directions all at the same time during a 61-yard touchdown run." Hirsch played himself in the 1951 biopic *Crazylegs*.

Crazy Ray

Wild West persona adopted by Dallas Cowboys **superfan** Wilford Jones, who served as a semi-official mascot of the team from 1962 until his death in 2007. A onetime pennant vendor at the Cotton Bowl, the boisterous African American Cowboys rooter was instantly recognizable on TV telecasts in his stereotypical western getup of chaps, blue leather vest festooned with white stars, and six-shooter. He was known for performing sleight-of-hand magic on the sidelines and leading the crowd in cheers of "Cowbooooyyys!" During Redskins games, he would engage in good-natured battles with **Chief Zee**, Washington's faux American Indian mascot. Although never officially hired by the team, Crazy Ray was provided with a complimentary parking space and an all-access pass at Texas Stadium. When he died of complications related to heart disease and diabetes in March of 2007, he had missed only three home games in 43 seasons.

Crews, Terry

Alan Hufana

Mediocre linebacker of the 1990s who parlayed a short-lived NFL stint into a lucrative second career as an actor and commercial spokesman. Crews is best known for playing musclebound lummoxes in films like *White Chicks*, *Friday After Next*, and the 2005 version of ***The Longest Yard***. He has also plied his trade on television, playing fathers on the canceled *Everybody Hates Chris* and the current TBS sitcom *Are We There Yet?* As a retired African American benchwarmer who went on to greater fame in the world beyond football, Crews fits into a tradition that stretches back to **Carl Weathers** and culminates in the national superstardom of "Old Spice Guy" **Isaiah Mustafa**.

Da Bears

Catchphrase commonly associated with a recurring *Saturday Night Live* sketch of the 1990s (officially known as The Superfans), concerning a group of morbidly obese, mustachioed Chicago sports fans who host a television program from a bar owned by Bears legend **Mike Ditka**. The brainchild of New York–born, Chicago-trained writer/performer Robert Smigel, The Superfans featured a rotating cast of regular *SNL* performers and special guests—most commonly Chris Farley, George Wendt, Joe Mantegna, and Smigel himself. The sketch's humor derived almost entirely from its stereotypical portrayal of Chicago fans as alcoholic, heart attack–prone gluttons who speak in thick Midwestern accents. Sketches typically climaxed with the Superfans raising their enormous beer glasses in a toast to their favorite team, "Da Bears."

Dallas Cowboys Cheerleaders

World-renowned cheerleading squad that revolutionized the world of sideline entertainment in the 1970s. For the first 12 years of the franchise's existence, Cowboys fans were entertained by the **CowBelles & Beaux**, a group of coed high school cheerleaders from the Dallas/Fort Worth area. In 1971, Cowboys general manager Tex Schramm decided to spice up the atmosphere at newly opened Texas Stadium with older, sexier, all-female entertainers. When his original idea of hiring professional models proved unworkable—they lacked the stamina to perform high-stepping dance routines in the Texas heat—Schramm brought in choreographer Texie Waterman to whip a dance team of knockouts into shape. Charged with bringing "New York–style jazz dancing to the 50-yard line," Waterman was responsible for creating many of the cheerleaders' memorable routines, including their world-famous hair toss. She also instituted a strict code of conduct, forbidding Cheerleaders to smoke, drink alcohol, chew gum, or fraternize with players on penalty of dismissal. To add more sizzle to the sideline show, the squad was outfitted in a midriff-baring star-spangled blouse, vest, and shorts combo by Dallas costumer Paula Van Waggoner. After making their debut in 1972, the Dallas Cowboys Cheerleaders became a local sensation. They did not receive significant national attention until 1975, however, when a roving camera zoomed in on one during a *Monday Night Football* telecast of a game between the Cowboys and the Chiefs in what would become known in years to come as a **honey shot**. With one wink, the cheerleader in question set off a nationwide hormonal rage. Requests for appearances by the troupe began flooding the Cowboys offices. Demand was so great that Schramm ordered his personal secretary,

Football by the Numbers | 18

Minimum age requirement for a Dallas Cowboys cheerleader.

Suzanne Mitchell, to work 24/7 on the Cheerleaders portfolio. By 1978, the Dallas Cowboys Cheerleaders were a full-fledged multimedia brand. They appeared on calendars, in network TV specials and shows like *The Love Boat* and *Family Feud*, and in their own eponymous TV movie. In the wake of their success, the aesthetic parameters of NFL cheerleading were forever changed, as teams rushed to replicate the combination of sexy attire and come-hither capering that had made the Dallas troupe so popular. Out went the demure high-steppers of yesteryear, replaced by the likes of the **Dolphin Starbrites**, the **Honey Bears**, and the **Embraceable Ewes**.

Davenport, Najeh

Mediocre NFL running back of the mid-2000s best known for defecating in the laundry basket of a college student at Barry University in 2002. According to police reports, coed Mary McCarthy was sleeping in her dorm room on April Fool's Night when she awoke to the sound of someone relieving himself. She investigated and found Davenport squatting inside her closet with feces dangling out of his sphincter. Charged with second-degree burglary and criminal mischief, Davenport protested his innocence on the grounds that the offending "manure" had been destroyed and could not be positively identified as his own. He accepted a sentence of 100 hours of community service in exchange for the dismissal of all charges. During a brief three-team stint in the NFL, Davenport was saddled with the derisive nicknames "Deuce," "Dookie," and "the Dump Truck."

Davis, Al

Swashbuckling **AFL** pioneer and longtime owner/head coach/general manager of the Oakland/Los Angeles Raiders. With his predilection for track suits, shades, and black leather outerwear, Davis has been an instantly recognizable icon of professional football since the 1960s. An architect of the vertical passing offense and onetime commissioner of the American Football League, he was an outspoken critic of the AFL/NFL merger and a perennial burr in the saddle of NFL commissioner Pete Rozelle throughout the 1970s and '80s. In the 1990s and 2000s, as age and decrepitude began to catch up with him, Davis became known for his increasingly bizarre personnel moves, including the routine hiring and firing of dubiously qualified head coaches. See also: **"Commitment to Excellence"**; **Irwindale**; **"Just Win Baby"**

Davis, Caitlin

Onetime New England Patriots cheerleader who was fired by the team in 2008 after photographs on a Facebook page apparently showed her drawing swastikas and penises on the body of a passed-out friend.

Legends of the Fall

The Oakland Raiders were originally known as the Oakland Señors after that name came in first in a newspaper-sponsored "name the team" contest in 1960. The names Admirals, Gauchos, Jets, and Dolphins were also considered, as were the Nuggets, Lakers, and Clippers—which would have been great if the team competed in the NBA Western Conference. In the end, negative public reaction to the Señors name—as well as suspicions that the contest may have been rigged—compelled the franchise to settle on Raiders instead.

Dawg Pound

Term coined in the 1980s to describe the end zone bleacher seats at Cleveland Browns games, a raucous redoubt populated by woofing, baying, dog mask–wearing Browns fans. **Hanford Dixon**, a **Pro Bowl** cornerback who played for the Browns in the 1980s, is widely credited with coming up with the appellation "Dawgs" and for barking like one in an effort to rev up his defensive teammates.

Karl Hassel Jr.

Inspired by his example, fans in the east end zone soon began showing up at games wearing canine paraphernalia. They were known for pelting opposing players with Milk-Bones and for smuggling kegs of beer inside the stadium hidden inside a makeshift dog house. **John "Big Dawg" Thompson**, a burly **superfan** in a bulldog mask, soon emerged as the unofficial leader of the pack. He would spearhead the fans' unsuccessful campaign to keep the Browns in Cleveland, and then to reconvene the Dawg Pound after the franchise was reconstituted by the NFL in 1999.

Dempsey, Tom

Legendary toeless placekicker, born with a deformed right foot, who set a longstanding NFL record with a 63-yard field goal. The previous record of 56 yards had stood for 17 years when Dempsey shattered it in the waning moments of a game between the New Orleans Saints and the Detroit Lions at Tulane Stadium on November 8, 1970. Dempsey relied on a special modified kicking shoe to help him achieve his uncanny accuracy, although he claimed it did not improve his distance. Nevertheless, the NFL instituted a

Audibles

> "I guess if not having any toes is an unfair advantage, I have an advantage."
>
> –Deformed field-goal kicker **Tom Dempsey**

rule—known informally as the "Dempsey Rule"—banning the use of unconventional footwear by kickers with prosthetic limbs. Dempsey's record boot stood unchallenged for 18 seasons, until Denver Bronco Jason Elam matched it on October 25, 1998.

Derrick Dolls

Official cheerleading squad of the Houston Oilers which performed at home games from 1978 until their mass firing in 1986. Named after an oil derrick, the Dolls mimicked the sexy sideline stylings of their western Texas counterparts, the **Dallas Cowboys Cheerleaders**. Their final years were marred by controversy. In 1985, three disgruntled Derrick Dolls sued the Oilers for $23.5 million in damages, claiming they were unjustly fired after fraternizing with players at a team party. The dismissed cheerleaders, who were African American, intimated in the press that their sackings may have been racially motivated. A court later ruled in favor of the team, citing a clause in the Dolls' contracts stating that "cheerleaders can be fired at will and without cause." With the suit wrapped up, Oilers owner Bud Adams formally disbanded the squad and terminated the rest of its members.

"Diddly Poo"

Fecal matter referenced by New Orleans Saints head coach **Jim Mora** during an infamous postgame press conference tirade on October 20, 1996.

Legends of the Fall

In September of 2008, 10 years after he helped make the **Dirty Bird** a national dance craze, photos surface on the Internet showing an apparently drunk and disheveled Jamal Anderson passed out on an Atlanta bar while inebriated pub crawlers do the Dirty Bird over his unconscious body.

Dirty Bird

Frenetic **end zone dance** developed by members of the 1998 NFC champion Atlanta Falcons that briefly gripped the imagination of football fans in the run-up to the team's appearance in Super Bowl XXXIII. Creation of the Dirty Bird is usually credited to Falcons running back Jamal Anderson, but tight end O.J. Santiago helped popularize the dance with a spirited rendition during a victory over the New England Patriots on November 8, 1998. The basic moves of the Dirty Bird are as follows:

Lift your right hand in the air in a "raise the roof" gesture, then bring it down across your chest to form a wing.
Perform the same motion with your left arm.
Flap both arms together as if attempting to fly.
Freestyle.

Dirty Bird mania reached its zenith at the NFC Championship Game on January 17, 1999, after which Atlanta's 55-year-old head coach Dan Reeves could be seen performing a painfully stiff version of the dance in celebration of the team's upset win over the Minnesota Vikings. At the height of the craze, an Atlanta seafood restaurant manager and Falcons season ticket holder beat the team to the punch by registering the Dirty Bird trademark, racking up more than $600,000 in T-shirt and other merchandise sales before the inevitable NFL lawsuit. An official Dirty Bird website was also set up. But the good times were not to last. The Falcons lost the Super Bowl and went 5–11 the following season. Two years later, Jamal Anderson was out of football entirely. In February of 2009, he was arrested on felony drug possession charges after he was found snorting cocaine off a toilet bowl in an Atlanta eatery.

Ditka, Mike

Hall of Fame tight end turned Chicago Bears coaching legend and one of only three men to win the Super Bowl as a player and a head coach. Pugnacious and media-savvy, a retired "Iron Mike" parlayed his colorful persona into a lucrative gig as a pregame commentator and national spokesman for the **Levitra** erectile dysfunction medication. He is one of a growing cohort of former NFL players to take up **winemaking**.

Dixon, Hanford

Pro Bowl cornerback of the 1980s credited with coining the term "**Dawg Pound**" to describe the east end zone redoubt of rabid Cleveland Browns fans at Cleveland Stadium.

Dobler, Conrad

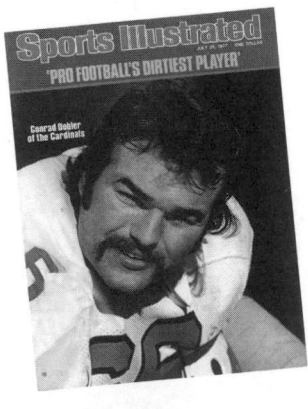

Hall of Fame offensive lineman whose name has become synonymous with vicious, nasty play. A 1977 *Sports Illustrated* cover story labeled Dobler "Pro Football's Dirtiest Player." The three-time **Pro Bowl** guard spent most of his career with the St. Louis Cardinals, where he developed a reputation for neutralizing defensive linemen by any means necessary—including punching, kicking, biting, and gouging at the eyes of

Doblerisms

The Wit and Wisdom of Conrad Dobler

"My hand at times has possibly slipped under the face masks." (on accusations he liked to claw at the flesh of his opponents)

"I wouldn't try to blind someone. Maybe blur their vision."

"I only bit one guy: Doug Sutherland of the Minnesota Vikings. He put his fingers through my face mask, and I don't think they were there to stroke my mustache. So I bite one finger in my life, and I don't even chew on it. The legend grew from there. It's almost like I'm worse than Jeffrey Dahmer."

"I see defensive linemen jump to knock a pass down. When that happened near me, I'd smack 'em in the solar plexus, and that got their hands down real quick."

"When I hit a guy, I'll hit him in the throat. He doesn't have any pads on his throat."

"I like tits. If women had three, it would be even better."

"If it flies, floats, or fucks, rent it."

"Some people get vasectomies. I used to give 'em."

"It's been 20 years since I played him, and I'm still on his fucking mind. And I like that!" (on **Merlin Olsen**, who had the words "Conrad Dobler: Gone, But Not Forgiven" etched on a tombstone for a graveyard scene on his 1980s TV drama *Father Murphy*)

"If I got turned down by girls as much as I was turned down by the NFL, I'd still be a virgin." (on his campaign to get disability benefits from the NFL)

his opponents. According to legend, one of Dobler's punches caused his victim to break down and cry on the field. Injury afforded no stay against Dobler's fury. On the contrary, he once spit in the face of Eagles safety Bill Bradley while Bradley was sprawled on the turf in agony. After slugging the Oakland Raiders' Phil Villapiano in the ribs, Dobler boasted that he only did it because he knew Villapiano's ribs were already injured. Nor would courtesy spare one from Dobler's wrath. At the end of the 1974 season, New York Giants rookie Jim Pietrzak made the mistake of wishing Dobler luck in the playoffs—and was rewarded with a punch in the throat. Dobler's signature move may have been his patented leg whip, a karate-style kick that took such a toll on his own body that he required more than 30 knee operations and 10 knee replacements after he retired. By the 2000s, Dobler had become so ravaged by injuries from his playing days—and the attendant medical bills—that he became something of a poster child for the campaign by NFL retirees to extract much-needed disability benefits from the league.

Dolfan Denny

Persona adopted by Miami Dolphins **superfan** Dennis Sym, a onetime BellSouth employee who led the cheers at team home games from 1966 to 2000. Known for his garish orange-and-aquamarine outfits—typically comprised of a loud, rhinestone-studded shirt, white shorts, glittering sombrero, and a matador cape—the Broward County resident started out by revving up the crowd with chants from his seat. His routines proved so popular that Dolphins owner Joe Robbie named him the team's semi-official sideline cheerleader in 1976. From that point on, Sym—who possessed a master's degree in electrical engineering—was paid $50 a game for his dancing, capering, towel-waving services. Fed up with the abuse he often received at the hands of drunken hecklers, Dolfan Denny retired from active rooting in 2000. He died of kidney disease in 2007.

Audibles

"Cheerleading is becoming nothing more than a battle of belly buttons, busts, and backsides."

–Bill Allen, director of the **Dolphin Dolls**, on the shift in public expectations about sideline entertainment in the late 1970s

Dolphin Dolls

Precision dance team that performed at Miami Dolphins home games from 1966 to 1978. The squad was composed of wholesome, well-scrubbed girls ages eight through 18 who were selected based on talent—specifically their ability to twirl a baton, perform drill team routines, dance, cheer, and do gymnastics—and not appearance. With the advent of the overtly sexy **Dallas Cowboys Cheerleaders**, such squads had become passé in the eyes of fans by the late 1970s. The Dolphin Dolls spent their final few seasons being pelted with refuse by horny Dolphins rooters. "We've been splattered with mustard, ketchup, and pickle relish," the leader of the squad complained to the press. Rumors abounded that NBC had informed the Dolphins they wouldn't show the Dolls on television unless the cheerleaders adopted skimpier costumes. The public outcry for more risqué cheerleading eventually grew so loud that the Dolphins public relations chief ordered the squad's director to begin recruiting older, sexier members. When the Dolls refused to comply, the troupe was disbanded and replaced with the go-go boot–clad **Dolphin Starbrites**.

Dolphin Starbrites

Official name of the Miami Dolphins cheerleading squad from 1978 to 1983. The Starbrites replaced the team's demure teenaged dance team the **Dolphin Dolls** in the wake of fan and media complaints that the original cheerleaders weren't sexy enough. Auditions were held for older, more

physically developed women who could adequately fill out the squad's standard uniform of one-piece bathing suits, hats, gloves, and go-go boots. For the first 12 years of their existence, the choreographer and director of the Starbrites was June Taylor, a Fort Lauderdale resident famous for her work with her namesake dance troupe on Jackie Gleason's TV variety show.

Donovan, Art

Thick-necked Hall of Fame defensive lineman of the 1950s who parlayed his old-school, crew-cut persona into a lucrative second career as a commercial pitchman and media icon in the 1980s and '90s. A two-time world champion as a member of the Baltimore Colts—widely known by the nickname "Bulldog"—Donovan developed a reputation in his later years as an engaging banquet speaker and one-stop anecdote factory for writers looking to conjure up the flavor of the NFL's olden days. His first brush with cult fame came in the mid-1980s after he made a series of popular guest appearances on *Late Night with David Letterman*. In the 1990s, he filled out his endorsement portfolio with local TV and radio commercials for breweries, automotive dealers, and the Maryland State Lottery, and a series of national promotional spots for ESPN.

Doomsday Defense

Eschatological nickname for the Dallas Cowboys defense of the 1960s, '70s, and '80s. The Doomsday Epoch is customarily subdivided into two eras: Doomsday I, roughly spanning the years 1966 through 1975; and Doomsday II, stretching from 1976 to 1982. Players associated with the Doomsday Defense include defensive linemen Bob Lilly, Randy White, and **Ed "Too Tall" Jones**, linebackers Chuck Howley and **Thomas "Hollywood" Henderson**, and defensive backs Mel Renfro, Cliff Harris, and Charlie Waters.

Field Guide to Zebras

Ben Dreith

Longtime NFL official, respected for his no-nonsense approach to adjudicating the game, who drew national attention for an unusual personal foul call during a 1986 game between the New York Jets and the Buffalo Bills. Explaining the penalty to the crowd, Dreith cited Jets defensive end **Mark Gastineau** (erroneously, as it turned out) for inappropriately pummeling Bills quarterback Jim Kelly. Or, as Dreith put it: "We have a personal foul on No. 99 of the defense. After he tackled the quarterback, he's giving him the business down there. That's a 15-yard penalty."

Drive, The

Commonly used term for the 15-play, 98-yard, game-tying touchdown drive engineered by quarterback John Elway that propelled the Denver Broncos to an overtime victory over the Cleveland Browns in the AFC Championship Game on January 11, 1987. A time traveler's ability to go back in time and predict the outcome of the Drive as it happened is a minor plot point in the 2010 film comedy *Hot Tub Time Machine*. See also: **Fumble, The (1988)**

"Drop Kick Me Jesus (Through the Goalposts of Life)"

Football-themed novelty song recorded by Ohio-born country-and-western singer Bobby Bare in 1976. The waltz-timed ditty peaked at No. 17 on the charts and received a Grammy nomination for Best Country Song. Composed by veteran Nashville songwriter Paul Craft, the lyrics conflate submission to God's will to a football being kicked through the uprights of a goalpost. "Drop Kick Me Jesus (Through the Goalposts of Life)" is reportedly one of former U.S. president Bill Clinton's favorite songs.

Audibles

Drop kick me, Jesus, through the goalposts of life,
End over end, neither left nor to right.
Straight through the heart of them righteous uprights
Drop kick me, Jesus, through the goalposts of life.

—chorus to Bobby Bare's 1976 hit "**Drop Kick Me Jesus
(Through the Goalposts of Life)**"

Dryer, Fred

Onetime All-Pro defensive end better known
to the general public for his post-NFL acting
career, principally as the star of the popular
TV police drama *Hunter*. Along with **Joe
Namath**, Dryer was one of two ex-gridiron
greats to miss out on the role of Sam
Malone on the long-running NBC sitcom
Cheers. Unlike Namath, who passed on
the part, Dryer actively auditioned for it
and was one of two finalists under
consideration. Non-athlete Ted Danson
eventually got the gig, although Dryer later scored a recurring guest role on
the series as sportscaster Dave Richards.

Days of Infamy | September 17, 1971

First-year Green Bay Packers coach Dan Devine breaks two major bones in
his leg when Giants guard Bob Hyland barrels into him on the sideline during
a 42–40 season-opening loss to the New York Giants at Lambeau Field.

E

Eaglettes

Former name of the Philadelphia Eagles cheerleading squad, now known simply as the Eagles Cheerleaders. From 1978 to 1983, the squad went by the name the **Liberty Belles**. The Eaglettes were on the field wearing elf costumes during the infamous **Santa Claus Incident** in 1968.

Einstein, Albert

Famed mathematician and physicist whose speculations on relativity foretold the development of the atomic bomb, although he took no part in its invention. Einstein's relationship to football history is somewhat less theoretical. He was once unexpectedly visited at his home in Princeton, New Jersey, by future Hall of Fame coach **George Allen**. The year was 1944 and Allen—then a young U.S. Navy midshipman—was immersed in a competitive checkers-playing phase. One Sunday morning, seized by the urge to challenge Einstein to a game of checkers, Allen rounded up a few of his dorm buddies and headed over to the 64-year-old professor's tastefully decorated home. After his wife graciously let the boys in, Einstein himself appeared, pipe in hand. He was cordial enough, but utterly uninterested in Allen's checkers challenge. "I don't play much checkers," Einstein told Allen. "I don't like it much." When Allen persisted, Einstein was forced to admit he

Audibles

"Nobody in football should be called a genius. A genius is a guy like Norman Einstein."

–Redskins quarterback turned ESPN analyst Joe Theismann

did not own a checkers board—at which point Allen and his buds agreed to leave the premises. Before they did, however, the man some called the father of the A-bomb left them with one important piece of information. World War II, he informed them, would soon be over. "A great boom," Einstein intoned, spreading his hands out wide to pantomime a mushroom cloud. And with that the jubilant young sailors returned home.

Electric Company, The

Nickname bestowed on the Buffalo Bills' offensive line of the 1970s by star running back **O.J. Simpson**, in recognition of the way their blocks "turned on the Juice." Fullback Jim Braxton, Paul Seymour, and Joe DeLamiellure were the most prominent members of the Electric Company.

Electric Football

Popular tabletop football game in which tiny plastic players compete for supremacy on a vibrating metal field. The original electric football game was invented in 1947 by Norman Sas, scion of the Tudor Metal

Charles Angell

Products company, a producer of toy piggy banks and other novelties. It was modeled on a vibrating car race game the company already had on the market. Tudor's Tru-Action Electric Football game first hit shelves in 1949, mesmerizing Cold War–era children with its violently tremulous, endlessly circling gridiron gladiators. The game was an immediate hit and by 1954, a competitor, Gotham Pressed Steel, emerged with a copycat game to challenge Tudor's market dominance. The two companies' competition fostered innovations and refinements of the game throughout the 1950s and

'60s, including the introduction of a scoreboard, photorealistic metal grandstand, and "sculp-action" poses on the figurines. In 1967, an NFL/**AFL** licensing agreement paved the way for players to be painted with official team colors and logos. As the NFL exploded in popularity over the course of the 1970s, so did that of Electric Football, prompting additional competitors like Coleco to get in on the action and making the game a staple of football-mad children's holiday wish lists throughout the decade. The Christmas morning giddiness that attended the receipt of an Electric Football board ordered out of the Sears catalog was invariably tempered by disappointment, however, as playing the game failed to deliver the exciting, realistic action promised in print ads and television commercials. In the 1980s, the advent of the video game era signaled the death knell for Electric Football as a mass market product. By 1989, sales of new game boards had slowed to a trickle. Today the game is played by a remnant of eccentrics fueled by childhood nostalgia. Miggle Toys, which acquired the rights to the Tudor product line in 1992, currently promotes regional and national electric football tournaments, where collectible geeks amass vintage figurines with the avidity of comic book hoarders and hobbyists pimp their tabletops in the manner of classic muscle car enthusiasts.

Electric Slide, The

Madcap **end zone dance** invented by Houston Oilers wide receiver Ernest Givins in the late 1980s. After scoring a touchdown, Givins would slide his foot across the turf and convulse his shoulders as if he were being electrocuted.

Electronic Quarterback

Popular handheld electronic football game marketed by Coleco Industries beginning in 1978. Invented by Coleco research and development chief Eric

Bromley, Electronic Quarterback (or "Coleco Football" as it was informally known) was designed to compete with Mattel Electronics' bestselling Football handheld. It was licensed for sale at Sears retail stores under the name Electronic Touchdown. An enhanced two-player version of the game, called **Head-to-Head Football**, began appearing in stores in 1980.

Elkjer, Thelma

Longtime secretary of NFL commissioner Pete Rozelle who is best known for her role in resolving the dispute over realignment that consumed the league in the wake of its merger with the **AFL**. In the spring of 1970, Rozelle tasked Elkjer with the job of picking one of five realignment proposals at random out of a cut-glass vase at NFL headquarters. She selected Plan 3, the only one that kept the Bears, Packers, Lions, and Vikings in the same division.

Embraceable Ewes

Name adopted by the Los Angeles Rams cheerleaders in 1978 and used officially throughout the 1980s. The alliterative moniker was chosen after the team discovered that the original name for the squad, the Ram Sundancers, was already taken.

Football by the Numbers | $14.12

Amount, after taxes, that the **Embraceable Ewes** and other cheerleading squads of the late 1970s received per game for their services

End Zone Celebration

Post-touchdown display of exuberance that has grown more elaborate since the invention of the spike by New York Giant **Homer Jones** in 1965. In response to an outbreak of taunting and choreographed, prop-driven end zone celebrations, the NFL has strictly regulated excessive celebration on penalty of a 15-yard unsportsmanlike conduct violation since 2006. See also: **Cell Phone Incident**; **Lambeau Leap**; **Mile High Salute**; **Sharpie Incident**

End Zone Dance

Display of end zone euphoria pioneered by wide receiver **Elmo Wright** in the early 1970s. See also: **Dirty Bird**; **Electric Slide, The**; **Funky Chicken**; **Ickey Shuffle**; **Row Your Boat**

Esiason, Norman Julius "Boomer"

Genial former **Pro Bowl** quarterback who parlayed his glib manner, distinctive nickname, and anodyne good looks into a lucrative post-retirement broadcasting career. A native Long Islander, Esiason enjoyed his

greatest success as a member of the Cincinnati Bengals, winning the 1988 NFL MVP and leading the team to a heartbreaking loss in Super Bowl XXIII. He retired after the 1997 season. Despite having little broadcasting experience, Esiason replaced the bombastic Dan Dierdorf as color commentator on **Monday Night Football** broadcasts in 1998. He was fired only two seasons in the role after repeated clashes with boothmate

Al Michaels. He has since reinvented himself as a morning drive-time radio host and studio analyst for CBS' *The NFL Today*. Esiason was given the nickname "Boomer" by his mother because he kicked so much in the womb. Products he's marketed under that name include Boomer's BBQ Sauce, an "award-winning" condiment, and the 1995 children's book *A Boy Named Boomer*.

ExtenZe

Brand-name penile enhancement supplement endorsed in television commercials by retired Dallas Cowboys head coach Jimmy Johnson.

F

Facenda, John

Baritone-voiced newscaster best known to football fans as the booming **"Voice of God"** behind innumerable **NFL Films** highlight packages. A fixture on Philadelphia radio throughout the 1930s, '40s, and '50s, Facenda first started narrating for NFL Films in 1967 following a chance meeting at a bar with the company's founder, **Ed Sabol**. His hiring faced stiff resistance from NFL team owners who were leery about his near-total ignorance of the game and preferred a seasoned sportscaster such as Jack Whitaker, Curt Gowdy, or Chris Schenkel. But Sabol, convinced his highlight films required a fresh voice, stuck to his guns. Facenda would remain with NFL Films until his death in 1984. Facenda's stentorian voice-overs provided a perfect match for the bombastic musical cues of longtime NFL Films composer **Sam Spence** and the rhapsodic copy supplied by Sabol and his son Steve.

Word of God

Selected Quotations from the Book of Facenda

"Lombardi. A certain magic still lingers in the very name."

"Do you feel the force of the wind? The slash of the rain? Go face them and fight them. Be savage again!"

"Excitement electrifies us, victory spikes the air, all sights are set on one glittering goal: the chance to play and win in the Super Bowl."

"Woe to he who goes against the charge of the oncoming lineman. Beware the drive block, the forearm shiver…It's one ton of muscle with a one-track mind."

"Hopes that were high in the heat of September can wilt and die in the chill of November."

"Through the chill of December the early winter moans. But it's that January wind that rattles old bones."

"The autumn wind is a pirate, Blustering in from sea

With a rollicking song he sweeps along, Swaggering boisterously….

The autumn wind is a Raider, Pillaging just for fun

He'll knock you 'round and upside down, And laugh when he's conquered and won."

Failure to Launch

Critically derided 2006 romantic comedy notorious among football fans for a disquieting nude scene involving Hall of Fame quarterback **Terry Bradshaw**. In the film, Bradshaw and Academy Award winner Kathy Bates play

Audibles

"Once I dropped my boxer shorts and exposed myself to the entire crew, it was kind of refreshing in a way. I was like, I can breathe."

—Terry Bradshaw, on his nude scene in *Failure to Launch*

concerned parents who hire a female relationship expert (Sarah Jessica Parker) to entice their ne'er-do-well son (Matthew McConaughey) out of their house. Bradshaw's character drops his pants at one point, leaving his bare behind visible for about 30 seconds.

Falconettes
Original name of the Atlanta Falcons cheerleading squad.

Fantasy Football
Wildly popular virtual competition in which participants draft and manage teams of NFL players. The participants' success is calibrated to the actual on-field performances of individual team members. While it did not reach its current heights of popularity until the advent of the Internet in the 1990s, Fantasy Football actually dates back to 1962. Its invention is usually credited to Wilfred Winkenbach, a part-owner of the Oakland Raiders who had previously created Fantasy Golf. Winkenbach first pitched the idea of a virtual football league to some sportswriter friends over dinner at the Milford Plaza Hotel in New York City. He helped organize the first eight-team fantasy league, the GOPPPL, or Greater Oakland Professional Pigskin Procrastinators League, and formulated the game's original rules and scoring system. Estimates vary, but it's thought that as many as 30 million Americans play Fantasy Football annually.

Father Murphy

Short-lived TV drama of the early 1980s starring former Los Angeles Rams defensive tackle **Merlin Olsen** as a bogus frontier priest. The erstwhile **Fearsome Foursome** stalwart played "Father" John Murphy, a kind-hearted drifter who poses as a clergyman to provide succor for a gaggle of ragamuffin orphans. Plots typically involved Father Murphy intervening in various interpersonal conflicts among his charges. In one episode, he got to meet Mark Twain. The family-friendly drama capitalized on the "good-natured goliath" persona that Olsen had developed on his previous series, *Little House on the Prairie*. However, it could not match that program's success. NBC excommunicated *Father Murphy* after just two seasons.

Favre, Brett

Quarterbacking legend of the 1990s who saw his once-sterling public image tarnished by scandal in the 2000s. After leading the Green Bay Packers to their first Super Bowl title in 29 years in 1997, the Kiln, Mississippi, native attracted a national following. His grizzled gunslinger persona made him a natural fit for lucrative sponsorship deals with Sears and Wrangler. Favre dabbled in film, appearing as a dim-witted janitor in teammate **Reggie White**'s 1996 magnum opus *Reggie's Prayer* and playing Cameron Diaz's boyfriend in the 1998 comedy *There's Something About Mary*. But his genial good ol' boy reputation suffered somewhat in the wake of his 2007 departure from Green Bay and seemingly annual retirement announcements. In 2010, Favre's image received an even more devastating blow when former New York Jets TV hostess **Jenn Sterger** accused him of "sexting" her digital images of his genitalia.

Fearsome Foursome

Nickname for a dominant defensive line, most commonly associated with the front four of the mid-1960s Los Angeles Rams. **Deacon Jones, Merlin**

Olsen, **Roosevelt "Rosey" Grier,** and Lamar Lundy were the original members of the Fearsome Foursome.

FieldTurf

Revolutionary brand of **artificial turf** that began to supplant **AstroTurf** as the NFL's preferred synthetic surface in the 1990s. Springier and more yielding than AstroTurf, FieldTurf is said to feel more like natural grass and is considered less conducive to injury.

Fight Song

See **"Another One Bites the Dust"**; **"Bear Down, Chicago Bears"**; **"Fly, Eagles Fly"**; **"Go! You Packers! Go!"**; **"Gridiron Heroes"**; **"Hail to the Redskins"**; **"Here We Go"**; **"Packarena"**; **"Purple and Gold"**; **"San Diego Superchargers"**; **"Skol, Vikings"**

Fireman Ed

Persona adopted by New York City firefighter Ed Anzalone, who has served as the New York Jets' marquee **superfan** since 1986. The longtime Jets season ticket holder wears a green-and-white fire helmet to games and leads the crowd in the famous "J-E-T-S!" chant, which he is widely credited with originating. In August of 2010, Anzalone was charged with assault after getting into a televised altercation with a New York Giants fan during the preseason opener at New Meadowlands Stadium. Charges were later dropped.

www.flickr.com/kowarski

1ˢᵗ & Ten

Raunchy football-themed situation comedy that aired on HBO from 1984 to 1991. Described by its makers as being "in the uproarious gridiron tradition of **North Dallas Forty** and **Semi-Tough**," *1ˢᵗ & Ten* chronicled the exploits of the California Bulls, a fictitious professional football team "more concerned with making passes than catching them." Future *Designing Women* fixture Delta Burke played the team's sassy owner, Diane Barrow, with *Dynasty*'s Geoffrey Scott as its perpetually horny quarterback, Bob Dorsey. Numerous retired NFL players also took part in the shenanigans, including Fran Tarkenton, Marcus Allen, Vince Ferragamo, and **John Matuszak**. In later seasons, **O.J. Simpson** joined the party as the Bulls' general manager, T.D. Parker. Simpson hanger-on **Al "A.C." Cowlings** was a frequent guest star. The ribald pay-cable series featured copious female nudity and was set to a braying laugh track. Game footage was filched from telecasts of the **USFL**'s Los Angeles Express, with little effort made to obscure that team's distinctive uniforms and logos.

Flea Flicker

Occasionally executed trick play invented by University of Illinois coaching legend Bob Zuppke while he was the head coach at Oak Park High School in 1910. While the flea flicker has many variations, the basic play calls for the quarterback to hand off or lateral the ball to a running back, then step back to receive a return lateral from that player before throwing a forward pass down the field. The play aims to deceive the defense into thinking a passing play is actually a running play. Zuppke, who also created the screen pass and the huddle, coined the term "flea flicker" to evoke the gyrations of a dog trying to dislodge a nettlesome flea. A high-risk, high-reward play, the flea flicker is attempted more often than other **trick plays** like the **quick kick** or the **Statue of Liberty Play** and has yet to be outlawed on any level, unlike the **fumblerooski**. The New York Giants successfully executed a flea flicker for a 44-yard gain against the Denver Broncos in Super Bowl XXI. Perhaps the most notorious and widely watched flea flicker occurred on November 18, 1985, when Washington Redskins quarterback Joe Theismann suffered a gruesome, career-ending broken leg when he was crushed by linebacker **Lawrence Taylor** during a blown flea flicker play in the second quarter of a nationally televised *Monday Night Football* contest against the New York Giants.

Flipper

Live bottlenose dolphin who served as a quasi-official mascot of the Miami Dolphins during the early years of the franchise. Flipper, whose permanent home was the Miami Seaquarium, was loaned out to the Dolphins for weekend home games in the late 1960s. He was known to cavort in a large fish tank in the east end zone at the Orange Bowl, doing flips and dives whenever the Dolphins scored a touchdown. Dolphins owner Joe Robbie "fired" Flipper in 1968, reportedly because the Seaquarium refused to pay for the upkeep of his tank or transporting the marine mammal to and from the stadium. A costumed dolphin named **T.D.** succeeded Flipper as team mascot in 1997.

Flutie, Doug

Diminutive quarterback of the 1980s best known for his collegiate achievements, including winning the 1984 Heisman Trophy and launching a memorable **Hail Mary** (or, as some called it, a "Hail Flutie") for the Boston College Eagles in a game against the Miami Hurricanes on November 23,

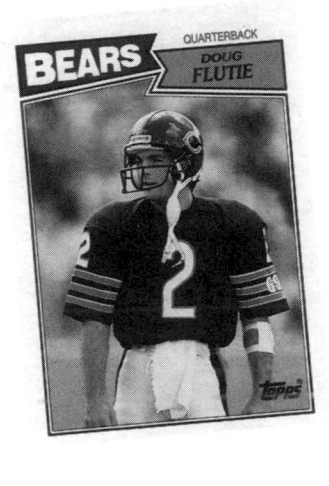

1984. As a professional, Flutie is remembered for being too short to make it in the NFL; for being one of the marquee stars of the **USFL**; and for crossing the picket line during the 1987 players' strike. He did his best work in the Canadian Football League, leading the Calgary Stampeders and Toronto Argonauts to three Grey Cup titles and capturing six Most Outstanding Player Awards. Flutie played himself in the 2002 TV movie *Second String*.

"Fly, Eagles Fly"

Official **fight song** of the Philadelphia Eagles, also known as "The Philadelphia Eagles Victory Song." Composed by Philadelphia ad men Charles Borrelli, Roger Courtland, and Ben Musicant, "Fly, Eagles Fly" dates back to the 1950s. Courtland himself used to lead a group of musicians in the performance of the song during Eagles home games. But the ditty never really caught on with fans until the late 1960s, when new Eagles owner Jerry Wolman commissioned a fresh arrangement from Arlen R. Saylor Sr., leader of the team's 110-piece marching band, The Philadelphia Eagles Sound of Brass. The peppier, brassier rendition—intended to evoke the charms of the Washington Redskins' **"Hail to the Redskins"**—got toes tapping all over the City of Brotherly Love but didn't sit well with the team's next owner, Leonard Tose. He had the brass band disbanded and the fight song mothballed in 1969. In recent years, "Fly, Eagles Fly" has made something of a comeback, serving as the musical prelude to the tribal fan chant "E-A-G-L-E-S, Eagles!"

Audibles

**"Hit 'em low
Hit 'em high
And watch our Eagles fly!"**

–lyrics to "Fly, Eagles Fly," which, if followed,
would result in a 15-yard penalty

Flying Elvis

Derisive term used by New England Patriots fans to refer to the team's current logo—so named because of its resemblance to Elvis Presley—which replaced football-snapping minuteman **Pat Patriot** on the team's helmets and insignia starting in 1993.

Fog Bowl

Infamous **bad weather game** played by the Philadelphia Eagles and the Chicago Bears on December 31, 1988, at Soldier Field in Chicago. The divisional playoff contest started out in seasonably cold, sunny weather, but by the end of the first half a weather anomaly ushered in a blanket of thick

AP Images

fog off of nearby Lake Michigan. The entire second half was played in a pea soup cloud that made seeing the ball nearly impossible beyond a 20-yard radius. Officials offered to delay the game, but both head coaches insisted that play continue. (The fog ended up lifting a half hour after the game concluded.) Thirty minutes of slapstick offensive football ensued, in which neither team could score a touchdown and the Bears' eight-point halftime lead held up. They won the game 20–12.

Football Movies

See *Any Given Sunday*; *Big Fan*; *Black Sunday*; *Brian's Song*; *Game Plan, The*; *Garbage Picking Field Goal Kicking Philadelphia Phenomenon, The*; *Gus*; *Heaven Can Wait*; *Invincible*; *Jerry Maguire*; *Leatherheads*; *Longest Yard, The*; *Monday Night Mayhem*; *North Dallas Forty*; *Number One*; *Reggie's Prayer*; *Saintly Switch, A*; *Second String*; *Semi-Tough*; *Something for Joey*; *Two-Minute Warning*

49er Nuggets

Popular San Francisco 49ers cheerleading squad first organized in 1970. The Nuggets straddled the era between the pom-pom-waving dance teams of the 1960s and the sexy cheerleading squads of the late 1970s. Consistent with the franchise's Old West iconography, they were typically outfitted in polyester hot pants, white felt cowboy hats, and white knee-high vinyl boots. A new cheerleading squad, the **San Francisco Gold Rush**, succeeded the Nuggets in 1983.

Franco's Italian Army

Boisterous paramilitary fan club devoted to Franco Harris, the Pittsburgh Steelers' half Italian American, half African American running back of the 1970s. Ukrainian American Steelers fans had already formed one ethnically

themed cheering section, **Gerela's Gorillas**, by the time Franco's Italian Army was mobilized in 1972. Army members were known for wearing battle helmets, waving small Italian flags, and smuggling wine, cheese, and other Italian delicacies into Three Rivers Stadium. Their battle cry was "Run, paisano, Run!" "Generalissimo" Tony Stagno, proprietor of one of Pittsburgh's most popular Italian bakeries, and local pizzaiolo Al Vento are widely credited with founding the fan club, which grew to include more than 20 members—including Frank Sinatra. See also: **Frenchy's Foreign Legion**

Freddie Falcon

Anthropomorphized bird of prey who has been the official mascot of the Atlanta Falcons since 1974. Often erroneously cited as the only mascot in Falcons history, Freddie is actually the second. A succession of live falcons named **Thor** had entertained home crowds during the franchise's inaugural season in 1966. With longevity have come copious extracurricular opportunities. Over the decades, Freddie has traveled across the United States and overseas to Japan, Egypt, Cuba, Puerto Rico, and Guam. Online videos have captured him frolicking in a shopping mall, going tubing, smashing a cheerleader in the face with a birthday cake, and dancing to Soulja Boy and MC Hammer. In the off-season, the costumed character charges $250 a pop for public appearances and corporate events.

Free Reign

Heavy metal band formed in 2008 by three Dallas Cowboys linemen. Billing itself as "heavier than metal," the group is comprised of three 300-pounders: Marc Colombo (lead singer and rhythm guitar), Leonard Davis (bass guitar), and Cory Procter (drums). Non-Cowboy Justin Chapman, a former high school offensive tackle, rounds out the head-banging combo on lead guitar. Free Reign released its debut CD *Tragedy* in 2010. Colombo has cited Metallica, Megadeth, Slayer, and Pantera as the band's major influences.

AP Images

Freezer Bowl

Commonly used term for the 1981 AFC Championship Game, a notorious **bad weather game** played between the San Diego Chargers and the Cincinnati Bengals on January 10, 1982, at Riverfront Stadium in Cincinnati. Game-time temperature was minus 9 degrees Fahrenheit, with a wind chill bottoming out at negative 59. (Chargers quarterback Dan Fouts famously had icicles forming in his beard at one point.) The favored Chargers saw their high-powered passing offense all but grounded by the frigid conditions, as the Bengals capitalized on four San Diego turnovers en route to a 27–7 victory.

Frenchy's Foreign Legion

Fan club formed by Pittsburgh Steelers rooters of the 1970s to cheer on the team's dapper running back, John "Frenchy" Fuqua. The flamboyant Fuqua, or "the French Count" as he preferred to style himself, was not actually French but a native of Detroit, Michigan. He was famous for wearing purple suits and see-through platform shoes with live goldfish in them. See also: **Franco's Italian Army**; **Gerela's Gorillas**

Frozen Tundra

Nickname given to Lambeau Field, home of the Green Bay Packers, in recognition of the often frigid field conditions, specifically during the infamous 1967 **Ice Bowl**. The term "Frozen Tundra" was coined by **NFL Films** scion **Steve Sabol** in his script for the 1967 Dallas Cowboys highlight film. Narrator Bill Woodson was the first to utter the phrase, although it is often erroneously attributed to NFL Films **"Voice of God" John Facenda**. (ESPN loudmouth **Chris Berman** is largely responsible for the misattribution.) According to Sabol, Packers coach Vince Lombardi objected to the term "Frozen Tundra" on grammatical grounds. The phrase was redundant, Lombardi charged, since a tundra by definition is always frozen.

Fumble, The (1978)

Term used by New York Giants fans to refer to an infamous turnover by quarterback Joe Pisarcik in the waning moments of a critical game against the Philadelphia Eagles on November 19, 1978, at Giants Stadium. The Giants were leading the game 17–12 with under a minute to play, poised to fall on the ball and run out the clock, when offensive coordinator Bob Gibson inexplicably called an off-tackle running play. Pisarcik and fullback Larry Csonka muffed the exchange, resulting in a fumble that bounced off the turf and was scooped up by blitzing Eagles cornerback Herman Edwards for the winning touchdown. The come-from-behind victory turned out to be the turning point in the playoff chase between the two rivals, as the Eagles went on to claim the NFC wild card by one game. (Not surprisingly, Philadelphia fans refer to the incident as the Miracle at the Meadowlands.)

AP Images

The Fumble is widely considered to be the nadir of a period of mediocrity in Giants football that lasted from the mid-1960s until the advent of the **Bill Parcells**/Phil Simms/**Lawrence Taylor** era in the early 1980s.

Fumble, The (1988)

Term used by Cleveland Browns fans to refer to a game-changing turnover that occurred in the final minutes of the AFC Championship Game between the Browns and the Denver Broncos on January 17, 1988, at Mile High Stadium in Denver. The Browns were down 38–31 and driving for the tying touchdown when running back Earnest Byner fumbled the ball on the 3-yard line. The Broncos recovered the ball, intentionally surrendered a safety, and sealed a 38–33 victory that propelled them to the Super Bowl for the second year in a row.

Fumblerooski

Seldom-used trick play invented by college football pioneer John Heisman in which the quarterback deliberately places the football on the ground to simulate a fumble. As the rest of the offense runs right, the right guard then picks up the ball and runs left, leaving the flummoxed defense scrambling in his wake. Banned in the NFL since the early 1960s and in college since 1992, the fumblerooski has rarely been executed successfully above the high school level. Fumblerooskis helped determine the outcomes of both the 1984 and 1988 Orange Bowls and the 1994 family comedy film *Little Giants*.

Fun Bunch

Nickname given to the receiving corps of the early 1980s Washington Redskins, known for their spirited **end zone celebration**. Touchdowns by members of the Fun Bunch invariably culminated in an exuberant group high-five. Membership in the Fun Bunch shifted over time, but at one time or another Art Monk, Virgil Seay, Rich Caster, Charlie Brown, Gary Clark, **Alvin Garrett**, Rick Walker, Donnie Warren, Clarence Harmon, and Otis Wansley counted themselves as members. See also: **Smurfs**

Funky Chicken

Dance craze inspired by Rufus Thomas' 1970 R&B hit "Do the Funky Chicken" and adapted by wide receiver **Billy "White Shoes" Johnson** for use as an **end zone dance**. Johnson began celebrating touchdowns with the Funky Chicken while a sophomore at Widener College, on a dare from one of his teammates. After he made it to the NFL, he rechristened the dance "the White Shoes Shuffle."

G

Game Plan, The

Crowd-pleasing 2007 Disney football movie starring former Miami Hurricane turned professional wrestler Dwayne "the Rock" Johnson. Johnson plays Joe "the King" Kingman, the conceited, Elvis-obsessed star

quarterback of the fictional Boston Rebels. When Kingman's well-ordered life is turned upside down by the appearance of the adorable eight-year-old daughter he never knew he had, heartwarming family comedy ensues. With its insistently peppy tone (Johnson flashes a manic rictus grin throughout), *The Game Plan* is best enjoyed by young children unfamiliar with football. In fact, the gridiron action takes a backseat to numerous scenes of children doing ballet. ESPN personalities Stuart Scott and Steve Levy have cameos, while **Monday Night Football** radio announcers Marv Albert and **Norman Julius "Boomer" Esiason** call the on-screen game action.

Garbage Picking Field Goal Kicking Philadelphia Phenomenon, The

Lightweight 1998 Disney Channel made-for-TV movie starring sitcom fixture Tony Danza as a placekicking prodigy for the Philadelphia Eagles. Danza plays Barney Gorman, a Philadelphia sanitation worker who has developed an uncommonly strong leg after years of kicking the hydraulic lift on his garbage truck. When he kicks a water jug at the city dump in the presence of an Eagles front office executive, he wins a tryout with the team. Barney makes the squad and becomes a nationwide sensation. In the film's highlight, Barney engages in a rib-eating contest with one of his new teammates to the strains of Ennio Morricone's famous title theme to *A Fistful of Dollars*. He also takes time to evangelize on behalf of straight-on kicking, as opposed to **soccer-style kicking**. Fred Stoller (Cousin Gerard from *Everybody Loves Raymond*) plays one of Barney's garbage man friends. Ray Wise (Leland Palmer on *Twin Peaks*) plays the Eagles' demanding new owner. Real-life Eagles owner Jeffrey Lurie has a cameo as a diner patron. **Chris Berman** of ESPN plays himself.

Garrett, Alvin

Diminutive African American wideout of the 1980s and a member of the Washington Redskins' **Smurfs** receiving corps who became the focus of a racial controversy that led to the departure of analyst **Howard Cosell** from the **Monday Night Football** broadcast booth in 1983. "Look at that little monkey run!" Cosell brayed as Garrett carried the ball during the September 5, 1983, *MNF* broadcast. The ill-chosen comment sparked a nationwide firestorm centered on animalistic depictions of blacks in the media, although Cosell later explained that he was only using a term of endearment that he often applied to his own white grandchildren.

Gastineau, Mark

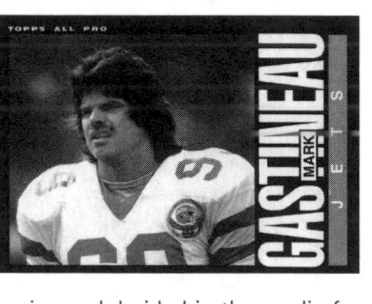

Flamboyant New York Jets defensive end of the 1980s and a charter member of the team's famed **New York Sack Exchange**. An innovator in the art of the **Sack Dance**, Gastineau was widely loathed around the NFL for his on-field posing and derided in the media for his spotlight-hogging marriage to Danish-born actress Brigitte Nielsen.

Gate D Party

Infamous halftime ritual perpetrated by drunken, rowdy New York Jets fans in the 2000s, in which women seeking egress from Gate D at Giants Stadium were exhorted to flash a crowd of male patrons ogling them from a looming spiral column. Women who refused to show their breasts were routinely groped, spit upon, verbally abused, and pelted with beer bottles and rubbish. The humiliating gauntlet of harassment only ceased after videos of some of the incidents were posted on YouTube in the fall of 2007.

Gatorade

Brand-name electrolyte-replenishing sports drink that has long been associated with collegiate and professional sports. (The name Gatorade derives from the nickname for the University of Florida football team, under whose auspices the drink was first developed.) The first NFL team to keep

Gatorade on its sideline was the 1969 Kansas City Chiefs. Their upset victory over the Minnesota Vikings in Super Bowl IV went a long way toward popularizing the product. By 1983, Gatorade was so prevalent it was named the Official Sports Drink of the NFL. Since 1984, the **Gatorade Shower** has been a celebratory postgame ritual leaguewide.

Gatorade Shower

Celebratory sideline tradition in which a team's head coach is ritually doused with a cooler full of **Gatorade** in the closing moments of a win. The Gatorade Shower is associated most strongly in the public mind with Hall of Fame linebacker Harry Carson of the New York Giants, who doused coach **Bill Parcells** after every one of the team's victories during its 1986 Super Bowl season. Giants nose tackle Jim Burt actually executed the first Gatorade Shower on Parcells the previous season in retaliation for Parcells' criticism of his blocking prowess. While most accounts still credit Burt with the ritual's invention, video evidence unearthed in 1999 by the *Chicago Daily Herald* proves conclusively that Chicago Bears defensive lineman Dan Hampton performed the dunk on head coach **Mike Ditka** on November 25, 1984—nearly a full year before Burt picked up the cooler. Gatorade Showers have since become a semi-regular postgame tradition at college and professional football games across the nation. At the peak of the trend in the late 1980s, Parcells reportedly received a $120,000 three-year endorsement stipend from The Quaker Oats Company, makers of Gatorade. While Parcells may have been the most celebrated recipient of the Gatorade Shower, legendary Washington Redskins coach **George Allen** was the most unlucky. In fact, his untimely death at age 72 has been widely attributed to a Gatorade bath he was administered on November 17, 1990. Allen's Long Beach State 49ers had just run out the clock on a season-ending 29–20 victory over UNLV when he was doused by jubilant players. Although there's some question about whether the substance in question was Gatorade or

Audibles

"It's like when you were in school and always used to pick on the chubby guys. That was sort of what we were doing: picking on the chubby guy."

—Gatorade Shower pioneer Jim Burt, on the dousing of Bill Parcells

ice water, coupled with the chilly 50-degree temperatures the liquid gave Allen a bad cold he never could shake. He was admitted to the hospital a few weeks later and died of ventricular fibrillation on New Year's Eve, just over a month after his ill-timed cold bath.

Gay Pirate
See **Bucco Bruce**

Gent, Peter
Iconoclastic Dallas Cowboys wide receiver of the 1960s best known as the author of the semi-autobiographical football novel ***North Dallas Forty***. The book, which exposed the drinking, drugging, pill-popping, and orgy-fueled excesses of the Cowboys under head coach Tom Landry, was later made into a motion picture starring Nick Nolte as a fictionalized version of Gent and country-and-western crooner Mac Davis as a thinly disguised version of quarterback **Don Meredith**.

George, Phyllis
Former Miss America and First Lady of Kentucky who enjoyed a controversial run as one of the founding co-hosts on CBS' ***The NFL Today*** pregame show from 1975 to 1983. Limited in her knowledge of football, the onetime beauty queen specialized in fawning player profiles, puff-piece human interest

Getty Images

stories, and warm-and-fuzzy interviews conducted in a manner reminiscent of Barbara Walters. Among her most celebrated "gets" was a 1975 sit-down with Dallas Cowboys quarterback Roger Staubach, during which the strait-laced former U.S. Navy midshipman rhapsodized about his sex life, comparing it favorably to that of **Joe Namath**. While George's work won her kudos as a pioneering female in the world of sports journalism, her softball approach did not endear her to her co-hosts—especially oddsmaker **Jimmy "the Greek" Snyder**, who repeatedly demeaned George in front of and away from the camera.

Gerela's Gorillas

Ape suit–clad affinity group founded by Pittsburgh Steelers fans of Ukrainian descent to honor the team's popular placekicker of the 1970s, Roy Gerela.

THE UNDERGROUND FOOTBALL ENCYCLOPEDIA

Gerela's Gorillas began decamping in the stands behind the west end zone at Three Rivers Stadium in 1972. Their mission was to cheer on Gerela and to intimidate the opposing team's kicker whenever he attempted a field goal—all while wearing gorilla masks. See also: **Franco's Italian Army**; **Frenchy's Foreign Legion**

Ghost to the Post

Nickname for a legendary pass play that set up the last-minute game-tying field goal in one of the longest games in NFL history—a double-overtime thriller between the Oakland Raiders and the Baltimore Colts played at Memorial Stadium in Baltimore on Christmas Eve, 1977. The "ghost" refers to Oakland tight end Dave Casper, who ran a post pattern and caught a 42-yard pass from quarterback Ken Stabler with time running out in regulation. Kicker Errol Mann's field goal then sent the game into overtime, where the Raiders emerged victorious. Along with the **Immaculate Reception** and the **Sea of Hands** play, Ghost to the Post is considered one of the most dramatic receptions in NFL postseason history.

Gifford, Frank

Freakishly telegenic New York Giants Hall of Famer who parlayed his good looks and association with gridiron glory into a 25-year post-retirement stint as one of the mainstays of the *Monday Night Football* announcing team. A versatile halfback/flanker, Gifford made eight **Pro Bowl**s and five championship games over the course of a 12-year NFL career. He replaced **Keith Jackson** as *MNF*'s lead play-by-play man in 1971, forming a formidable power trio with analysts **Howard Cosell** and **Don Meredith**. In 1986, the arrival of new play-by-play man Al Michaels relegated Gifford to analyst duties. Gifford's squeaky-clean public image received a mortal blow in 1997 when the 66-year-old husband and father was caught on film by a supermarket tabloid in the arms of Suzen Johnson, a buxom flight attendant who bore no resemblance to his wife, perky TV chat show hostess Kathie Lee Gifford. Although "Giff" later claimed he was set up by the paparazzi, the indiscretion was but one of several reasons cited for his exile from the *Monday Night Football* broadcast booth in 1998. (The dreadful on-air chemistry between Gifford and fellow analyst Dan Dierdorf was another.) In a misguided attempt to spare their onetime marquee star from any further embarrassment, *MNF* producers moved Gifford into a nebulous co-hosting role on a new 20-minute pregame show, *Monday Night Blast*, a raucous sports bar party hosted by loud-mouthed ESPN anchor **Chris Berman**. But Gifford looked spectacularly ill at ease in his new assignment and was summarily removed from the broadcast entirely after just one season.

Glanville, Jerry

Colorful NFL head coach of the 1980s and '90s known for his all-black wardrobe and his obsession with Elvis Presley. For years, Glanville would leave two tickets for the King at the will-call window before every game. Before becoming a head coach, Glanville first earned notoriety as the architect of the Atlanta Falcons' Grits Blitz defense of the late 1970s. He also lent his name to *Jerry Glanville's PigSkin Footbrawl*, a bizarre 1990 video game for the Sega Genesis system that features a no-holds-barred, rugby-style version of football played by medieval avatars.

Audibles

"I haven't heard from Elvis since his daughter married Michael Jackson. I think it killed him."

–Jerry Glanville, on why he stopped leaving tickets for Elvis Presley

God of Sod

See **Toma, George**

Gogolak, Pete

Hungarian-born placekicker of the 1960s who is primarily responsible for introducing **soccer-style kicking** to the NFL. Before Gogolak joined the Buffalo Bills in 1964, placekickers invariably approached the ball head-on from directly behind the holder, kicking with a special flat-toed shoe. Gogolak, who had grown up in Budapest watching and playing European "football," approached from the side and kicked with his instep. Gogolak's technique was derided by many at first, but it was eventually popularized by his more stylish successors like Norwegian Jan Stenerud. By the late 1970s, soccer-style kicking had all but displaced straight-ahead kicking from the professional game.

Golden Girls

Old-school, pom-pom waving Green Bay Packers cheerleading squad that entertained crowds at Lambeau Field with choreographed skits, dance routines, twirls, tumbles, and acrobatics from 1961 to 1972. Comprised entirely of clean-cut female dance students from northwestern Wisconsin and attired demurely in one-piece sequined swimsuits and high-heeled boots (reportedly at the behest of Vince Lombardi, who detested short skirts), the squad was organized and led by onetime national baton champion Mary Jane Van Duyse, the inamorata of legendary Packers coach Earl Louis "Curly" Lambeau. Their name is an homage to Packers great "Golden Boy" **Paul Hornung**.

"Good Ol' Days"

Sentimental "We Are the World"–style **music video** recorded by retired members of the Dallas Cowboys as part of a 1986 Christmas video package. "Good Ol' Days" celebrates the golden years of "Staubach and Pearson and Hayes" through the use of vintage game footage, while the actual stars from that era harmonize with headphones cupped to their ears in the manner of Band-Aid's "Do They Know It's Christmas." See also: **"Christmas in Dallas"**

Goodyear Blimp

Branded airship that has flown over American sports venues since 1932. Since 1960, the Goodyear Blimp has been outfitted with cameras in order to provide aerial views of events like the Super Bowl. The blimp is featured prominently in the football-themed movies *Black Sunday* and *Two-Minute Warning*.

"Go! You Packers! Go!"

Official Green Bay Packers **fight song** performed at the team's home games since 1931. It is the oldest professional football fight song in the world. Exhorting the team to "fight and bring the bacon home to old Green Bay," the lyrics came from Eric Karll, a Milwaukee commercial jingle writer who would go on to pen "Welcome, Mr. Roosevelt," a song commemorating President Franklin Delano Roosevelt's 1934 visit to Wisconsin. For many years, the rights to "Go! You Packers! Go!" were owned by bandleader Lawrence Welk, forcing the team to pay the "champagne music" impresario a royalty every time the song was played. See also: **Packer Lumberjack Band**

> "My jump was excellent. It was my landing
> I needed to work on."
>
> **—Bill Gramática**, on the freak jumping accident that
> resulted in a season-ending ACL injury in 2001

Gramática, Bill

Successful Argentine placekicker of the 2000s known for his exuberant, leaping celebrations after made field goals. One such display, in December of 2001, resulted in a torn anterior cruciate ligament that ended Gramática's season. Bill is the younger brother of **Pro Bowl** placekicker Martin "Automatica" Gramática. Together with their younger brother Santiago, they own and operate Gramática SIPS International, an insulated panel manufacturing company based in Sarasota, Florida.

Greatest Show on Turf

Phrase commonly associated with the St. Louis Rams' passing offense of the late 1990s and early 2000s, in reference to the frenetic, circus-like pace set by offensive coordinator Mike Martz. The nickname had originally been bestowed on the run-and-shoot attack of the early 1990s Houston Oilers (and was in fact the title of that team's 1992 highlight film) but today is used almost exclusively to refer to the St. Louis offense under quarterback Kurt Warner, running back Marshall Faulk, and wide receivers Torry Holt and Isaac Bruce.

Green Bay Sideliners

Name used by the Green Bay Packers cheerleaders from 1977 to 1986. Formerly known as the **Packerettes**, the squad was officially disbanded and has never been replaced.

Greene, "Mean" Joe

Hall of Fame defensive lineman of the 1970s who gained additional national exposure through his appearance in one of the most famous Coca-Cola TV commercials of all time. A cornerstone of the Pittsburgh Steelers' famed **Steel Curtain** defense, Greene moonlighted as an actor throughout the late 1970s and early 1980s. He appeared as himself in 1980's *Smokey and the Bandit II* and in a TV movie based

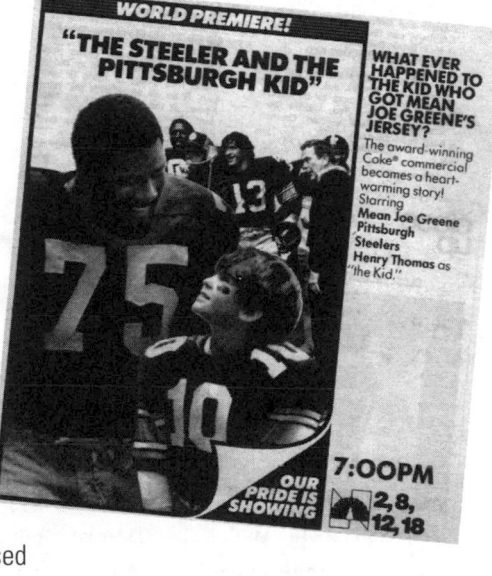

on the life of Steelers teammate Rocky Bleier. But he scored his biggest breakthrough in 1979 when he played off his ornery persona in a popular 60-second Coca-Cola ad that ran during the Super Bowl telecast. In the spot, a scowling, sweat-soaked Greene accepts a postgame bottle of Coke from a wide-eyed nine-year-old boy, played by child actor **Tommy Okon**. The soft drink's miraculous rejuvenative powers quickly put a smile back on Mean Joe's face. In return, he tosses the tyke his game-worn jersey. The

Football by the Numbers | 18

Number of 16-ounce bottles of Coca-Cola **"Mean" Joe Greene** drank on the final day of shooting of his classic 1979 commercial

Field Guide to Zebras

Johnny Grier

Trailblazing NFL official who became the first African American referee in league history in 1988.

commercial proved so popular that it was later expanded into a full-length TV movie, *The Steeler and the Pittsburgh Kid*, with Greene playing himself and *E.T.: The Extra Terrestrial* star Henry Thomas replacing Okon. The 1981 film told the story of the making of the ad and its aftermath.

"Gridiron Heroes"

Official team **fight song** of the Detroit Lions sung at home games every time the Lions score. "Gridiron Heroes" was composed in 1934 on commission from Lions owner G. A. Richards by Graham T. Overgard, leader of the Wayne State University marching band. Overgard, who later became the Lions' director of entertainment, is also the author of "Force of Freedom," the official anthem of the Peace Corps.

Grier, Roosevelt "Rosey"

Pro Bowl defensive tackle of the 1950s and '60s and a member of the Los Angeles Rams' celebrated **Fearsome Foursome** who in retirement earned a reputation as an exceptionally well-rounded "gentle giant." Grier's eclectic interests included acting, singing, community service, and needlepoint. A close personal friend and sometime bodyguard to Senator Robert F. Kennedy, the 6'5", 300-pound Grier was the man who subdued RFK's assassin, Sirhan Sirhan, in the aftermath of the fatal shooting at the Ambassador Hotel in Los Angeles on June 5, 1968. After guest starring on numerous television shows

ROSEY GRIER'S NEEDLEPOINT for men

Audibles

"If you take a look into some needlepoint stores, you'll be in for quite a surprise. Examine the designs, and you'll find that they're bold and free, with designs that range from traditional floral and woods scenes to things that are abstract or even surreal. I've also seen American Indian designs reproduced on canvas. Men are attracted to the more modern geometrics and bold colors—and the more of us who do it, the greater the demand will be for designs with masculine appeal, and the more designs there'll be."

–from the introduction to *Rosey Grier's Needlepoint for Men*

throughout the late 1960s, Grier took up movie acting in the 1970s, appearing in the low-budget sci-fi shocker **The Thing with Two Heads** and the Billy Crystal comedy *Rabbit Test*, among other features. Despite his enormous size, he successfully cultivated the image of a sensitive hulk—in part because of his passion for macramé, which he touted in a 1973 book *Rosey Grier's Needlepoint for Men*. He briefly headlined his own syndicated television variety series, *The Rosey Grier Show*, and crooned a song, "It's All Right to Cry," on the children's album/TV special *Free To Be…You and Me*. After being ordained a Pentecostal minister in 1983, Grier dedicated the remainder of his life to community service and motivational speaking. He played a kindly reverend in fellow Christian sack machine **Reggie White**'s 1997 religious feature **Reggie's Prayer**.

Ground Chuck

Nickname used to describe the conservative, run-first offenses of longtime NFL head coach Chuck Knox.

Gumbo

Affable St. Bernard who has been one of two official **mascots** of the New Orleans Saints since the team's inception in 1967. (The other is **Sir Saint**.) The original Gumbo was a live dog, a gift to the team from the Louisiana Restaurant Association, in recognition of both St. Bernard Parish, Louisiana, near where the Saints play, and the city's signature Cajun stew. Big Easy trumpet legend Al Hirt (a minority owner of the franchise whose nickname, oddly enough, was Jumbo) personally serenaded Gumbo I, as he came to be known, at a welcome luncheon before the team's first home game on September 17, 1967. For the next 18 seasons, Gumbo I and his three descendants roamed the sideline, decked out in Saints apparel or swathed in blankets festooned with the team's fleur-de-lis logo. But the good times did not roll for long. Gumbo I ran away after just four seasons on the job. Gumbo II died suddenly of a mysterious intestinal disorder in 1975. She is remembered primarily for running onto the field of play and chasing Pittsburgh Steelers quarterback **Terry Bradshaw** as he dashed for the end zone during a Monday night game in 1974. Gumbo III took to falling asleep during games and developed a nasty habit of defecating on the carpet at the Louisiana Superdome—a predilection the fourth and final Gumbo inherited and expanded upon. "Every time we brought her onto the field, she'd always take a crap," cackled Larry Dale, the incontinent canine's owner and handler. It was no surprise then when Saints management opted to fire Gumbo midway through the 1985 season. (Dale went on to sue the team for wrongful termination.) New owner Tom Benson later brought back the character— this time in a more controllable costume form—in 1994.

Gus

Tiresome 1976 Disney children's film about a
mule that can kick field goals. *Gus* stars teen
heartthrob Gary Grimes, five years removed
from his star-making role in *The Summer of '42*,
as a dim-witted Yugoslavian goatherd whose
pet mule kicks like the dickens whenever he
hears the shouted command "Oyage!" Ed
Asner plays the owner of the fictional
California Atoms, perennial NFL also-rans
who ride Gus' magic hoof all the way to the

Super Bowl. Don Knotts is woefully miscast as the team's head coach,
with Liberty Williams as Grimes' love interest and Tom Bosley and Tim
Conway as a pair of bumbling ex-cons who attempt to kidnap the mule
before the big game. The film climaxes with an interminable chase sequence
in which Gus rampages through a supermarket. Chicago Bears legend Dick
Butkus has a small role as Grimes' romantic rival, with Johnny Unitas as a
television commentator and Dick Enberg as the Atoms' PA announcer.

"Guy in the Glass, The"

Obscure inspirational poem written by American radio performer Dale
Wimbrow in 1934 and occasionally quoted by legendary NFL coach **Bill
Parcells**. The poem, often mistakenly identified as "The Man in the Glass,"
urges the reader toward a frank and honest self-assessment by the act of
metaphorically looking in the mirror. It concludes with the lines:

> You can fool the whole world down the pathway of years,
> And get pats on the back as you pass,
> But your final reward will be heartaches and tears
> If you've cheated the guy in the glass.

Parcells invariably reads it aloud in the locker room to his teams immediately after announcing he has stepped down as head coach. Al Groh, a Parcells disciple who succeeded him as coach of the New York Jets in 2000, read it to his charges when he quit as head coach at the University of Virginia in December of 2009.

H

Hail Mary

Term typically applied to a long-yardage pass thrown at the end of a game or a half. While such desperation heaves have always been a part of football, the term "Hail Mary" did not come into vogue until the mid-1970s, after Dallas Cowboys quarterback Roger Staubach successfully executed a game-winning, last-minute touchdown pass in a playoff game against the Minnesota Vikings on December 28, 1975. A devout Roman Catholic, Staubach himself coined the term "Hail Mary" in remarks to reporters after the game, when he cited the Ave Maria as the prayer he recited in the huddle before uncorking the 50-yard bomb to wide receiver Drew Pearson.

"Hail to the Redskins"

Official **fight song** of the Washington Redskins played at the team's home games since 1938. It is the second-oldest professional football fight song in the world (only **"Go! You Packers! Go"** is older) and arguably the most well known. "Hail to the Redskins!" goes the chorus to the song. "Hail Victory! Braves on the warpath. Fight for old D.C.!" The original lyrics were somewhat more politically incorrect. The words were written by Corinne Griffith, wife of Redskins founder and owner George Preston Marshall, a ravishing onetime Oscar-nominated silent film actress known as "the Orchid Lady of the Screen." The music was composed by the team's band leader

Audibles

> Hail to the Redskins! Hail to victory!
> Braves on the war path! Fight for old Dixie!
> Scalp 'em, swamp 'em, We will take 'em big score!
> Read 'em, weep 'em, touchdown, We want heaps more!
> Fight on...Fight On...Til you have won, Sons of Washington!
>
> **—lyrics to "Hail to the Redskins"**

Barnee Breeskin, who swiped the melody from an old Christian hymn titled "Yes, Jesus Loves Me." Breeskin retained the rights to the song until the 1950s when he sold them to Clint Murchison, a Texas oil tycoon and would-be NFL owner. Murchison used the rights to the tune as a bargaining chip in his successful quest to extract Marshall's approval for an expansion franchise in Dallas. The Dallas Cowboys would go on to forge a bitter rivalry with the Redskins in the decades to come.

Haley, Charles

Emotionally volatile All-Pro NFL linebacker of the 1980s and '90s known for his reputedly enormous penis and attendant penchant for exhibitionism. According to journalist Jeff Pearlman's tell-all book about the 1990s Dallas Cowboys, *Boys Will Be Boys*, Haley was an inveterate locker room masturbator with a "fire hose"–sized phallus that he enjoyed waving in the faces of teammates. "It got to the point of ejaculation," reported one eyewitness who remembered seeing Haley stroking himself in a meeting while talking openly about having sex with other players' wives. Fittingly, Haley crowned himself with the nickname "the Last Naked Warrior." The five-time Super Bowl champion had other behavioral problems that went beyond his tendency toward exposing himself. As a member of the San Francisco 49ers, he once wiped his sphincter in a team meeting and threw the resulting wad of used toilet paper at defensive line coach John Marshall.

Halftime Shows
See **Jackson, Janet**; **Up With People**

Handley, Ray

Respected NFL assistant whose disastrous two-year stint as the head coach of the New York Giants in the early 1990s epitomized the pitfalls of replacing a living legend. Handley, the Giants' offensive coordinator, was selected over his defensive counterpart **Bill Belichick** to replace the departing **Bill Parcells** in 1991, just months after he led the Giants to their second Super Bowl title. Belichick would go on to a Hall of Fame coaching career with the New England Patriots. By contrast, Handley compiled a 14–18 record over two seasons, presided over a needless quarterback controversy, and had numerous run-ins with the media. Giants fans turned on him, serenading him with chants of "Ray Must Go" and holding up signs that read "From the Super Bowl to the toilet bowl. Thanks, Ray." Handley was fired at the end of the 1992 season and disappeared from football entirely.

Hard Knocks

Popular HBO reality series in which cameras are trained on a single NFL team for the duration of its training camp. The program debuted in 2001 with a look at the preseason preparations of the defending Super Bowl champion Baltimore Ravens. The series achieved new heights of publicity buzz in 2010, a season that featured the New York Jets and a series of profane outbursts by head coach **Rex Ryan** that provided weekly talk radio fodder.

Audibles

"Let's go eat a goddamn snack!"

–New York Jets head coach **Rex Ryan**,
in a memorable scene from the 2010 edition of *Hard Knocks*

HC of NYJ

Inventive shorthand employed by notoriously terse defensive coordinator **Bill Belichick** on the resignation letter he wrote following a one-day stint as head coach of the New York Jets in 2000. Belichick was the Jets' choice to replace the departing **Bill Parcells** that January, but he reportedly got cold feet over the impending sale of the team. Moments before taking the podium at a press conference to announce his hiring, Belichick hastily scrawled the words "I resign as HC of NYJ" on a sheet of looseleaf paper. He then baffled the assembled media with a long, rambling monologue about his reasons for quitting—none of which made any sense. Jets linebacker coach Al Groh eventually replaced him as head coach.

He Hate Me

Distinctive nickname used by journeyman special teams player Rod Smart during his days in the **XFL**. Emboldened by the lack of uniform restrictions in wrestling impresario **Vince McMahon**'s fledgling "extreme" football

league, Smart decided to put the nom-de-gridiron "He Hate Me" on the back of his jersey in a kiss-off to everyone who had doubted his ability over the years. As a running back for the Las Vegas Outlaws in 2001, Smart received copious national television exposure and quickly emerged as the public face of the XFL. The He Hate Me jersey became one of the short-lived league's top sellers. When the XFL folded, Smart leveraged his fame into a five-year career in the NFL. He played in Super Bowl XXXVIII—under his real name—as a member of the Carolina Panthers.

Head-to-Head Football

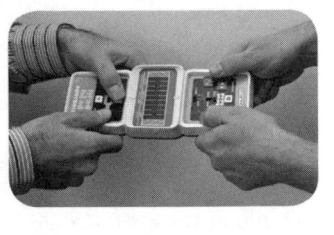

Two-player version of Coleco Electronics' popular handheld football game **Electronic Quarterback**. Released in 1979 as part of a line of two-player handhelds that also included Baseball, Hockey, Basketball, and Soccer, it was billed as the first handheld football game to offer "real competition." A character can be seen playing Coleco Head-to-Head Football in the 1981 stoner comedy *Cheech and Chong's Nice Dreams*.

Heaven Can Wait

Critically acclaimed 1978 romantic comedy starring Warren Beatty as a deceased backup quarterback for the Los Angeles Rams. Beatty plays Joe Pendleton, a saxophone-tooting second-stringer who is spirited away from a gruesome auto accident by an overeager angel who doesn't realize that Pendleton isn't scheduled to die for another five decades. Deprived of his true destiny, Pendleton is given a second chance at life in the body of billionaire industrialist Leo Farnsworth. He makes the most of the opportunity by romancing a visiting Brit, played by Julie Christie, and enlisting a Rams trainer to help arrange a tryout with the team in time for the upcoming Super

Bowl. Several retired Rams, including **Deacon Jones** and Jack Snow, have cameos in the Oscar-nominated film. NFL broadcasters Dick Enberg, Curt Gowdy, Al DeRogatis, and Bryant Gumbel (sporting an enormous Afro) also appear as themselves. Field and locker room footage was filmed at the Los Angeles Coliseum before a **Monday Night Football** game between the Rams and the Minnesota Vikings on October 24, 1977. A remake of the 1941 non-football film *Here Comes Mr. Jordan, Heaven Can Wait* was remade again—this time with Chris Rock playing the lead character as a stand-up comic—as *Down to Earth* in 2001.

"Heavy Action"

Full title of the instrumental theme music to ABC/ESPN's **Monday Night Football** telecast, whose majestic "duh duh duh DUH" hook has become a competitive call to arms the world over. The quintessential American sports theme was actually composed by an Englishman, Johnny Pearson, whose other notable credit is the title theme to the twee veterinary drama *All Creatures Great and Small*. Pearson wrote "Heavy Action" in 1970 on commission for the BBC sports competition series *Superstars*. In 1971, ABC acquired the rights to the theme and began using it on the opening credits of its *Monday Night Football* broadcasts. The music was also heard underneath analyst **Howard Cosell**'s popular halftime highlights segment. While almost universally beloved as the authoritative *MNF* title theme, since the early 1990s "Heavy Action" has played second fiddle to **Hank Williams Jr.**'s grating country rock rave-up **"All My Rowdy Friends Are Here for Monday Night."** Veteran TV theme composer Edd Kalehoff updated the arrangement of "Heavy Action" when *MNF* moved to ESPN in 2006.

Heidi Game

Infamous 1968 **AFL** telecast that was marred by NBC's ill-starred decision to cut away from the thrilling final moments of a critical game between the New York Jets and the Oakland Raiders to show the opening minutes of the heart-warming family TV movie *Heidi*. The Jets were leading 32–29 with less than a minute to play in a crucial contest played at the Oakland-Alameda County Coliseum on November 17, 1968. The Raiders had the ball and quarterback Daryle Lamonica was fading back to pass when the game feed suddenly disappeared from television sets across the country. After a station break, *Heidi*, starring Jennifer Edwards as the lovable pigtailed pixie from Johanna Spyrie's children's book series, began to unspool to howls of outrage from football fans (and anxious bettors) everywhere. A flood of angry phone calls—estimated at more than 10,000—well-nigh melted the NBC switchboard. Network sports executives were left scrambling to get in touch with technicians who were acting under strict orders to cut out of any game that exceeded its three-hour time window, for fear of alienating Timex, *Heidi*'s sponsor. As it turned out, the football audience had way more to gripe about. The Raiders ended up winning the game in a remarkable comeback that saw them score two touchdowns in just 19 seconds. Fallout from the Heidi Game prompted the NFL to revise its agreement with the broadcast networks to ensure that every game remained on the air to its conclusion. And thanks to the loud public display of annoyance, AFL rooters came away with documentary evidence that their league was no longer the weak sister to the NFL when it came to generating television interest. As a result, NBC was able to raise its ad rate for AFL telecasts to bring it closer to parity with the rate charged for CBS NFL telecasts.

Henderson, Mark

Massachusetts burglar who famously cleared a path for New England Patriots placekicker John Smith during the controversial **Snowplow Game** in 1982.

Henderson, Thomas "Hollywood"

Flamboyant, trash-talking, cocaine-snorting Dallas Cowboys linebacker of the 1970s renowned for his high opinion of his own game and his lack of regard for his opponents. The self-described "best linebacker ever to play pro football" once observed of Steelers quarterback **Terry Bradshaw** that he "couldn't spell cat if you spotted him the 'c' and the 'a.'" He drew the ire of Cowboys coach Tom Landry for partying with the Pointer Sisters before games and sniffing vaporized cocaine out of a nasal inhaler on the sideline during them. After retiring from the NFL in 1980, Henderson served more than two years in prison for having sex with underage girls. He would eventually clean up his act and publish a tell-all memoir, *Out of Control: Confessions of an NFL Casualty*, in 1990.

"Here We Go"

Bass-driven novelty song, composed in 1994 by Richland, Pennsylvania, real estate investor Roger Wood and adopted by Pittsburgh Steelers fans as the team's unofficial **fight song** ever since. "Here we go, Steelers, here we go," goes the song's simplistic but irresistibly catchy chorus. "Pittsburgh's goin' to the Super Bowl." "Here We Go" has sold more than 150,000 copies since its initial release, making it one of the top-selling locally produced singles of all time. Wood regularly updates the lyrics to reflect changes in the team's personnel.

Audibles

"I can listen to the song again and again. It is like a Christmas carol. You never, ever get sick of it."

—Roger Wood, composer of the unofficial national anthem of Steelers Nation, "Here We Go"

Audibles

"Let's go out with some dignity and show 'em we're not a bunch of horses' asses!"

—Leon Hess, in an address to his 2-9 Jets before a 1995 game against the Seattle Seahawks

Hess, Leon

Elderly gas station magnate who served as principal owner of the New York Jets from 1977 until his death in 1999. Although he was a minority owner during the Jets' **Joe Namath**–led glory years of the late 1960s and early '70s, Hess came to be associated in the public mind with the franchise's long stretch of futility under head coaches like Joe Walton, Bruce Coslet, and Rich Kotite. One of the last of the old-school paternalistic owners, his hands-off management style endeared him to players and team employees.

Hogettes

Band of cross-dressing, pig nose–wearing Washington Redskins **superfans** who have led the cheering section at the team's home games since November of 1983. Originally there were 11 Hogettes, organized by the

Field Guide to Zebras

Ed Hochuli
Highly regarded NFL official, easily recognized by television viewers for his surprisingly buff physique which he accentuates with his penchant for wearing extremely snug shirts. Hochuli's bulging biceps, the product of a rigorous four-day-a-week weightlifting regimen, have won him a large online cult following, as exemplified by the website WhatWouldEdHochuliDo.com. His nickname around the league is "Hochules."

group's founder, **Michael "Mikey T." Torbert** (also known as Boss Hogette), who got the idea to don women's clothing at an especially ribald Halloween party. He soon began recruiting friends and family members to join him in the stands at Redskins games, attired in frowsy

polka-dot dresses and pig snouts chosen to honor the team's vaunted offensive line, known as the **Hogs**. Protected from imitation by a registered trademark, the Hogettes continue to appear regularly at charity events in the Washington, D.C., area.

Hog Heaven

List of Current and Former Hogettes

Michael "Boss Hogette" Torbert
Ralph "Grandpaw Hogette" Campbell
Michael "Big Macette" McCartney
Joe "Joevette" Varnadore
George "Big Georgette" Maxfield
Bruce "Porkchop" Lindsay
Edward J. "Edette" Heid III
William J. "Stoneyette" Stoner Sr.
Howard "Howiette" Churchill
David "Spiggy" Spigler
Eddie "Hog Ed" Souder
Nick "Nickette" Nerangis
David D. "Davette" Torbert
Michael "P Wee" Wright
Michael D. "Mikette" Wade
Mike "Hollywood Hillbilly" Gardner

Hogs

Nickname for the Washington Redskins offensive line of the early 1980s, a legendarily porcine group of blockers comprised of tackles Joe Jacoby and George Starke, guards Russ Grimm and Mark May, center Jeff Bostic, and tight ends Don Warren and Rick Walker. The term "Hogs" was coined by offensive line coach Joe Bugel, who strode around the team's practice facility one morning in 1982 exhorting his charges to hit the blocking sleds harder with shouts of "Okay, you Hogs, let's get running down there." Bruising running back **John Riggins** was considered by many to be an honorary Hog.

Holtz, Lou

Legendary college coach whose lone disastrous season in the NFL became a template for subsequent failed transitions to the professional ranks, like those of Steve Spurrier and Nick Saban. After successful stints at William & Mary and North Carolina State, Holtz went 3–10 with the 1976 New York Jets and established a reputation as an eccentric martinet. He slept in a cot in his office, lined up his players by size during the National Anthem, and distributed sheet music for a proposed team **fight song**, which players summarily tossed in the garbage. Convinced that his rah-rah style would never work in the NFL, Holtz quit with one game left on the schedule, saying "God did not put Lou Holtz on this earth to coach in the pros." Twelve years later, returned to his natural element, he led Notre Dame to its 11th national championship.

Audibles

Win the game, fight like men, We're together win or lose, New York Jets go rolling along...And where e'er we go, We'll let the critics know, That the Jets are here to stay.

–lyrics to **Lou Holtz**'s proposed New York Jets **fight song**, sung to the tune of "The Caissons Go Rolling Along"

Holy Roller

Infamous "forward fumble" play that resulted in a controversial victory for the Oakland Raiders over the San Diego Chargers in a game played at San Diego Stadium on September 10, 1978. Trailing by six points with seconds left, the Raiders were facing a second down deep in San Diego territory when quarterback Ken Stabler avoided a game-ending sack by purposely fumbling the ball forward. Running back Pete Banaszak and tight end Dave Casper then pretended to try to pick up the football, batting it over the goal line and into the end zone, where Casper recovered it for a game-tying touchdown. Errol Mann's extra point at the end of regulation sealed the win for the Raiders. After howls of protest from Chargers backers—in San Diego, the play is known as the Immaculate Deception—the NFL instituted a rules change forbidding teams from advancing fumbles in this manner during the last two minutes of a game.

Honey Bears

Official cheerleading squad of the Chicago Bears from 1977 to 1985. The Honey Bears were the brainchild of franchise owner **"Papa Bear"** George Halas, who wanted his team to have a bodacious dancing pep squad to compete with the **Dallas Cowboys Cheerleaders**. In 1985, two years after Halas' death, the Bears' new owners announced plans to disband the Honey Bears after the season. They gave their final performance at Super Bowl XX in January of 1986, dancing to Prince's "Baby, I'm a Star." The fact that the Bears have not won a Super Bowl since has led to the dissemination of an urban legend that a "Honey Bear Curse" now afflicts the franchise.

Honey Shot

Term of art used by television directors to refer to a close-up of a pom-pom-waving cheerleader or an attractive woman in the stands at a football game. Most historians credit the invention of the honey shot to ABC's **Andy**

Getty Images

Sidaris, a onetime *Wide World of Sports* director pressed into service on the network's college football telecasts in the mid-1970s. The use of honey shots, which has since become widespread on NFL telecasts, is widely credited with sparking the worldwide celebrity of the **Dallas Cowboys Cheerleaders**. One of the first honey shots to inspire national water cooler conversation occurred on November 10, 1975, during a ***Monday Night Football*** game between the Kansas City Chiefs and the Dallas Cowboys. In the middle of that telecast, Sidaris reportedly ordered his cameramen to pan Texas Stadium looking for especially well-endowed cheerleaders, using the barked command "Okay, find the honeys!" The director then repeatedly returned to shots of one cheerleader in particular, a winking blonde whom he claimed was "having sex with the camera." A similar shot, this time of a winking brunette, captivated audiences during CBS' coverage of Super Bowl X between the Cowboys and the Pittsburgh Steelers in January of 1976. **Jenn Sterger**, a future object of **Brett Favre**'s attention, was also introduced to America by a honey shot during a Florida State–Miami college football game in 2005.

Hook and Lateral

Rarely executed trick play in which a receiver runs a "hook" pattern, catches a forward pass, and then immediately laterals to a teammate streaking down the field to the consternation of would-be tacklers. Often erroneously referred to as a "hook and ladder," the play relies on precise timing between the two offensive players handling the ball. Consequently, there is a high risk of turnover. One of the most memorable hook and laterals in NFL history occurred on January 2, 1982, during an AFC divisional playoff game between the San Diego Chargers and the Miami Dolphins. Dolphins wideout Duriel Harris and running back Tony Nathan successfully executed the lateral exchange, which capped a dramatic first-half Miami comeback.

Hopper, Dennis

Late maverick Hollywood filmmaker of the 1960s who entertained football fans of the 1990s with a series of bizarre Nike commercials in which he played **Stanley Craver**, a deranged, jock-sniffing NFL referee.

Horn, Joe

See **Cell Phone Incident**

Hornung, Paul

Hall of Fame halfback of the 1950s and '60s known as "the Golden Boy" for his blond hair and movie star looks. A versatile fixture of the Green Bay Packers in their Kennedy Era glory years, Hornung excelled running coach Vince Lombardi's unstoppable power sweep. Off the field, he cultivated a libertine persona, famously telling Lombardi at one point he preferred being a playboy to a football player. That lifestyle finally caught up to him in 1963, when Hornung and pal **Alex Karras** were suspended by NFL commissioner Pete Rozelle for admitting that they occasionally bet on football games. The two players were reinstated after 11 months of league probation.

I

I Am Third

Autobiography by Hall of Fame running back Gale Sayers published in 1971. The memoir's depiction of the unlikely friendship between Sayers and his terminally ill Chicago Bears teammate Brian Piccolo provided the basis for the acclaimed "guy cry" television movie ***Brian's Song***.

Ice Bowl

Popular term for the 1967 NFL Championship Game, the most famous **bad weather game** in NFL history, played between the Dallas Cowboys and the Green Bay Packers at Lambeau Field in Green Bay on December 31, 1967. The ambient air temperature at game time was 13 degrees below zero with a wind chill of minus 48 degrees Fahrenheit. Referee Norm Schachter's whistle froze to his lips before the opening kickoff. Due to the malfunctioning of a vaunted underground heating system installed at the behest of Green Bay head coach Vince Lombardi, the entire game was played on rock-hard frozen turf that resembled an ice skating rink. The inability of running backs to find purchase for their cleats ended up factoring in the outcome of the game, when Packers quarterback Bart Starr elected to attempt a goal-line quarterback sneak instead of a handoff in the final seconds with the home team trailing by three. The Packers prevailed 21–17 and went on to win their second Super Bowl title.

Ickey

Nickname bestowed in childhood on Elbert Woods, Cincinnati Bengals running back of the 1980s, by his older brother Rodney. The distinctive moniker reflected young Rodney's inability to pronounce the name Elbert, which he routinely vocalized as "Eeee-eee," and which the boys' parents later recast as "Ickey."

Ickey Shuffle

Whimsical **end zone dance** that made rookie running back Elbert "**Ickey**" Woods of the Cincinnati Bengals a national folk hero in 1988. Woods performed the first Ickey Shuffle during a game against the Cleveland Browns on September 25, 1988, at Riverfront Stadium in Cincinnati. "My Prerogative" by Bobby Brown was at the top of the pop music charts at the time and Woods had worked out a few dance steps to go with the song. With his mother

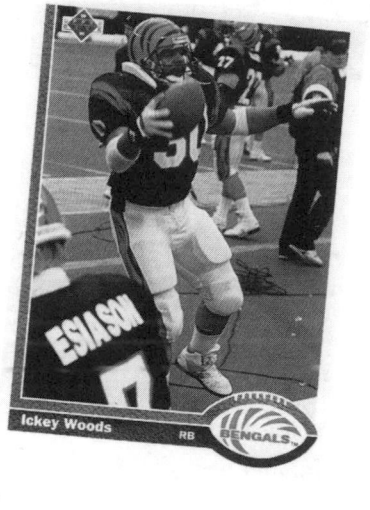

Ickey Woods   RB

in town to watch him play in an NFL game for the first time, he decided to break out his new moves the next time he scored a touchdown. The resulting Shuffle consisted of an alternating sequence of left-right steps, followed by three hops, a spike of the football, and a finger twirl accompanied by the refrain "Woo woo woo!" Woods wound up performing his touchdown dance 15 times that season as he rushed for 1,066 yards and led the Bengals to the Super Bowl. While some detractors criticized the Ickey Shuffle for its perceived lack of rhythm—one wag derided it as "unblack"—it quickly became a nationwide sensation. NASCAR driver Darrell Waltrip did an Ickey

Audibles

He shakes it to the left
He shakes it to the right
He dances in the end zone
Like his underwear's too tight

–lyrics to a novelty song inspired by the **Ickey Shuffle**

Shuffle in victory lane after winning the Daytona 500. A Cincinnati restaurant started serving an Ickey Shake. And the Arthur Murray Dance Studio added the dance to its curriculum. The next year, Woods tore his anterior cruciate ligament in the second game of the season and all but vanished from football. He retired in 1991 at the age of 25 and became a door-to-door salesman for Omaha Steaks. According to published reports, he occasionally performed the Ickey Shuffle for prospective customers.

Immaculate Deception
See **Holy Roller**

Immaculate Reception

Nickname given to the miraculous play that ended the divisional playoff game between the Oakland Raiders and the Pittsburgh Steelers at Three Rivers Stadium in Pittsburgh on December 23, 1972. The Raiders led 7–6 with 22 seconds to go when Pittsburgh quarterback **Terry Bradshaw** threw a desperate fourth-down pass to John "Frenchy" Fuqua from his own 40-yard line. Oakland safety **Jack "the Assassin" Tatum** collided with Fuqua just as the ball arrived, sending the carom floating high into the air and into the waiting arms of running back Franco Harris, who galloped in for the winning touchdown. The Raiders protested that the ball had deflected

Audibles

"If a defensive player touches pass first, or simultaneously with or subsequent to its having been touched by only one eligible offensive player, then all offensive players become and remain eligible."

–passage from the 1972 NFL rulebook that would have negated the **Immaculate Reception**

off of Fuqua, negating the reception, but officials ruled that it was last touched by Tatum. Although the Steelers lost the AFC Championship Game to the Miami Dolphins the following week, the Immaculate Reception is widely credited with ushering in their four–Super Bowl golden era of the 1970s. Coinage of the nickname, a play on the Roman Catholic doctrine regarding the supposed sinlessness of the Virgin Mary, is attributed to Pittsburgh-area leather goods purveyor Michael Ord, who led a postgame toast to Harris' score at a local tavern with the words "From here on, this day will forever be known as the Feast of the Immaculate Reception."

Invincible

Inspirational 2006 feature film loosely based on the exploits of 30-year-old Philadelphia Eagles rookie **Vince Papale**. Erstwhile Funky Buncher Mark Wahlberg plays Papale, who rose from the obscurity of semipro football to became a folk hero in Philadelphia after he unexpectedly made the city's NFL squad in 1976. Curiously, the movie alters a number of key details of Papale's life in an effort to give his story an even more *Rocky*-like, against-

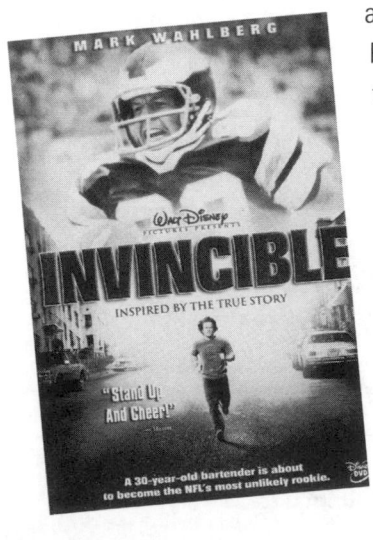

all-odds arc. It eliminates any mention of Papale's considerable playing experience in the **WFL** and elsewhere and substitutes a fictitious all-comers open tryout for the private workout with head coach Dick Vermeil that Papale actually received. Despite the liberties taken, Wahlberg's earnest performance and the inspired casting of Greg Kinnear as Vermeil make *Invincible* one of Disney's more successful football films—especially when compared to the execrable *Gus*.

Ironhead

Distinctive nickname bestowed on Craig Heyward, a **Pro Bowl** running back of the 1980s and '90s, in recognition of his exceedingly large, hard head. The punishing back wore a size 8¾ helmet, with which he became notorious for bludgeoning the abdomens of would-be tacklers. Legends abounded about the supposed hardness of Heyward's noggin, including one that claimed he had once been struck over the head with a pool cue— breaking the cue in half.

Irsay, Bob

Miserly, dyspeptic longtime owner of the Baltimore Colts, reviled in that city for moving the team to Indianapolis in the middle of the night. In the wee morning hours of March 29, 1984, moving trucks rolled into the Colts' Owings Mills, Maryland, headquarters to spirit away all the franchise's equipment and assets to its new home in Indiana. The audacious move, the product of secret negotiations between Irsay and city leaders in Indianapolis, represented the culmination of a five-year dispute between the owner and the Maryland state legislature over requested improvements at dilapidated Memorial Stadium. It came just two months after an apparently inebriated Irsay appeared at a press conference, vowing to keep the Colts in Baltimore and declaring "This is my goddamn team."

Irwindale

Blighted Southern California city that was fleeced out of $10 million by Los Angeles Raiders owner **Al Davis** as part of a mid-1980s franchise relocation boondoggle. The municipality, home to numerous abandoned gravel pits, successfully wooed Davis into accepting a $105 million stadium deal in 1987—contingent on little else beside his word that he would move his team out of the Los Angeles Coliseum and into one of the disused quarries. The deal eventually unraveled in a flurry of lawsuits and accusations that saw Davis pocket a nonrefundable $10 million check granted to him by the city as a good faith gesture. The peripatetic owner eventually relocated the Raiders back to their original home in Oakland.

Isotoner

Brand of winter gloves endorsed by Hall of Fame quarterback Dan Marino in a popular series of television commercials from the 1990s. The ads depicted a grinning Marino doling out fleecy mittens to his offensive linemen and concluded with the tagline, "Take care of the hands that take care of you."

J

Jackson, Bo

Legendary two-sport star of the 1980s and '90s and the first man ever to achieve All-Star status in both baseball and football. A running back selected first overall in the 1986 NFL Draft, Jackson considered football a hobby, although he arguably received more notoriety for one ***Monday Night Football*** performance than for his eight seasons of success in Major League Baseball. That showcase game came on November 30, 1987, when Jackson ran for 221 yards for the Los Angeles Raiders in a victory over the Seahawks at the Kingdome in Seattle. The evening's highlight came on Jackson's third and final touchdown, when he bulldozed overhyped draft bust **Brian Bosworth**—an outspoken critic of Jackson's who spent the week leading up to the game talking trash about him. The hit cemented Jackson's status as a pop icon and ground into fine powder what little remained of Bosworth's credibility as an athlete. Although his NFL career came to an abrupt end as the result of a hip injury in 1990, Jackson's legend lived on in the form of the ubiquitous "Bo Knows" ad campaign of the early 1990s. Jackson's digital avatar, Tecmo Bo, was a dominant figure in the popular football video game ***Tecmo Super Bowl***.

Jackson, Janet

Scion of a pop music dynasty who famously scandalized the planet by exposing her right breast during a halftime performance at Super Bowl XXXVIII on February 1, 2004. Jackson was performing a duet of "Rock Your Body" with Justin Timberlake when the onetime N'Sync heartthrob turned Caucasian funkmeister reached out and peeled back a portion of her bustier, allowing her nipple-shielded teat to pop free. The so-called "Wardrobe Malfunction" ignited a national firestorm. CBS, which televised the Super

AP Images

Bowl that year, was inundated with complaints from viewers—35,000 of whom reportedly signed up for the TiVo recording service so they could document their outrage through endless replayings. Jackson later apologized for the incident, calling it "an accident."

Jackson, Keith

Folksy Georgia-born play-by-play man best known for his work on ABC college football telecasts. Jackson, whose prior professional football broadcasting experience was limited to calling several **AFL** games in the early 1960s, was also behind the mike for the inaugural season of ***Monday Night Football*** in 1970. He got the assignment only after **Frank Gifford** couldn't extricate himself from his contract with CBS. Jackson lasted just one season on the ABC prime-time showcase, a tenure lowlighted by the night **Howard Cosell** set his pants on fire with a carelessly discarded cigarette butt. After being replaced by Gifford in time for the 1971 season, Jackson confined himself to college football, basketball, and baseball telecasts for the rest of the 1970s. In the 1980s, he re-emerged as the lead play-by-play man on ABC's telecasts of the **USFL**. His catchphrase is "Whoa Nelly!" Actor Shuler Hensley played Jackson in the 2002 made-for-cable television movie ***Monday Night Mayhem***.

Jacksonville ROAR

Official name of the Jacksonville Jaguars cheerleading squad, which has revved up the crowd at home games since the franchise's inception in 1995.

Jaxson de Ville

Trash-talking, sunglass-wearing, anthropomorphized big cat who has been the official mascot of the Jacksonville Jaguars since 1996. Known informally as the bad boy of NFL **mascots**, Jaxson de Ville has often courted controversy with his penchant for antagonizing the Jaguars' opponents.

During a game against the Atlanta Falcons in 1996, the yellow-and-teal feline could be seen shaking the goalposts before a Morten Andersen field-goal attempt that would have eliminated the Jaguars from the

Michelle Smith

playoffs. Andersen ended up missing the kick. Two years later, in a game against the Steelers, the irritating mascot put on a veritable clinic of bad sportsmanship. He repeatedly trespassed on the field of play while the Steelers were in their offensive huddle, taunting the players, and, at one point, pummeling and stomping on a life-sized mannequin of Steelers quarterback Kordell Stewart, who was just a few feet away. At another point, the irritating mascot mimed wiping his behind and armpits with the Steelers' venerable **Terrible Towel**. A 2007 confrontation with members of the Indianapolis Colts prompted Colts president Bill Polian to lodge an official complaint with the league about Jaxson's antics. The NFL responded by adopting a rule stipulating that team mascots must stay behind the six-foot white sideline border at all times during the game "and they are prohibited from engaging in any acts of taunting opposing players, coaches, or game officials." Besides getting under opposing players' skin, Jaxson de Ville has become famous for his theatrical and sometimes dangerous entrances into Jacksonville's EverBank Field. At various times he has bungee jumped off a bank of lights, rappelled down from the scoreboard, and parachuted onto the field of play. On at least two occasions, the mascot's flair for the dramatic has put life and limb in jeopardy. While charging out of the locker room with the Jaguars before a game with the Tennessee Titans in 2008, Jaxson de Ville got a little too close to a pyrotechnic display, causing his ears to catch on fire. In 2009, he got caught suspended upside down over the 50-yard line for several minutes while attempting to zip-line across the stadium. He had to be lowered down by stadium security.

Jerry Maguire

Oscar-nominated, catchphrase-laden romantic comedy about a floundering sports agent and the single mother who loves him. Tom Cruise plays the titular player representative, whose roster of clients dwindles to one after he has an outbreak of conscience. Cuba Gooding Jr. won the Academy Award for Best Supporting Actor for his portrayal of Rod Tidwell, the cocky Arizona Cardinals wide receiver who sticks with Maguire as his agent's fortunes decline. Several lines from the film—"You had me at hello," "Help me help you," and, most notably, "Show me the money!"—became national conversational touchstones. (Sadly, others, like "I didn't shoplift the pootie," did not.) The 1996 film features multiple cameos by NFL personalities of the era, including Troy Aikman, Drew Bledsoe, Wayne Fontes, and the then–*Monday Night Football* announcing crew of **Frank Gifford**, Al Michaels, and Dan Dierdorf.

Jerry-Tron

Nickname bestowed by the media on the 9,000-square-foot high-definition video display board at Cowboys Stadium in Dallas. The name is a winking reference to Cowboys owner Jerry Jones, who came up with the idea while attending a Celine Dion concert at Caesar's Palace in Las Vegas. The 72-foot-high, 160-foot-long center-hung screen, said to be the world's biggest in-stadium video board, weighs more than 1 million pounds and cost $40 million to install—more than it cost to build the entire facility the Cowboys used to call home, Texas Stadium. The Mitsubishi-manufactured monstrosity, which debuted with the opening of the Cowboys' new stadium in 2009, began to generate controversy almost immediately. During the preseason,

Arthur LeBon

Football by the Numbers | **30,000,000**

Number of light bulbs required to illuminate **Jerry-Tron**

several punts caromed off Jerry-Tron, prompting NFL commissioner Roger Goodell to issue an edict declaring that any down disrupted by the board would be replayed.

Joe Namath Show, The

Short-lived primetime talk show hosted by New York Jets star quarterback **Joe Namath** that aired on some 45 syndicated television stations starting on October 10, 1969. Chainsmoking sports journalist Dick Schaap—often clad in loud plaid slacks—served as second banana on the alcohol-fueled chatfest, which saw Namath schmoozing it up with various athletic and literary VIPs while sipping whiskey out of a poorly disguised coffee mug. (The tinkle of ice in Broadway Joe's cup was routinely captured by the microphones.) Miniskirted actress/model Louisa Moritz was on hand to provide jiggle in the manner of Goldie Hawn on *Laugh-In*. Notable guests included Woody Allen, Muhammad Ali, Truman Capote, and Maximillian Schell. Discussions often centered on Namath's favorite topics: booze, "broads," the ethical problems posed by sports gambling (Namath discerned none), and whatever publication or sportswriter had written something unkind about the quarterback that week. Namath's obvious discomfort on

Audibles

"We were the drinkingest show in television."

–Larry Spangler, producer of *The Joe Namath Show*

camera proved both a blessing and a curse. *The New York Times* praised the half-hour for its "amateurish naturalness," while *Time* magazine found it "infuriatingly engaging." Sadly, the show lasted only 15 weeks, although it has gained a cult following thanks to repeated airings on the retro-themed sports cable channel ESPN Classic.

John 3:16

Biblical verse often cited on signage by fans at professional football games. The full text of the verse, from the Gospel According to John in the King James version, reads as follows: "For God so loved the world, that he gave his only begotten Son, that whosoever believeth in him should not perish, but have everlasting life." Bewigged born-again Christian Rollen Frederick Stewart, better known to the world as **Rainbow Man**, is widely credited with popularizing the display of John 3:16 signs at arenas nationwide.

Johnson, Billy "White Shoes"

Popular NFL wide receiver and kickoff returner of the 1970s, famed for his alabaster footwear and innovation in the art of the **end zone dance**. A native of Boothwyn, Pennsylvania, Johnson first began dying his cleats white in high school. When his coach asked him why, he claimed they made him run faster. Though undersized at 5'9", he was drafted in the 15th round by the Houston Oilers in 1974. He caught 29 passes for 388 yards in his rookie season and quickly emerged as one of the league's most dangerous return specialists. But he did not achieve folk hero status until he made the decision to entertain bored Astrodome fans by dancing his so-called rubber legs dance, a variation on cape-

wearing soul man Rufus Thomas' **Funky Chicken**, in the end zone after each touchdown. Eventually rebranded "the White Shoes Shuffle," it was the first true end zone dance, paving the way for such successors as the Washington Redskins' **Fun Bunch**, the Atlanta Falcons' **Dirty Bird**, and the choreographed gyrations of Cincinnati Bengal Chad **Ochocinco**.

Johnson, Bob

Onetime mule wrangler for the Kansas City A's baseball team who enjoyed a long tenure as the Indian regalia-clad rider of **Warpaint**, the Kansas City Chiefs' live paint horse mascot.

Johnson, Chad

See **Ochocinco**

Johnson, Suzen

See **Gifford, Frank**

Jones, Deacon

Hulking Hall of Fame defensive end, nicknamed "the Secretary of Defense," who cultivated a short-lived acting and singing career in the 1960s and '70s. Born David Jones, the 6'5", 260-pound Florida native christened himself "Deacon" for no other reason than, he said, "nobody would ever remember a player named David Jones." Considered one of the most prolific pass

---

Audibles

"I've got to be the baddest dude I know of."

–Deacon Jones

rushers in NFL history, Jones innovated in his use of the head slap to bewilder and annoy his opponents. He is widely credited with coining the term "quarterback sack," an homage, he said, to the devastation caused by the sacking of Rome by Barbarian tribes. Like his fellow linemen **Roosevelt "Rosey" Grier** and **Bubba Smith**, Jones had a brief brush with Hollywood fame in his post-NFL days, appearing on the television shows *Bewitched*, ***The Brady Bunch***, *ALF*, and ***The Odd Couple***, and in several feature films. He was one of the original **Lite All-Stars** and briefly fronted the L.A. funk combo Night Shift (later known as WAR).

Jones, Ed "Too Tall"

Towering All-Pro defensive end of the 1970s and a cornerstone of the second edition of the Dallas Cowboys' famed **Doomsday Defense**. At 6'9" the aptly nicknamed Jones was nearly half a foot taller than linemates Harvey Martin, Larry Cole, and Randy "the Manster" White.

Jones, Homer

Middling wide receiver of the 1960s widely credited with ushering in the era of **end zone celebration** through his invention of the touchdown spike in 1965. Jones' original idea was to celebrate a score by throwing the ball into the stands in emulation of his New York Giants teammates **Frank Gifford** and Alex Webster. But he feared being fined by the NFL and opted to drive the football into the turf instead.

Jones, Wilford

See **Crazy Ray**

Juranitch, Joseph

See **Ragnar**

K

Kalas, Harry

Late Philadelphia sports broadcaster who succeeded **John Facenda** as the voice of **NFL Films** after Facenda's death in 1984. The beloved longtime radio voice of baseball's Philadelphia Phillies, "Harry the K" also supplied the narration for the highlight packages run on HBO's *Inside the NFL* from 1977 to 2008. From 2005 to 2009, he served as the host of Animal Planet's Puppy Bowl—a canine competition programmed annually opposite the Super Bowl telecast.

Kapp, Joe

Journeyman Mexican American professional quarterback of the 1960s and '70s best known for being proclaimed the NFL's "toughest Chicano" on the cover of a 1970 issue of *Sports Illustrated*. Kapp led the Minnesota Vikings to their first Super Bowl appearance in 1970, becoming the only player ever to appear in the Rose Bowl, the Super Bowl, and Canada's Grey Cup. After retiring from the NFL in 1971, Kapp made frequent cameo appearances in football movies throughout the decade, including **The Longest Yard**, **Two-Minute Warning**, and **Semi-Tough**. In the 1980s, he gave up acting and entered the college coaching ranks. In 1986, he was fired from his post as head coach at the University of California for exposing himself during a press conference.

Kardiac Kids

Collective nickname for the 1980 Cleveland Browns in recognition of the young team's penchant for heart attack–inducing come-from-behind victories. Led by head coach Sam Rutigliano and quarterback Brian Sipe, the 1980 Browns also staved off numerous comeback attempts en route to an 11–5 record and their first division title since 1971. They were in position to notch another last-second victory in the divisional playoff game against the Oakland Raiders until Rutigliano's infamous **Red Right 88** play call resulted in the interception that ended the Browns' Cinderella season.

Karras, Alex

Pro Bowl defensive tackle of the 1960s who later pursued a career as an actor, most notably as **Mongo**, the slow-witted strongman in the 1974 Mel Brooks comedy *Blazing Saddles*. A first-round draft pick of the Detroit Lions in 1958, Karras moonlighted as a professional wrestler during the early years of his pro football career. In 1963, he was suspended by the league for one season for betting on NFL games along with Green Bay Packers star **Paul Hornung**. After retiring in 1970, Karras tried his

hand at broadcasting (he spent three years as an analyst on *Monday Night Football*) and show business (debuting as himself in the 1968 movie adaptation of George Plimpton's **Paper Lion**). He had guest starring roles on the TV sitcoms *M*A*S*H* and *The Odd Couple* and was a longtime regular on the 1980s chestnut *Webster*, playing a wealthy white ex-NFL star who adopts a growth-stunted black child. Karras' actress wife Susan Clark co-starred with him on that series and in the 1982 sex comedy *Porky's*.

K.C. Wolf

Chris Phillips

Costumed wolf who has served as the official mascot of the Kansas City Chiefs since 1989. K.C. Wolf replaced **Warpaint**, the team's beloved live pinto horse mascot, upon Warpaint's retirement. (A less well-liked mascot, the costumed Native American caricature **Cassie Chief**, had briefly patrolled the sideline in the mid-1980s.) The lupine mascot, who some say resembles a raccoon more than a wolf, was named after the Wolfpack, a group of raucous Chiefs fans who used to occupy the temporary bleachers at the team's old home at Municipal Stadium. In 2006, K.C. Wolf became the first mascot inducted into the Mascot Hall of Fame. In the off-season, he enjoys a lucrative second career on the motivational speaking circuit. He makes more than 350 personal appearances a year, appearing at children's parties, store openings, business meetings and conventions, schools, and nursing homes. He's even walked two brides down the aisle on their wedding days. In February of 2010, Woofie, as he is affectionately known, was the featured speaker at the "True Love Waits" abstinence rally in Raymondville, Missouri.

Kemp, Jack

Journeyman quarterback of the 1960s—one of the only men ever to play in the NFL, **AFL**, and **CFL**—who went on to a long and successful political career. The 1965 AFL MVP and affable supply-side evangelist served nine terms in the House of Representatives and was the Republican Party's candidate for vice president in 1996.

Killer Bees

Collective nickname for the Miami Dolphins defense of the early 1980s, several members of which—including Bill Barnett, Bob Baumhauer, Lyle Blackwood, Kim Bokamper, and Bob Brudzinski—had last names that started with the letter "B."

Kimmel, Jimmy

Schlubby late-night television talk show host of the 2000s who rocketed to stardom based in part on his regular appearances on the FOX NFL pregame show. From 1999 to 2002, Kimmel headlined "Jimmy's Picks," a popular segment of *FOX NFL Sunday* in which he made game-day picks from a man-cave redoubt. Impressionist **Frank Caliendo** occasionally appeared alongside Kimmel in the humorous sketches that accompanied the selections.

Kissing Suzy Kolber

Humorous NFL blog founded and run by refugees from the comment boards at the popular sports blog Deadspin, including Drew "Big Daddy" Magary. The site's name commemorates the celebrated 2003 incident in which a drunken **Joe Namath** announced his desire to kiss ESPN sideline reporter **Suzy Kolber** on national television.

King, Peter

Beefy sports journalist who rose to national prominence in the 1990s, first as a pro football columnist for *Sports Illustrated*, and later as a ubiquitous talking head on pregame and postgame highlight shows. A knowledgeable NFL insider in the tradition of Pete Axthelm and Will McDonough, King is the closest thing football has to baseball's sagacious wise man Peter Gammons.

Audibles

"I wanna kiss you. I couldn't care less about the team strugg-a-ling. What we know is we can improve. Chad Pennington, our quarterback, missed the first part of the season, and we struggled. We're looking to next season, we're looking to make a noise now and...I wanna kiss you!"

—**Joe Namath**, expressing his true feelings to sideline reporter **Suzy Kolber**, in 2003

Kolber, Suzy

ESPN sideline reporter best known for being on the receiving end of an unwanted amorous advance by Hall of Fame quarterback **Joe Namath**. Kolber was interviewing Namath from the sideline of a Saturday night game between the New England Patriots and the New York Jets at Giants Stadium on December 20, 2003, when the apparently inebriated 60-year-old repeatedly stated his desire to kiss her. The next day, a chastened Namath apologized for his behavior, blaming it on an overabundance of "Christmas cheer." He later admitted to having an alcohol problem and checked himself into rehab. The popular NFL blog **Kissing Suzy Kolber** is named after the incident.

Kopay, Dave

Journeyman running back of the late 1960s and early 1970s best known for being the first ex-NFL player to publicly disclose his homosexuality. Kopay came out of the closet in a interview with the *Washington Star* in December of 1975, two years after he hung up his jock following an unspectacular nine-year career with the 49ers, Lions, Redskins, Saints, and Packers. His 1977 memoir *The David Kopay Story*, which included revelations about other

Audibles

"He's an idiot."

—**Dave Kopay**, on famously homophobic defensive end **Reggie White**

gay players and insights into the pervasive homophobia inside NFL locker rooms, was a *New York Times* best seller. While it raised his profile, it may have led to his being blackballed by the league. Unable to secure a coaching job, Kopay returned to his hometown of Los Angeles to help run his family's floor-covering business, Linoleum City. In a 1998 interview with *GQ* magazine, he was quoted as saying that he fantasized about having sex with Dallas Cowboys quarterback Troy Aikman on the Sunset Strip.

the coming-out story that made football history
BY DAVID KOPAY AND PERRY DEANE YOUNG

Kornheiser, Tony

Bald sportswriter turned ESPN talking head who parlayed his unlikely media fame into a short-lived, polarizing stint as a game analyst on ***Monday Night Football***. The longtime *Washington Post* columnist and host of the popular basic cable sports debate program *Pardon the Interruption* joined the *MNF* booth in 2006, with a mandate to provide the kind of unpredictable stream-of-consciousness commentary previously supplied by comedian **Dennis Miller**. But Kornheiser proved ill-suited to the traditional **Howard Cosell** "wild card" role, routinely phoning in a veritable word salad of off-topic observations on everything from his dry cleaning travails to the composition of his personal **fantasy football** team, and openly irritating broadcast partner Joe Theismann. When Kornheiser left the booth after three seasons, his departure from the program was attributed to his purported fear of flying. He was replaced by former NFL head coach Jon **"Chucky"** Gruden in 2009.

Kronz, Gregory

Suburban Pittsburgh ninth-grader who coined the term "**Steel Curtain**" for the fabled Steelers defense of the 1970s. Since 1992, Kronz has been the Rector of St. Luke's Episcopal Church in Hilton Head, South Carolina.

L

Ladd, Ernie "the Big Cat"

Mammoth **AFL** defensive tackle of the 1960s who is equally well known for his second life in **professional wrestling**. Nicknamed "the Big Cat" for his surprising agility, Ladd was one of the largest players of his era: 6'9" and 315 pounds, with a 52-inch chest, 39-inch waist, 20-inch biceps, 19-inch neck, and size 18D shoes. Drafted in the 15th round by the San Diego Chargers in 1961, he spent eight seasons in the AFL and helped lead the Chargers to the league title in 1963. After a knee injury prompted his retirement from football in 1970, Ladd turned to his second love—wrestling. He enjoyed a 16-year career in the WWF, grappling with the likes of Bruno Sammartino, Gorilla

Football by the Numbers | **124**

Number of pancakes consumed by **Ernie "the Big Cat" Ladd** at a charity flapjack-eating contest in 1965

Monsoon, and Bobo Brazil. One of the sport's first African American villains, Ladd became notorious for his ongoing feud with André the Giant (whom he derided in interviews as "André the Dummy"). He died of colon cancer in 2007. To date, the Big Cat is the only man elected to both the AFL Hall of Fame and the World Wrestling Entertainment Hall of Fame.

Lambeau Leap

Traditional Green Bay Packers **end zone celebration** in which a player leaps into the arms of fans in the stands after scoring a touchdown. The Leap was invented by safety LeRoy Butler and popularized by wide receiver Robert Brooks. Butler executed the inaugural Lambeau Leap on December

Scott Byrne

26, 1993, during the fourth quarter of a game against the Los Angeles Raiders. Defensive end **Reggie White** recovered a Raiders fumble and lateralled the ball to Butler, who ran the final 25 yards for the score that sealed a 28–0 Packers victory and clinched the franchise's first playoff spot in 11 years. To celebrate his first-ever NFL touchdown (and to burn off enough energy to combat the minus-22-degree wind chill), Butler leapt into the arms of the south end zone faithful. Two seasons later, the Packers' skill players, led by Brooks, took up the tradition, which remains to this day and is imitated at several other NFL venues. Both players involved in pioneering the Lambeau Leap successfully cashed in on the innovation. Butler published a 2003 memoir, *The LeRoy Butler Story: From Wheelchair to the Lambeau Leap*, while Brooks recorded a Leap-themed rap single titled "Jump in the Stands."

Lange, Jeffrey

Snowball-tossing miscreant who ignited a national media firestorm during the waning moments of a game between the New York Giants and the San Diego Chargers at Giants Stadium on December 23, 1995. The 26-year-old administrative assistant from Bridgewater, New Jersey, helped instigate a wild snowball-tossing melee that left 25 people injured. One of the icy projectiles struck Chargers equipment manager Sid Brooks and knocked him unconscious. Lange became a poster child for unruly fan behavior at NFL games after his anonymous photo was published in the New York City tabloids. The Giants offered a bounty of $1,000 to anyone who could identify him. Lange was eventually arrested and charged with disorderly conduct. His lengthy rap sheet—including a prior burglary arrest and a conviction for assaulting police officers—brought further embarrassment upon the P.R.-conscious Giants franchise, which issued a public apology to the people of San Diego. In the end, Lange was found guilty and ordered to pay a $500 fine and $150 in court costs. In the aftermath of the controversy, Lange unsuccessfully sued the New Jersey Sports and Exposition Authority, which operates Giants Stadium, claiming he had been fired from his job and exposed to "ridicule, public humiliation, and public scorn"—including the indignity of having snowballs thrown at him by strangers.

Last Naked Warrior, The

See **Haley, Charles**

Leaf, Ryan

Surly, unmotivated quarterback of the late 1990s widely considered to be the biggest draft bust in NFL history. Selected with the second overall pick by the San Diego Chargers in 1998, Leaf distinguished himself with his poor play (14 touchdowns and 36 interceptions over parts of four seasons) and his unpleasant personality. In a celebrated locker room incident, Leaf was caught on camera cursing out a San Diego newspaper reporter. He was mercilessly booed by Chargers fans and had numerous run-ins with hecklers, prompting the team to cut him following the 2000 season. After a failed comeback attempt with the Dallas Cowboys, Leaf retired in 2002 at the tender age of 26. In 2008 he resigned from his coaching position at West Texas A&M after allegedly soliciting a pain pill from one of his players.

Leatherheads

Unbearably tedious 2008 screwball comedy set during the "leather helmet" glory days of professional football in the 1920s. George Clooney stars as Jimmy "Dodge" Connelly, the two-fisted captain of the fictional Duluth Bulldogs, with *The Office* heartthrob John Krasinski as the team's hotshot young college recruit, a character loosely based on Red Grange. The two men brawl with opponents,

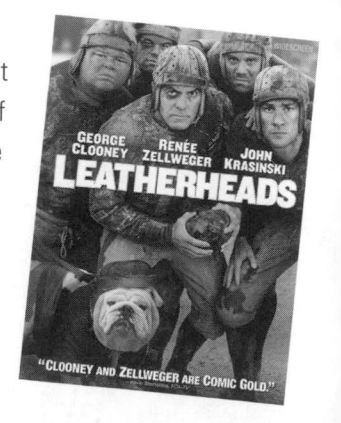

bicker with each other, and vie for the affections of a feisty newspaper reporter played by **Jerry Maguire**'s Renée Zellweger. The dismal screenplay was co-written by onetime *Sports Illustrated* "humorist" Rick Reilly. Despite the best efforts of its big-name stars, *Leatherheads* bombed at the box office, foreclosing the possibility of another old-time football movie for at least a generation.

"Let's Ram It"

Infamous **music video** recorded by the 1986 Los Angeles Rams. "If you ram it just right, you can ram it all night," instructs the verse to the nearly six-minute-long ditty, which piles on endless double entendres playing off the notion of "ram" as a verb, along with nearly 100 repetitions of "Let's ram it" in the chorus. The weirdly compelling video features such mid-1980s Rams stalwarts as Eric Dickerson, Nolan Cromwell, and Jackie Slater rapping in an empty stadium. (Highlight: Cromwell informing us that "I like to ram it as you can see. 'Cause nobody likes ramming more than me.") The idea for "Let's Ram It" came from Rams cheerleader and future **Monday Night Football** sideline reporter Lisa Guerrero, who was inspired by the success of the Chicago Bears' "**Super Bowl Shuffle**." (Guerrero also has a brief cameo in the video.) Quarterback Jim Everett was the only Rams starter who refused to participate. A half-hour documentary about the video, *The Making of "Let's Ram It": Behind The Scenes*, was filmed simultaneously.

Levitra

Popular impotence drug that has become associated with professional football through the seemingly incessant airing of commercials touting its efficacy during NFL telecasts, especially the Super Bowl. The first of the so-called boner pills to take on industry leader Viagra, Levitra's makers, Glaxo and Bayer, cultivated a relationship with the NFL from the very beginning. In 2003, the companies signed a three-year, $20 million deal that granted Levitra the right to use the NFL logo in its advertising. Former Chicago Bears coach **Mike Ditka** was enlisted to appear in a series of ads as the face of the erectile dysfunctional male. Another popular Levitra ad depicted a presumably impotent man attempting to throw a football through a tire swing.

Lewis, Ray

Hard-hitting All-Pro linebacker of the 1990s and 2000s best known to the general public for successfully dodging murder charges following an Atlanta nightclub killing on the night of Super Bowl XXXIV. Lewis was attending a postgame party when a dispute with some fellow clubgoers escalated into a violent stabbing that left two men dead. Lewis was initially charged with two counts of murder, but later pleaded down to misdemeanor obstruction of justice in exchange for testimony against two of his compatriots. In 2010, Lewis completed the unlikely rehabilitation of his public image when he succeeded **Isaiah Mustafa** as the national spokesman for Old Spice Body Wash.

Liberty Belles

Name used by the Philadelphia Eagles cheerleading squad from 1979 to 1983. They were formerly known as the **Eaglettes**.

Great Moments in Cheerleaders Scandal

In 1979, freelance photojournalist Gene Puskar was banned from covering the Eagles after he snapped three pictures of a **Liberty Belles** cheerleader with her breast out. The offending mammary became exposed while the Belles were high-stepping to disco music during a pregame rehearsal at Veterans Stadium. "They were doing the one-two on the high kicks...I just noticed there was a possibility something might be popping up," Puskar said. "I saw it about to happen and it did happen." Puskar later sold the photographs to *Playboy*.

Limbaugh, Rush

Right wing radio host, rabid Pittsburgh Steelers fan, and all-around football aficionado whose controversial views on race may have cost him a chance at becoming an NFL team owner. Although he occasionally talked football on his daily radio gabfest, Limbaugh's connection to the pro game did not become widely known until 2000, after he emerged as a finalist to replace **Norman Julius "Boomer" Esiason** as a *Monday Night Football* analyst on ABC. Various newspaper reports pegged him as executive producer **Don Ohlmeyer**'s first choice for the gig, before **Dennis Miller** edged him out. In the fall of 2003, Limbaugh was hired by ABC's sister network, ESPN, to serve as a commentator on its *NFL Sunday Countdown* pregame show. But the outspoken opponent of affirmative action sparked a nationwide controversy when he derided the ability of African American quarterback Donovan McNabb, claiming on air that the **Pro Bowl** signal caller was "overrated...because he's black." In the wake of the ensuing media firestorm, Limbaugh resigned from the program. Six years later, that incident came back to haunt Limbaugh when the conservative firebrand joined an ownership group attempting to purchase the St. Louis Rams. Limbaugh was eventually forced to drop his bid after many players, including McNabb, objected.

Lite All-Stars

"AFTER A NICE, CIVILIZED GAME OF TENNIS, THERE'S NOTHING LIKE A COUPLE OF LITE BEERS."

LITE BEER FROM MILLER.
EVERYTHING YOU ALWAYS WANTED IN A BEER. AND LESS.

All-pro roster of jocks assembled by the Miller Brewing Company in the 1970s to provide a macho public face for its low-calorie beer, Lite Beer from Miller. **John Madden**, Dick Butkus, **Bubba Smith**, and **Roosevelt "Rosey" Grier** were just a few of the NFL icons to appear in television commercials touting the great-tasting, less-filling brew. The campaign's tagline was "Everything you always wanted in a beer. And less."

Longest Yard, The

Popular 1974 film comedy about a prison football team assembled by a down-on-his-luck former NFL quarterback. Mustachioed matinee idol Burt Reynolds plays Paul "Wrecking" Crewe, a sneering wastrel who left the pro game in disgrace in the aftermath of a point-shaving scandal and now lives the life of a gigolo in central Florida. When his latest sugar mama kicks him out, Crewe smacks her around, steals her car, and ends up in state prison. There the sadistic warden (former *Green Acres* star Eddie Albert) orders him

to recruit and train inmates to play in a rigged exhibition game against a team of corrections officers. Onetime NFL stars Ray Nitschke and **Joe Kapp** appear as football-playing guards in director Robert Aldrich's film, which became an unlikely box office hit and precipitated a spate of raunchy sports comedies in the late 1970s (*The Bad News Bears*, *Slap Shot*, *__North Dallas Forty__*). The totally unnecessary 2005 remake sands most of the rough edges off Aldrich's original, replacing Reynolds with the vapid Adam Sandler. A distasteful gay panic subplot, courtesy of comic Tracy Morgan, makes the retrograde sexual politics of the original film look positively progressive by comparison. Michael Irvin gets the NFL cameo in the new version, with ESPN personality Dan Patrick hilariously awkward as a highway patrolman.

Longley, Clint

Journeyman backup quarterback of the 1970s best known for leading the Dallas Cowboys to victory in a memorable **Thanksgiving Day** game against the Washington Redskins in 1974. Longley, a rattlesnake-rustling free spirit nicknamed "**the Mad Bomber**," subbed for the injured Roger Staubach and threw two touchdown passes in the come-from-behind 24–23 win. Cowboys offensive lineman Blaine Nye famously described Longley's performance as "the triumph of an uncluttered mind." The game cemented Longley's status as a folk hero in Dallas, though it did little to endear him to Staubach, who loathed him for his open and obnoxious campaign to take away his starting job. Their feud culminated in an infamous brawl at a team practice in 1976, where Longley reportedly sucker punched Staubach and the former Navy standout responded by knocking Longley to the ground and raining blows upon him in an effort to make good on a promise to "knock his Bugs Bunny teeth in." Soon after the incident, Longley was traded to the San Diego Chargers.

Lousiannes

Short-lived name for the original New Orleans Saints dance team, which entertained home crowds during the team's inaugural season in 1967. Organized by Saints halftime show impresario Tommy Walker, the longtime entertainment director of Disneyland, the squad had to be renamed the Saints Dancers after just one preseason game when it was discovered that the name "Lousiannes" had already been copyrighted by a local high school.

Love Boat Scandal

Commonly accepted shorthand term for a controversial maritime orgy indulged in by members of the 2005 Minnesota Vikings. The floating debauch took place during a team-organized charter boat trip on Lake Minnetonka in October of 2005 and involved numerous strippers, prostitutes, and public sex acts—many of them caught on camera. Seventeen Vikings were implicated in the scandal. Quarterback Daunte Culpepper and three others were hit with misdemeanor public indecency charges. The outlandish nature of the players' indiscretions—cornerback Fred Smoot allegedly employed a purple double-dong dildo on one of the female partygoers—scandalized the franchise and became fodder for sports radio hosts across Minnesota (many of whom played the theme to TV's *The Love Boat* during their reports).

"Luv Ya Blue"

Catchphrase, **fight song**, and promotional campaign associated with the Houston Oilers of the late 1970s, a period that saw the previously moribund franchise compete with the Pittsburgh Steelers for dominance of the AFC. "Luv Ya Blue" fever can be traced back to November 20, 1978, when the

Field Guide to Zebras

Phil Luckett

Respected NFL official who earned eternal ignominy in Pittsburgh for his botched coin toss before the overtime period in the 1998 **Thanksgiving Day** game between the Pittsburgh Steelers and the Detroit Lions. Although Steelers team captain Jerome Bettis distinctly called "tails," and the coin landed "tails" up, Luckett inexplicably awarded the toss to the Lions, who elected to receive and promptly marched down the field for a game-winning field goal.

Oilers defeated the Miami Dolphins 35–30 on ***Monday Night Football*** behind a bruising 199-yard, four-touchdown rushing performance by rookie running back Earl Campbell. That night, more than 50,000 Oilers fans filled the Houston Astrodome, all waving pom poms in the team's powder blue-and-white color scheme. "Luv Ya Blue" quickly became the Oilers' rallying cry, with local banks and other businesses enlisted by the team to promote the phrase across the city. An area songwriter, Mack Hayes, was commissioned to record a song extolling the "Luv Ya Blue" ethos. Heartbreaking Oilers losses in the 1978 and 1979 AFC Championship Games at Pittsburgh were capped by massive "Luv Ya Blue" pep rallies at the Astrodome, where blue-face-painted fans gathered in the tens of thousands to sing the song and shower praise on Campbell, head coach Bum Phillips, and the rest of their homecoming heroes.

Audibles

Look out football, here we come, Houston Oilers, Number One.
Houston has the Oilers, the greatest football team.
We take the ball from goal to goal like no one's ever seen.
We're in the air, we're on the ground...always in control
And when you say the Oilers, you're talking Super Bowl.
'Cause we're the Houston Oilers, Houston Oilers, Houston Oilers, Number One.
Yes, we're the Houston Oilers, Houston Oilers, Houston Oilers, Number One.
We've got the offense. We've got the defense.
We give the other team no hope. 'Cause we're the Houston Oilers, Houston Oilers,
You know we're gonna hold the rope.

—lyrics to **"Luv Ya Blue"** by Mack Hayes and the Luv Ya Blue Band

Mad Bomber, The

Nickname bestowed upon Oakland Raiders quarterback Daryle Lamonica by *Monday Night Football* analyst **Howard Cosell** in recognition of Lamonica's propensity for throwing long passes. The Mad Bomber was also the nickname of cult favorite Cowboys quarterback **Clint Longley**.

Madden Curse

Supposed hex that befalls any NFL player who appears on the cover of NFL coaching legend **John Madden**'s eponymous line of football video games. Like the **Chunky Soup Curse**, the Madden Curse afflicts its victims with injuries and diminished performance.

Madden, John

Beefy, ebullient Hall of Fame head coach turned broadcaster, commercial pitchman, and video game pioneer. Madden spent 10 seasons as the head man of the Oakland Raiders, leading the team to its first Super Bowl title in 1977. After retiring from the game at the tender age of 42, he began a long and lucrative second career in television, compiling 15 Emmy Awards as the lead NFL analyst for all four major broadcast networks. Known for his ability to break down an increasingly complex game into sound bites accessible to the layman, Madden forged a personal connection with the audience unlike anything seen on sports television since the days of the widely despised **Howard Cosell**. When he wasn't embellishing football telecasts with proprietary exclamations like "Boom!" and "Doink" or exhorting the nation to try **Turducken** on **Thanksgiving Day**, Madden was amassing an enviable portfolio of commercial endorsements. Burly and excessively enthusiastic—sometimes scarily so—"Big John" could be seen throughout

Curses!

Five Purported Victims of the Madden Curse

1999

San Francisco 49ers running back Garrison Hearst breaks his right fibula in an NFL divisional playoff game. He sits out the next two full seasons and never fully recovers.

2003

St. Louis Rams running back Marshall Faulk sustains an ankle injury, fails to regain his form, and never again rushes for 1,000 yards in a season.

2004

The day after *Madden NFL 2004* is released, cover subject **Michael Vick** of the Atlanta Falcons breaks his leg in the preseason and misses 12 games.

2005

Perennial **Pro Bowl** linebacker **Ray Lewis** fails to record a single interception for the first time in his career. A late-season wrist injury keeps him on the sideline for the Baltimore Ravens' playoff run.

2006

Philadelphia Eagles quarterback Donovan McNabb suffers a sports hernia in the first game of the season.

the 1980s and '90s bursting through backdrops in high-energy TV spots for Miller Lite, Ace Hardware, and ("Boom!") Tough Actin' Tinactin, among other products. Since 1998, he has lent his name to a state-of-the-art football video game that is annually one of the medium's best sellers.

Mademoiselles
See **Mam'selles**

Mad Stork, The
Distinctive nickname bestowed on 6'7", 220-pound linebacker Ted Hendricks during his time at the University of Miami. The moniker pays tribute to the future NFL Hall of Famer's long arms and bird-like mien, although Hendricks' Oakland Raiders teammates reportedly preferred to call him "Kick 'Em in the Head Ted" for his aggressive tackling style.

Audibles

"Ted's elevator doesn't go all the way to the top."

–John Madden on Ted **"the Mad Stork"** Hendricks

Mam'selles
Sideline dance team that entertained crowds at New Orleans Saints home games from 1968 to 1971. Originally called the Mademoiselles, the choreographed cheerleading squad was dragooned into service as hostesses during the 1968 Republican National Convention in Miami Beach under the name "the Nixon Dancers." After the Mam'selles disbanded in 1971, the Saints went without an official dance team until 1975, when the **Bonnes Amies** debuted.

Man in the Hat, The

Commonly used nickname for Hall of Fame head coach Tom Landry, who was famous for wearing a matching suit and fedora on the sideline.

Marinaro, Ed

Middling NFL running back of the mid-1970s better known for his post-retirement acting career. Marinaro played Officer Joe Coffey on the groundbreaking NBC police drama *Hill Street Blues* from 1981 to 1986. The onetime Cornell standout also portrayed lumpy Long Island lothario Joey Buttafuoco in the 1992 TV movie *Amy Fisher: My Story.*

Marshall, Jim

Two-time **Pro Bowl** defensive end of the 1960s and '70s remembered less for his standout play as a member of the Minnesota Vikings' **Purple People Eaters** defense than for his legendary wrong-way run on October 25, 1964. In the fourth quarter of a game at San Francisco's Kezar Stadium, Marshall scooped up a fumble by 49ers halfback Billy Kilmer and rumbled 66 yards into the wrong end zone, whereupon he tossed the ball into the stands for a safety. The Vikings ended up winning the game 27–22, but Marshall never lived down the incident, which he called the most humiliating moment of his 20-year NFL career.

Field Guide to Zebras

Jerry Markbreit
Respected NFL official of the 1970s, '80s, and '90s best known for botching the coin toss before Super Bowl XVII in 1983. Markbreit called "tails" even though the coin clearly landed on "heads." After huddling with the other officials, he corrected his error. After the game, Markbreit explained that he had been bewildered by the coin's design.

Martyball

Name, often used derisively, given to the run-first, conservative brand of offensive football preferred by former Browns, Chiefs, Redskins, and Chargers head coach Marty Schottenheimer.

Mascots

See **Billy Buffalo**; **Blitz**; **Blue**; **Boltman**; **Bucco Bruce**; **Captain Fear**; **Cassie Chief**; **Gumbo**; **Miles**; **Pat Patriot**; **Poe**; **Ragnar**; **Rampage**; **Ramster**; **Roary**; **Rowdy**; **Sir Purr**; **Sir Saint**; **Sourdough Sam**; **Staley Da Bear**; **Swoop**; **T.D. (Browns mascot)**; **T.D. (Dolphins mascot)**; **Thor**; **Thunder**; **Toro**; **T-Rac**; **Trapper**; **Vikadontis Rex**; **Viking, the**; **Viktor the Viking**

Masters of the Gridiron

Bizarre sword-and-sorcery film made by members of the 1986 Cleveland Browns and distributed exclusively in northeastern Ohio. The 18-minute, shot-on-video, *Lord of the Rings*–inspired epic has the Browns, clad in barbarian warrior costumes, dispatched by a mysterious robed wizard on a quest to retrieve a championship ring of power. The "Clan of Modella"—a reference to team owner **Art Modell**—includes such mid-1980s Browns stalwarts as Ozzie Newsome, Earnest Byner, and Clay Matthews. Rotund 1960s relic Tiny Tim, outfitted in a fright wig and mascara, plays their nemesis, the sinister Lord of the League. While short on plot, *Masters of the Gridiron* is rich with terrible wordplay. (Warriors are recruited from the "Hills of Linebackus," "Village of Receivus," "Hamlet of Interceptus," and so on.) Cleveland-area wimp rockers The Michael Stanley Band provide musical accompaniment in the form of the video's theme song, "Hard Die the Heroes."

Matuszak, John

Hard-living defensive end of the 1970s, known as "the Tooz," who pursued a successful post-NFL acting career before dying of a drug overdose in 1989. The first pick in the 1973 NFL Draft, Matuszak spent his best years as a member of the Oakland Raiders, where his outlaw reputation

PORTRAIT OF A FRIENDLY MONSTER

and appetite for liquor, firearms, and painkillers barely stood out in a locker room full of misfits and party animals like Ted **"the Mad Stork"** Hendricks and **Jack "the Assassin" Tatum**. The generation of children who grew up in the 1980s know Matuszak less for his athletic achievements than for his role as **Sloth**, the kind-hearted grotesque, in the 1985 adventure comedy *The Goonies*. His tell-all autobiography, *Cruisin' with the Tooz*, was published in 1987.

Mayhem on a Sunday Afternoon

Cinema verité–style football documentary, directed by future Oscar winner William Friedkin (*The French Connection*, *The Exorcist*), which aired on ABC on November 15, 1965. Friedkin sewed wireless microphones inside the shoulder pads of players on the Cleveland Browns and commissioned an original jazz score from organist Jimmy Smith to create a jagged, gritty portrayal of NFL game action as seen from gridiron level. Billed as a "definitive history of the game from 14th century England to the present day," the David L. Wolper production built on techniques pioneered in the 1960 football documentary *The Violent World of Sam Huff*.

McDaniel, Wahoo

Popular **AFL** linebacker of the 1960s known for his distinctive nickname, his American Indian heritage, and his post-retirement career in **professional wrestling**. Born Edward McDaniel, the part Chickasaw, part Choctaw Oklahoma native was called Wahoo after his father, who loved to fish (a wahoo is an especially ferocious variety of fighting fish). McDaniel played parts of nine seasons with the Oilers, Broncos, Jets, and Dolphins and became a crowd favorite. In the off-season, he wrestled to supplement his income, which led to a lucrative second career inside the squared circle. Clad in a traditional Native American headdress, McDaniel traveled across the south grappling on the NWA and AWA circuits, where he became known as the master of the Indian Strap Match. He died of complications from diabetes in 2002.

McKernan, Tim

See **Barrel Man**

McMahon, Jim

Free-spirited, headband-wearing quarterback of the 1980s and '90s best known for leading the Chicago Bears to their only Super Bowl title in 1985. Partial to spiky pseudo-punk hairstyles and 24/7 sunglasses (necessitated, he claimed, by a childhood accident in which he stabbed himself in the eye with a fork), McMahon routinely irked NFL officials with his outspoken proclamations and outrageous behavior. He wore unauthorized headbands bearing corporate logos and extolling the virtues of acupuncture. He famously mooned a media helicopter in the run-up to Super Bowl XX. And he brought the "**Super Bowl Shuffle**" to a screeching halt with some of the most inartful rapping ever recorded.

McMahon, Vince

Pumped-up **professional wrestling** impresario and founder of the **XFL**.

Mean Machine

Name of the fictional football team of prison inmates in both the 1974 and 2005 versions of *The Longest Yard*.

Meeds, Hub

See **Viking, The**

Meredith, Don

Laconic, witty, Texas-born quarterback of the 1960s best known as one of the original *Monday Night Football* commentators, alongside **Keith**

The Tao de Dandy Don

Pearls of Wisdom from the Mouth of Don Meredith

"Fair Hooker? I haven't met one yet."—on the first *Monday Night Football* telecast in 1970, commenting on the Cleveland Browns' oddly named wide receiver Fair Hooker

"They're number one."—referring to a fan giving the camera the finger during a 1972 game in Houston

"Welcome to the Mile High City—and I really am."—before a 1973 game in Denver

"Mother Love's Traveling Freak Show."—Meredith's term for the *MNF* announcing trio of himself, **Frank Gifford**, and **Howard Cosell**

"That was sick, Howard."—to Cosell, after the ponderous analyst praised the "commitment and dedication" of a player who had just vomited out of his helmet

Jackson and **Howard Cosell**. The jovial leader of the underachieving Dallas Cowboys teams of the pre–Roger Staubach era, Meredith proved a natural fit for the broadcast booth, where his penchant for liquor and down-home *bon mots* enlivened many a prime-time blowout. His trademark sign-off was on off-key rendition of "The Party's Over" by country crooner Willie Nelson. Meredith's hayseed mannerisms occasionally got under the skin of the urban sophisticate Cosell, whom he followed out of the *Monday Night Football* booth in 1984. When not calling games, Meredith occasionally moonlighted as an actor. In the 1980s, he became the commercial spokesman for Lipton Iced Tea. Country-and-western star turned actor Mac Davis played a thinly disguised "Dandy Don" analog named Seth Maxwell in the 1979 film ***North Dallas Forty***.

Miami Pound Machine

Distinctive nickname bestowed on the Miami Dolphins defense of the 1980s in homage to the chart-topping Miami Sound Machine led by Cuban American songstress Gloria Estefan.

Mile High Salute

Military-style **end zone celebration** associated with the Denver Broncos since the mid-1990s, when it was first popularized by the team's star running back Terrell Davis. The salute is directed at the crowd by a player standing in the end zone after scoring a touchdown, and was originally intended as a tribute to Davis' father, who was serving in the military at the time. The NFL banned the Mile High Salute in the mid-2000s as part of its crackdown on excessive celebration.

Miles

Terrifying man/horse hybrid who has been the official mascot of the Denver Broncos since 2001. Essentially a lithe human poured into a form-fitting Broncos uniform and topped with a white horse's head, Miles gestated for two years between the announcement of his advent as team mascot and his first live on-field appearance. He's been known to wear a Speedo and to tool around Invesco Field at Mile High on a motorcycle. Until the retirement of **Barrel Man** in 2007, Miles was essentially third in the Broncos mascot hierarchy behind the team's live Arabian horse, **Thunder**.

Miller, Dennis

Allusive right-wing comedian, best known for his stint as the "Weekend Update" anchor on *Saturday Night Live* during the 1980s, who irritated football fans for two seasons as the third wheel in the ***Monday Night Football*** broadcast booth from 2000 to 2002. Miller's hiring was the brainchild—if that is the word for it—of *MNF* producer and **O.J. Simpson** hanger-on **Don Ohlmeyer**, an old friend from Miller's days at NBC. After two soporific seasons of the **Norman Julius "Boomer" Esiason** Experience, Ohlmeyer was desperate to inject a little **Howard Cosell**–type wild card energy into the moribund *Monday Night* franchise. According to reports, Miller beat out conservative radio gabber **Rush Limbaugh**, newspaper columnist (and future *MNF* defiler) **Tony Kornheiser**, ex-quarterback Steve Young, and comic actor Billy Crystal for the plum position alongside play-by-play fixture Al Michaels and stolid X's and O's analyst Dan Fouts. While he succeeded in generating off-season buzz for the 2000 season, Miller alienated nearly as many viewers as he electrified with his irreverent, stream-of-consciousness in-game commentary. Constant references to Michaels as "Albino" were leavened with head-scratching allusions drawn from history, classic literature, and popular

Miller Time

A Selection of Representative Dennis Miller Zingers from his Time on *Monday Night Football*

"**George Toma** is to turf what Sy Sperling is to fake hair."

"The ref is whipping out that flag like it's the only lighter at a crack house."

"I haven't seen anyone rely on the ground game this much since the Battle of Verdun."

"Look at all the shadows on the field. This place is lit like a Bergman film."

"The Giants are thinner than Kate Moss at certain positions."

"[Mike] Shanahan's tendencies are harder to read than Angelina Jolie's."

"When the hell is Warren Moon going to retire? I mean, this guy is older than the cuneiform in Nebuchadnezzar's tomb."

"**Jim Mora** had a complete Krakatoa flameout yesterday. Jimmy goes off every five years."

culture to no discernible comic effect. The major television critics panned Miller's performance from the get-go, while fans failed to groove on whatever Cosell-esque "guy you love to hate" frisson the new analyst was intended to provide. After two desultory years behind the microphone, Miller was dismissed and replaced by living legend **John Madden**.

Miracle at the Meadowlands
See **Fumble, The (1978)**

Modell, Art

Longtime owner of the Cleveland Browns who is reviled in that city after moving the team to Baltimore in 1996.

Monday Night Football

Game-changing prime-time NFL telecast that has successfully blurred the line between sports and entertainment for more than 40 years. As originally conceived by NFL commissioner Pete Rozelle, *Monday Night Football*—which aired on the ABC network from 1970 to 2005, and thereafter on the basic cable sports channel ESPN—was a weekly prime-time showcase for the fast-growing professional game. ABC Sports, under the stewardship of producer Roone Arledge, turned it into a ratings behemoth and pop cultural touchstone. *MNF* debuted on September 21, 1970, with a game matching the New York Jets against the Cleveland Browns. Eschewing the two-man approach used on most football telecasts, it was the first national sports program to place three men in the enclosed space of the broadcast booth. **Keith Jackson** provided the play-by-play that first season, with color commentary from the unlikely duo of **Don Meredith** and **Howard Cosell**. Meredith, a folksy former quarterback, was soon nicknamed "Dandy Don" by the acerbic Cosell, a onetime lawyer whose pomposity was matched only by his verbosity. The oil-and-water team became a mainstay of the early *Monday* telecasts. When ex-Giants great **Frank Gifford** replaced Jackson in 1971, the crew that would dominate the program's glory years was in place. The weekly broadcast was an instant ratings success, attracting beaucoup media buzz over the ensuing decades through the addition of celebrity guests (John Lennon and Ronald Reagan shared the booth on one memorable broadcast in 1974), a country rock theme song (a reworked version of the **Hank Williams Jr.** hit "All My Rowdy Friends (Have Settled Down)" began assaulting viewers' eardrums beginning in 1989), and innovative promos (such as a controversial 2004 intro featuring wide receiver **Terrell Owens** and a scantily clad **Nicollette Sheridan** of ABC's *Desperate Housewives*). The telecast lost much of its "must-see" cachet with the acrimonious departure of Cosell in 1983. Attempts to replicate his "annoying guy who was never a jock" schtick by new hires **Dennis Miller** and **Tony Kornheiser** proved disastrous. In 2005, the telecast was shunted off the network to ESPN and saddled with a less compelling slate of games—in which diminished state it languishes to this day. See also: **"All My Rowdy Friends Are Here for Monday Night"**; **Berman, Chris**; **Esiason, Norman Julius "Boomer"**; **Garrett, Alvin**; **"Heavy Action"**; *Monday Night Mayhem*; **Williamson, Fred "the Hammer"**

Monday Night Mayhem

TNT television film based on journalist Bill Carter's 1987 book about the first 25 years of *Monday Night Football*. John Turturro—a decade too young and 50 pounds too light to be playing **Howard Cosell**—nevertheless delivers a weirdly mesmerizing performance, with able support from erstwhile *Cheers* regular Jay Thomas as NFL commissioner Pete Rozelle and John Heard as *MNF* impresario Roone Arledge. Relative unknowns portray **Frank Gifford**, **Keith Jackson**, and **Don Meredith**, to less discernible effect. The highly episodic 2002 telefilm depicts several signature moments in *Monday Night Football* history, including the infamous **Alvin Garrett** "monkey" incident and Cosell's on-air announcement of the death of John Lennon. But the real highlights come in scenes where Turturro is allowed to chew the scenery—such as a sequence showing Cosell boogying down to "Takin' Care of Business" by Bachman-Turner Overdrive. Spike Lee's longtime cinematographer Ernest Dickerson directed. The choogling period soundtrack was assembled by onetime Beach Boys collaborator Van Dyke Parks.

Mongo

Dim-witted buffoon played by former Detroit Lions great **Alex Karras** in Mel Brooks' 1974 comedy *Blazing Saddles*. Karras had previously appeared in 1968's *Paper Lion*.

Monsters of the Midway

Nickname adopted by the Chicago Bears of the early 1940s and revived to apply to their 1985 Super Bowl team. It was originally used to describe the University of Chicago football team, whose campus incorporated a stretch of parkland known as the Midway Plaisance.

Mora, Jim

Irascible NFL head coach of the 1980s, 1990s, and early 2000s who gained national notoriety for his profane postgame press conference meltdowns. Mora's rhetorical reputation rests on three main pillars: the "Could've, Would've, Should've" address he delivered to the assembled media following a heartbreaking loss to the San Francisco 49ers on October 25, 1987, in which he decried excuse-making by the media on behalf of the 3–3 New Orleans Saints; the celebrated **"Diddly Poo"** tirade he unleashed on October 20, 1996, following a Saints loss to the Carolina Panthers that dropped their record to 2–6 (Mora resigned as head coach the following day); and the infamous **"Playoffs?"** rant on November 25, 2001, that followed a 40–21 pasting of Mora's Indianapolis Colts, once again by the 49ers. This last jeremiad is considered something of a Gettysburg Address of postgame press conference meltdowns and has been sampled in a popular Coors Light TV commercial that began airing in 2006.

The Best of Jim Mora

The "Could've, Would've, Should've" Speech

They're better than we are. We're not good enough. We shouldn't be thinking about beating these 49ers. We shouldn't be talking about it, 'cause the Saints ain't good enough. And you guys shouldn't write about us being a playoff team and all that bullstuff—that's malarkey. We ain't good enough to beat those guys and it was proven out there today. It's that simple. We're not good enough yet. We've got a long way to go. We've got a lot of work to do. We're close, and close don't mean shit. And you can put that on TV for me. I'm tired of coming close, and we're gonna work our asses off until we ain't close anymore, and it may take some time. We're gonna get it done. We aren't in their—we aren't good enough. They're better than us— black and white, simple, fact! "Could've, would've, should've" is the difference in what I'm talking about! The good teams don't come in and say "Could've." They get it done! All right? It's that simple! I'm tired of saying "Could've, should've, would've." That's why we ain't good enough yet! 'Cause we're saying "Could've" and they ain't! I'm pissed off right now. You bet your ass I am. I'm sick of could've, would've, should've, coming close, if only.

The "Diddly Poo" Tirade

Well, what happened was, that second game, we got our ass kicked. In the second half, we just got our ass totally kicked. We couldn't do diddly poo offensively, we couldn't make a first down, we couldn't run the ball, we didn't try to run the ball, we couldn't complete a pass—we sucked. The second half, we sucked. We couldn't stop the run. Every time they got the ball, they went down and got points. We got our ass totally kicked in the second half—that's what it boiled down to. It was a horseshit performance in the second half. Horseshit. I'm totally embarrassed and totally ashamed. Coaching did a horrible job. The players did a horrible job. We got our ass kicked in that second half. It sucked. It stunk.

The "Playoffs?" Rant

Well, I'll start out saying this: do *not* blame that game on the defense, okay? I don't care who you play, whether it's a high school team, a junior college team, a college team, *much* less an NFL team. When you turn the ball over five times—four interceptions, one for a touchdown, three others in field position to set up touchdowns—you ain't going to beat anybody I just talked about. Anybody. All right? And that was a disgraceful performance in my opinion. We threw that game. We gave it away by doing that. We gave them the friggin' game. In my opinion, that sucked. You know? You can't turn the ball over five times like that. Holy crap! I don't know who the hell we think we are when we do something like that. Unbelievable. Five turnovers. One of them for...we've thrown four interceptions for touchdowns this year. That might be an NFL record! And we've still got six games left, so there's no telling how many we'll have. That's pitiful! I mean, it's absolutely pitiful to perform like that. Pitiful!

[Reporter asks about the possibility of the Colts rallying to secure a playoff berth]

What's that? Ah—*Playoffs?* Don't talk about—*playoffs?!* You kidding me?! *Playoffs?!* I just hope we can win a game! *Another* game!

Mr. Irrelevant

Name bestowed annually since 1976 on the final pick in the NFL draft, a mocking reference to the supposed insignificance of any college player selected that low. The godfather of Mr. Irrelevant was former NFL wide receiver Paul Salata, who himself enjoyed a mostly irrelevant career with the 49ers and Colts in the early 1950s. Each summer after the draft, Salata hosts "Irrelevant Week" in Newport Beach, California, where the unlucky selectee is feted with a roast, golf tournament, and regatta and handed the coveted "Lowsman Trophy"—a parody of the Heisman that depicts a player fumbling a football. The term "Mr. Irrelevant" is now often applied retroactively to final picks who pre-date its 1976 coinage. Notable Mr.

Days of Infamy | February 8, 1936

University of Chicago halfback Jay Berwanger, the first Heisman Trophy winner, becomes the first pick in the first NFL draft. He also becomes the first bust. Drafted by the Philadelphia Eagles, Berwanger never played a down in the NFL.

Irrelevants of the past include Marty Moore, the 222nd pick of the 1994 draft who in 1997 became the first Mr. Irrelevant to play in a Super Bowl; Jim Finn, a well-regarded fullback for the Bears, Colts, and Giants in the early 2000s; and the aptly named Dud Parker.

Mud Bowl

Generic term used to describe a notable **bad weather game** played in muddy field conditions. Notable Mud Bowls include the playoff game in December of 1977 between the Los Angeles Rams and the Minnesota Vikings at the Los Angeles Coliseum, in which days of Southern California rain turned the field into quicksand-like muck that severely hampered the Rams' running game, resulting in a 14–7 win for the underdog Vikings; and the 1982 AFC Championship Game between the New York Jets and the Miami Dolphins, where the Jets' speed game was negated by the muddy track at the Orange Bowl in Miami. The Dolphins defense wound up dominating the game as Miami won 14–0 and advanced to the Super Bowl. After the game, Jets officials blamed Dolphins head coach Don Shula for deliberately leaving the tarp off the field during the three-day rainstorm.

Music City Miracle

Commonly used term for the dramatic kickoff return for a touchdown that ended the playoff game between the Tennessee Titans and the Buffalo Bills at LP Field in Nashville on January 8, 2000. The Bills had just scored on a field goal to take a 16–15 lead with 16 seconds left in the contest. Titans fullback Lorenzo Neal accepted the ensuing kickoff and handed the ball to tight end Frank Wycheck, who in turn lateralled to teammate Kevin Dyson. Dyson then scampered 75 yards for the winning touchdown in one of the most shocking reversals of fortune in NFL playoff history.

Music Video

Short film made by or on behalf of professional football teams in an effort to energize fans and foster team unity. See also: **"Buddy's Watching You"**; **"Christmas in Dallas"**; **"Let's Ram It"**; **"Masters of the Gridiron"**; **"New England, the Patriots, and We"**; **"Seahawks Locker Room Rock, The"**; **"Silver and Black Attack"**; **"Super Bowl Shuffle"**; **"Team of the '80s"**; **"Thanks to the 12th Man"**; **"U Can't Touch Us"**, **"We Are the 49ers"**; **"Who Dey Rap"**

Mustafa, Isaiah

Onetime wide receiver whose brief NFL career was but a prelude to fame as the star of a popular series of Old Spice shower gel commercials, "The Man Your Man Could Smell Like." The ad campaign, which started running in 2010, features Mustafa— who played for four NFL teams plus the World League's Barcelona Dragons between 1997 and 2000— as a towel-clad stud extolling the life-changing effects of Old Spice Body Wash.

Don L. Ancheta

N

Namath, Joe

Iconic quarterback of the 1960s and '70s and one of professional football's first multimedia superstars. Heavily recruited out of the University of Alabama, Namath elected to sign with the **AFL**'s New York Jets over the NFL's St. Louis Cardinals in 1965, in part because of the allure of playing in the nation's media capital. "Broadway Joe," as he came to be known, made the leap to national folk hero following his brash but accurate prediction of a victory by the Jets over the heavily favored Baltimore Colts in Super Bowl III. Afforded unprecedented celebrity for a professional football player, Namath soaked up the spotlight. He grew a weirdly mesmerizing Fu Manchu moustache, hosted his own boozy nighttime talk show, and tweaked the NFL authorities by consorting with shady characters in a mobbed-up nightclub venture, **Bachelors III**. He also embarked on a ludicrously counterintuitive entertainment career. From a cringe-inducing **Beautymist** Pantyhose commercial to the amateurish biker movie *C.C. and Company*, Namath never let his lack of acting ability stand in the way of his Hollywood dreams. He continued on that path after retiring from the NFL in 1977, headlining the misbegotten TV sitcom *The Waverly Wonders* and bringing nothing to the table in a mercifully short-lived stint as a *Monday Night Football* analyst. In 1983, Broadway Joe finally made his Broadway debut, assuming the role of Lt. Stephan Maryk, a disloyal Navy officer, in a well-received production of Herman Wouk's *The Caine Mutiny Court-Martial*. It was to prove the high point of a stage career that otherwise consisted of summer stock runs of *Damn Yankees* and other B-grade musicals. From there, Namath largely faded into toupeed obscurity. Widespread suspicions of alcoholism were given credence by a bizarre televised apparition in 2003,

Legends of the Fall

Joe Namath passed on the role of Sam Malone in the long-running TV sitcom *Cheers*.

during which the leering legend woozily attempted to kiss ESPN reporter **Suzy Kolber**. In 2010, a seemingly sobered-up Namath mounted another mini-comeback, appearing in high-waisted pants as an advisor to Jets quarterback Mark Sanchez on an episode of HBO's **Hard Knocks** and launching his own satellite radio show, *The Broadway Blitz with Joe Namath*, on SIRIUS NFL Radio.

"New England, the Patriots, and We"

Inane Super Bowl **fight song** commissioned by Boston-area music video channel V66 in honor of the 1985 AFC champion New England Patriots. Intended as a response to the Chicago Bears' **"Super Bowl Shuffle,"** "New England, the Patriots, and We" features Boston mayor Raymond Flynn, local TV and radio personalities, and ordinary citizens all bopping along to a synthesizer-driven pop song concocted by work-for-hire V66 house band The Studio Soundtrack Singers. Violent imagery pervades throughout. An unhinged anchorman is shown pointing a gun at the head of a child's stuffed bear. Later, Boston dock workers throw a refrigerator off the side of a building. Several members of the Patriots appear, out of uniform, and identifiable only by their incongruous MTV logo baseball caps. The unbelievably annoying song includes no fewer than 27 repetitions of the title chorus.

Great Moments in Cheerleaders Scandal

In October of 1978, a staff assistant hired by the **New Orleans Saints Angels** was arrested on drug possession charges. Although neither the dancers nor their choreographer were implicated in the scandal, the ensuing media firestorm prompted the Saints to disband the squad.

New Orleans Saints Angels

Short-lived New Orleans Saints cheerleading squad of the late 1970s. The Angels were essentially a reorganized and renamed version of the team's popular mid-1970s dance team the **Bonnes Amies**. Their troubled reign in the Big Easy lasted less than a full season.

New York Football Giants

Official legal name of the franchise colloquially known as the New York Giants, so called to distinguish it from the baseball team of the same name—even after that team moved to San Francisco in 1958.

New York Sack Exchange

Distinctive nickname bestowed on the New York Jets' defensive line of the early 1980s, one of the NFL's most prolific and flamboyant front fours. **Mark Gastineau**, Joe Klecko, Marty Lyons, and Abdul Salaam formed the core of the original Sack Exchange—so named by a Jets fan who showed up at a game with the moniker scrawled across an old bed sheet. In November of 1981, the sack-dancing quartet solidified their association with New York City's financial markets by ringing the ceremonial opening bell at the New York Stock Exchange.

NFL Films

Legendary highlight film production company, founded by the father-son tandem of Ed and **Steve Sabol**, which revolutionized the way sports is presented on film. **Ed Sabol** was a 45-year-old Philadelphia overcoat salesman and aspiring filmmaker when he secured the rights to film the 1962 NFL Championship Game. NFL commissioner Pete Rozelle was so impressed with his work that he appointed Sabol the league's official documentarian. In 1964, with seed money from the NFL, NFL Films was born. Over the next several decades, the company helped transform the stodgy gray image of professional football through the innovative use of state-of-the-art filmmaking techniques. Showcased in annual Super Bowl and team highlight films and on television shows like HBO's *Inside the NFL* and the syndicated *NFL Game of the Week*, NFL Films highlight packages relied on dramatic camerawork, portentous narration from **"Voice of God" John Facenda**, and the bombastic music cues of composer **Sam Spence** to make even the most one-sided blowout seem like a gripping life-or-death struggle. Since its inception, NFL Films has collected more than 100 Emmy Awards.

NFL Today, The

Groundbreaking CBS pregame show that revolutionized the form through its unique mix of innovative production techniques and colorful on-air personalities. Although it existed in an embryonic form as far back as the early 1960s, the modern version of *The NFL Today* dates back to 1975, when host Brent Musburger, resident jock Irv Cross, and erstwhile Miss America **Phyllis George** (reporting human interest stories) set the template for all pregame shows that came in its wake. The addition of wiseguy/oddsmaker **Jimmy "the Greek" Snyder** in 1976 completed the classic lineup and helped generate the interpersonal friction that fueled publicity buzz throughout the 1980s.

Nigerian Nightmare, The

Imposing nickname bestowed on Christian Okoye, an African-born running back of the 1980s, by his Kansas City Chiefs teammate Irv Eatman, in recognition of the Enugu, Nigeria, native's physical running style.

Nixon, Richard

Disgraced 36th president of the United States, known football fanatic, and a onetime benchwarmer on the Whittier College football team. Nixon was an avowed Washington Redskins fan, though as a native Californian who spent his winters in South Florida he also harbored soft spots for the Los Angeles Rams and the Miami Dolphins. As president, he developed a reputation for kibitzing with the head coaches of the teams for which he rooted. In 1971, he famously suggested a play to Redskins coach **George Allen** during a visit to practice a few days before a playoff game with the San Francisco 49ers. The play—a flanker reverse dubbed "Nixon's Play" in the press—resulted in a 13-yard loss and helped seal the Redskins' 24–20 defeat. A week later, Nixon was at it again, telephoning Dolphins coach Don Shula at his home in Florida at 1:30 in the morning to suggest a play to be run in the upcoming Super Bowl. The Dallas Cowboys pounded the Dolphins 24–3 and Nixon's play—a pass to Paul Warfield—was nearly intercepted by Cowboys cornerback Mel Renfro, who cracked "Nixon's a great strategist, isn't he?"

Audibles

"I want to thank the president for offering not to send in any more plays."

–Dolphins coach Don Shula, after his team won Super Bowl VII without any help from offensive coordinator-in-chief **Richard Nixon**

No Fun League

Derogatory term for the NFL, a reference to the league's perceived overzealousness in penalizing, fining, and suspending players for seemingly minor infractions involving excessive celebrations and uniform violations.

No-Name Defense

Nickname for the Miami Dolphins defense of the early 1970s, so called because it was devoid of big-name stars. The first use of the nickname is usually attributed to Dallas Cowboys coach Tom Landry.

North Dallas Forty

Critically acclaimed 1979 film based on the tell-all novel of the same name by ex-Dallas Cowboys wide receiver **Peter Gent**. *North Dallas Forty* chronicles the travails of Gent's fictionalized stand-in, Phil Elliott, a pill-popping, pot-smoking bench player for the North Dallas Bulls, played by Nick Nolte. Country-and-western star Mac Davis plays Elliott's best friend Seth Maxwell, a playboy quarterback clearly modeled on the Cowboys' high-living signal caller **Don Meredith**.

Character actor G.D. Spradlin is the team's humorless martinet of a head coach, B.A. Quinlan, a thinly veiled Tom Landry analog. Oakland Raiders star **John Matuszak**, in his first major movie role, plays an outspoken defensive lineman. Like Jim Bouton's baseball tell-all *Ball Four*, *North Dallas Forty* outraged some in the tight-lipped NFL community with its frank portrayal of rampant drug use and sexual escapades in professional football. Several ex-players who served as technical advisors on the film were quietly blacklisted by their teams, although NFL commissioner Pete Rozelle steadfastly denied any involvement.

Number One

Commercially unsuccessful, critically derided 1969 film starring Charlton Heston as a quarterback for the New Orleans Saints. Heston himself developed the idea for a dramatic feature about an NFL star on his way out, which he claimed was inspired by Morris Berman's iconic photograph of New York Giants quarterback Y.A. Tittle, on his knees, dazed and bloody, in the second quarter of a 1964 game against the Pittsburgh Steelers. Journeyman Tom Gries directed, from a script by David Moessinger with strong input from the gravel-voiced star. Heston plays Ron "Daddy Cat" Catlan, an aging superstar going through a midlife crisis at home and pondering retirement from the gridiron. To prepare for the role, Heston worked out five days a week on the Harvard University football field with former Los Angeles Rams turned actors Mike Henry and **Roosevelt "Rosey" Grier**. Serving as the actor's personal quarterback coach was onetime USC standout Craig Fertig, who was astonished by Heston's total lack of athletic aptitude. "I was in physical condition for it, but brought no football skills to the job," Heston would later admit. "I had no talent whatsoever for what I was trying to learn." It shows. The scenes where Heston attempts to throw forward passes are painful to watch, as is the rest of this overwrought melodrama, which also stars Bruce Dern, Jessica Walter, and Diana Muldaur. Factual errors—the Saints are depicted as having been in existence since the early 1960s—also undermine the film's credibility. Good luck finding it on television. *Number One* is rarely shown and has never been released on DVD.

N.W.A.

Compton, California-based hip-hop "gang"—the initials stand for "Niggaz with Attitude"—whose adoption of Los Angeles Raiders uniform garb in the late 1980s helped spur the explosion in NFL apparel sales in the 1990s.

Ochocinco

Nom-de-gridiron adopted by Cincinnati Bengals wide receiver Chad Johnson in the mid-2000s. "Ocho Cinco," or "eight five" in Spanish, is an erroneous translation of his jersey number, 85. At first, Ocho Cinco was little more than a colorful nickname, used by ESPN anchors eager to hype one of the more flamboyant players in the NFL. Then, before a game against the Atlanta Falcons in October of 2006, Johnson altered the back of his jersey to read "Ocho Cinco" instead of "C. Johnson." Although he did not wear the altered jersey during the game, the NFL fined him $5,000 for violating the league uniform policy. In response, Johnson had his name legally changed to "Chad Javon Ochocinco" in August of 2008. In 2011, Ochocinco announced he would be changing his name back to Johnson.

O'Connor, Sandra Day

Trailblazing female Supreme Court justice known for her moderate judicial philosophy, her introduction of Jazzercise classes to the Court, and for her unfortunate run-in with legendary Washington Redskins running back **John Riggins** in 1985. O'Connor and Riggins were seated next to each other at the Washington Press Club's annual black-tie Salute to Congress dinner when the hulking former Super Bowl MVP, who'd apparently been overserved, sidled up to the very married jurist with unseemly familiarity. After she rebuffed his suggestion that she pose for a pin-up poster, Riggins told her, "Come on, Sandy Baby, loosen up. You're too tight," and then proceeded to pass out on the floor. According to newspaper reports, Riggins lay there for several minutes while the wait staff served dessert to the mortified VIPs. To his credit, Riggins repented of his conduct the next morning and sent roses to O'Connor by way of an apology. For her part, O'Connor was more amused than annoyed by the wasted pigskinner's boorish come-on. She was soon outfitting her Jazzercise classmates in T-shirts reading "Loosen up at the Supreme Court." Several years later, after Riggins had retired from football and was trying to make a go of it as an actor on the D.C. theater circuit, O'Connor even showed up on opening night of one of his plays and gave *him* a dozen roses for his curtain call.

Odd Couple, The

Classic TV sitcom of the 1970s that featured a number of football-themed episodes, pegged to main character Oscar Madison's career as a New York City sportswriter. In the first-season episode "The Hideaway," a coveted Eskimo quarterback recruit turns out to be a gifted cellist, causing conflict between aspiring sports agent Oscar and his persnickety aesthete roommate, Felix Unger. In Season Two's "Win One for Felix," Felix becomes coach of his son's peewee football team, using old recordings of Knute Rockne locker room speeches for inspiration. By Season Three, the show had begun to rely increasingly on big-name guest stars, including several from the world of professional football. Former Detroit Lions standout **Alex Karras** dropped by for a 1973 episode, "That Was No Lady," playing a thinly veiled version of himself. That same year, All-Pro defensive end **Bubba Smith** appeared as himself in "Take My Furniture Please," revealing a heretofore hidden affinity for French Provincial interior decor. And **Fearsome Foursome** stalwart **Deacon Jones** memorably menaced Oscar in "Felix's First Commercial," about the portrait photographer's attempts to film a shaving cream ad. Controversial commentator **Howard Cosell** also appeared in two *Odd Couple* episodes, the second of which—1975's "Your Mother Wears Army Boots"—had Oscar desperately scheming to land an analyst's gig on ***Monday Night Football*** (which, coincidentally, also aired on ABC).

AP Images

Ohlmeyer, Don

Imperious, pinkie ring–wearing network TV executive best known among NFL fans as the architect of such misbegotten broadcasting experiments as the 1982 **announcerless game** and the controversial hiring of logorrheic comedian **Dennis Miller** as an analyst on *Monday Night Football*. Late-night host David Letterman once remarked that Ohlmeyer "couldn't create gas if he ate a bean dinner." For many years, Ohlmeyer was also known as a close friend and mentor to accused double murderer **O.J. Simpson**.

Okon, Tommy

Child actor who played opposite **"Mean" Joe Greene** in a classic 1979 Coca-Cola commercial. Okon was passed over for the role of "The Kid" in the follow-up 1981 made-for-TV movie *The Steeler and the Pittsburgh Kid*, in favor of future *E.T.: The Extra Terrestrial* star Henry Thomas. He currently owns a stone-importing business in Queens, New York.

Olivo, Frank

Diminutive 19-year-old Philadelphia Eagles fan who was pelted with snowballs by the crowd at Franklin Field while dressed up as Santa Claus during a notorious halftime incident in 1968. See also: **Santa Claus Incident**

Olsen, Merlin

Hall of Fame defensive lineman of the 1960s and '70s, a member of the Los Angeles Rams' fabled **Fearsome Foursome**, and known to TV viewers for his memorable roles on the family dramas *Little House on the Prairie* and *Father Murphy*. The 6'5", 270-pound Mormon cultivated a "gentle giant" persona that held him in good stead as a celebrity spokesman for FTD Florists. He also worked as the lead analyst on NBC football telecasts from 1978 to 1988.

Olson, Lisa

Onetime *Boston Herald* sportswriter whose 1990 sexual assault at the hands of several members of the New England Patriots generated a nationwide debate on the sexual harassment of female sports reporters. The 26-year-old Olson was working the Patriots locker room after a team practice on September 17, 1990, when she was accosted by a gaggle of naked players making lewd comments and gestures. A subsequent report commissioned by the NFL indicated that tight end Zeke Mowatt waved his genitals in Olson's direction, asking, "Is this what you want?" (Mowatt was later fined $12,500 by the NFL for his role in the incident.) In the aftermath of her public revelation of the assault, Olson was besieged with death threats, obscene phone calls, and hate mail from irate Patriots fans. Her tires were slashed, her apartment was burglarized, and a note was sent to her demanding that she "leave Boston or die." Unapologetic Patriots owner Victor Kiam even joined in the abuse, calling her "a classic bitch." The sportswriter was forced to flee to Australia for several years to escape further harassment. Olson eventually filed a civil harassment suit against the Patriots, which was reportedly settled for $250,000.

One-Bar Helmet

Throwback headgear that reminds fans of a certain age of the gridiron heroes of their youth. Legendary NFL coach Paul Brown is credited with inventing the facemask on the fly in 1953 in an effort to keep quarterback Otto Graham on the field after he suffered a gash across his face. The ever-resourceful Brown soon entered into a consultation with the Riddell sporting goods company, instructing its engineers to develop a permanent solution to the epidemic of face-stomping. "Give me something that will fit across the front of a helmet and will be about as big as my little finger," he instructed Riddell designers. "I want it so it can withstand a stray foot, or a deliberately thrown fist or elbow, and take away the inclination to punch someone. But keep it light enough to weigh less than an ounce." The result was the BT-5 (for "bar tubular, version 5"), football's first mass-produced facemask (a boon, as it turned out, to Brown's bank account; he earned royalties on every facemask sold). Single-bar helmets would remain prominent into the 1970s, especially for offensive skill players for whom visibility was paramount. Concerns about safety caused the one-bar to fall out of favor in the 1980s, although kickers and punters continued to prefer it. Washington Redskins quarterback Joe Theismann was

AP Images

Football by the Numbers | 85.8

Percent of NFL players who revealed that they did not wear protective cups in a 1978 survey

the last non-kicker to wear the single-bar, considering it a means to goad his defensive opponents (one of whom, New York Giants linebacker **Lawrence Taylor**, ended his career by sacking him and breaking his leg in 1985). The NFL banned the single-bar facemask in 2004. Journeyman punter Scott Player was the last player to wear one, earning him the nickname "Punty McOnebar."

"One for the Thumb in '81!"

Rallying cry of the 1980 Pittsburgh Steelers, coined by defensive lineman **"Mean" Joe Greene** in an effort to spur his teammates on to collect a fifth Super Bowl ring ("for the thumb") in January of 1981. T-shirts bearing the slogan were printed and a novelty song, "One for the Thumb in '81," was recorded by John Zovath and Tom Perry. Sadly, the Steelers' thumb was to remain unadorned for another 25 seasons. The team went 9–7 in 1980 and failed to make the playoffs.

Orange Crush

Nickname bestowed on the defensive unit of the 1977 AFC champion Denver Broncos—a reference to the team's loud orange uniforms.

Original Whizzinator, The

Drug-masking kit employed by Minnesota Vikings running back **Onterrio Smith** in a 2005 scheme to circumvent an NFL-mandated urine test.

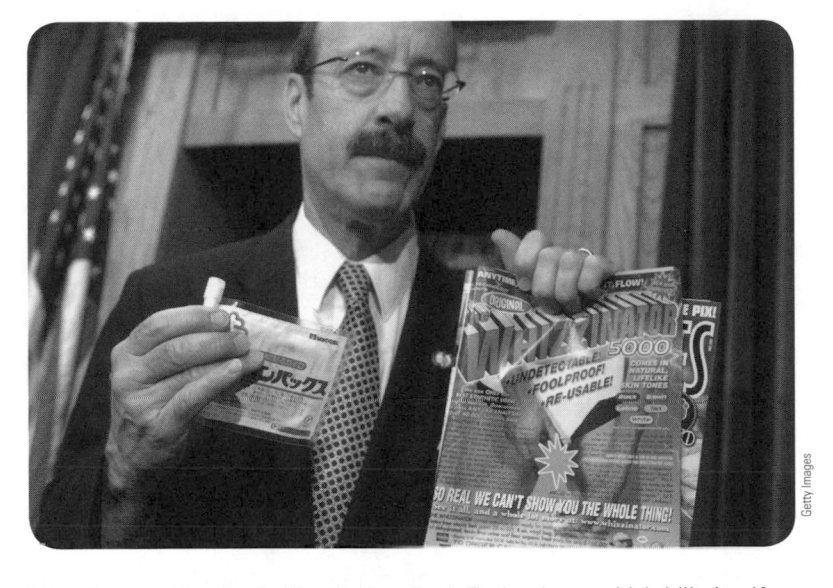

Getty Images

Manufactured by the California firm Puck Technology, which bills itself as "the undisputed leader in synthetic urine," the Whizzinator consists of a four-inch-long prosthetic phallus affixed to a jockstrap and a plastic bladder. Using a syringe, the user fills the bag with a solution of powdered urine and water and proceeds to "urinate" in front of the drug test observer by releasing a tiny valve, producing a stream of undetectably clean urine. If the user remembers to cough at the right moment to mask the sound of the valve opening, the ruse is nearly foolproof. It's unclear whether Smith ever used the Whizzinator successfully. His apparatus was confiscated during a search of his luggage after a tube of toothpaste set off security alarms at the Minneapolis–St. Paul International Airport on April 21, 2005. Later that year, the NFL suspended Smith for the entire 2005 season for his third violation of the league's substance abuse policy. The offending prosthesis was later sold at auction for $750 to a sports bar owner and memorabilia collector from Mankato, Minnesota.

Over-the-Hill Gang

Team nickname bestowed upon the Washington Redskins of the early 1970s in recognition of the advanced age of many of the team's starters during the reign of veteran-loving head coach **George Allen**. Allen's "future is now" mandate set off an orgy of front office wheeling and dealing that saw Washington spin off draft picks in exchange for seasoned players like Billy Kilmer, Richie Petitbon, Jack Pardee, and Boyd Dowler. Spurred on by their cagey veteran core, the Over-the-Hill Gang steamed to the NFC championship in 1972 before running out of gas in Super Bowl VII in a 14–7 loss to the undefeated Miami Dolphins. See also: **Fun Bunch**; **Hogs**; **Smurfs**

Owens, Terrell

Brash, outspoken, All-Pro wide receiver of the 1990s and 2000s, known informally as "T.O." A third-round pick of the San Francisco 49ers in 1996, Owens has repeatedly courted controversy (and worn out his welcome with five different teams) with his penchant for trash-talking, excessive **end zone celebration**, and bizarre postgame pronouncements. See also: **Sharpie Incident**; **Sheridan, Nicollette**

"Packarena"

Parody version of the Los Del Rio dance hit "The Macarena" recorded by Milwaukee radio host Jane Matenaer in honor of the 1996 Green Bay Packers. On February 16, 1997, "Packarena" became the first NFL-themed novelty song to be played in space when astronauts on board the Space Shuttle *Discovery* used it as a wake-up call for their Wisconsin-born payload commander, Mark C. Lee.

Packerettes

Erstwhile cheerleading squad of the Green Bay Packers. The Packerettes gave way to the **Golden Girls**—named after Packers great **Paul Hornung**—from 1961 to 1972 and were rechristened the **Green Bay Sideliners** in 1977.

Packer Lumberjack Band

Legendary Green Bay Packers marching band that entertained at the team's home games and select road contests from 1921 until well into the 1950s—at which point it lost its "lumberjack" designation and became simply the Green Bay Packer Band. Members were clad in traditional lumbering garb: rubber boots, plaid woolen jackets, and matching hunting caps.

Pac-Man

Nickname bestowed in early childhood on Adam Jones, a talented but troubled cornerback/kick return specialist of the 2000s. The moniker was coined by his mother Deborah in recognition of the avidity with which he sucked on his bottle as an infant. Jones' tenure in the NFL has been marred by numerous run-ins with the law and league officials. NFL commissioner Roger Goodell suspended him for a year in 2007 following an incident in which members of the then–Tennessee Titan's entourage allegedly fired into the crowd during a melee at a Las Vegas strip club, resulting in the irreversible paralysis of bouncer Tommy Urbanski. In an effort to rehabilitate his image, Jones announced plans in 2008 to retire his "Pac-Man" nickname—requesting that sportswriters refer to him exclusively as Adam or "Mr. Jones." He is one of numerous NFL stars to embark upon a secondary career in **professional wrestling**.

Palmer, Jesse

*See **Bachelor, The***

Papa Bear

Nickname of Hall of Fame head coach, Chicago Bears paterfamilias, and longtime NFL *macher* George Halas. Jack Warden won an Emmy for his portrayal of Halas in the 1971 made-for-TV movie ***Brian's Song***.

Papale, Vince

Philadelphia Eagles special teamer of the mid-1970s whose exploits supplied the inspiration for two football films: the 1998 made-for-television movie ***The Garbage Picking Field Goal Kicking Philadelphia Phenomenon***, starring Tony Danza, and the 2006 theatrical feature ***Invincible***, starring Mark Wahlberg. A Philadelphia native and part-time schoolteacher, Papale was an accomplished semipro player when newly hired Eagles coach Dick Vermeil permitted him a private tryout in 1976. When he subsequently made the squad, Papale became one of the NFL's oldest rookies ever at the age of 30. He played effectively on special teams and occasionally at wide receiver before an injury curtailed his career in 1979. Papale's nickname was "Rocky."

Paper Lion

Acclaimed 1966 nonfiction book by journalist and bon vivant George Plimpton, documenting his experiences as a "last-string quarterback" in training camp with the 1963 Detroit Lions. One of the seminal works of the "participatory journalism" fad of the 1960s, *Paper Lion* focuses mainly on Plimpton's athletic ineptitude and does not contain much in the way of behind-the-scenes insights into NFL culture of the period. It does contain Plimpton's characteristically droll portraits of numerous Lions stalwarts, including cornerback Dick "Night Train" Lane and defensive lineman **Alex**

Karras, who would later name his son after Plimpton. In 1968, the book was made into a feature film starring Alan Alda as Plimpton and featuring cameos by Karras, **Frank Gifford**, and Vince Lombardi—all playing themselves. *Paper Lion* was the only feature film in which Lombardi ever appeared.

Parcells, Bill
See **Tuna**

Pat Patriot

Fictitious Revolutionary War minuteman who has served as the official mascot of the New England Patriots since 1961. The original rendering of Pat Patriot, a ticked-off militia member in a tri-cornered hat snapping a football, actually dates back to the late 1950s. Before the then–Boston Patriots even took the field, *Boston Globe* cartoonist Phil Bissell was commissioned to create a logo that represented the team. In 1961, miserly Patriots owner Billy Sullivan convinced the newspaper to hand over all rights to the character for free, compensating Bissell a total of $100 for his efforts. Pat Patriot went on to grace the team's helmets, stationery, pennants, and other paraphernalia for more than three decades. In 1993, the snapping patriot logo was discontinued and replaced by the team's current **Flying Elvis** insignia. The name Pat Patriot was retained, but the mascot was given a makeover in Flying Elvis' image. Now more mischievous than angry, the newfangled mascot was often compared unfavorably to his predecessor. He attracted all the wrong kinds of headlines in December of 2009 when Pat Patriot portrayer Robert Sormanti was busted by police for soliciting a prostitute via Craigslist during an undercover sting operation at a Rhode Island hotel.

Perry, William "the Refrigerator"

Gargantuan defensive tackle of the 1980s best known as the public face of the 1985 Chicago Bears. A first-round draft pick out of Clemson, Perry earned his nickname during his college years when a friend saw him stepping out of an elevator and likened his carriage to a walking refrigerator. At his heaviest, "the Fridge" weighed nearly 400 pounds and was nearly impossible to move, prompting Bears coach **Mike Ditka** to insert him on offense at fullback on occasion. (In one of the many oddities of Super Bowl XX, Perry scored a rushing touchdown while Hall of Fame running back Walter Payton did not.) Perry was so immense that he had to have his Super Bowl ring custom made. At size 25, it is more than twice as big as a typical man's ring and by far the largest in Super Bowl history. A significant Reagan Era folk hero and a vital cog in the Bears' Shufflin' Crew, Perry was the subject of not one but two tribute rap songs: "Frig-O-Rator" by Roq-In' Zoo and "Refrigerator" by Hard Machine.

Pisarcik, Joe

See **Fumble, The (1978)**

Playmakers

Controversial television drama that aired on ESPN from 2003 to 2004 depicting life behind the scenes in a fictionalized version of the NFL. Real-life players objected to the series' portrayal of professional football locker rooms as cesspools of sex, drug use, and criminal activity. Despite solid ratings and positive reviews, the all-sports network was pressured to cancel the show after just 11 episodes.

"Playoffs?"

Shouted interrogative that served as the rhetorical climax of an infamous postgame tirade by Indianapolis Colts coach **Jim Mora** on November 25, 2001, footage from which was later featured in a popular Coors Light television commercial.

Plimpton, George

See **Paper Lion**

Poe

Costumed perching bird who has served as an official mascot of the Baltimore Ravens since 1996. Poe was originally one of three raven **mascots** named in honor of the city of Baltimore's most famous resident, Edgar Allan Poe. The literary triad was famously "hatched" from enormous eggs before a preseason game between the Ravens and the Philadelphia Eagles on August 24, 1998. They were, in order of emergence, Edgar, a "tall, strong, competitive Raven with long, flowing feathers, and sharp, pointy eyes;" Allan, a "short, skinny, and agile" bird; and Poe, the "chubby, lazy, but undeniably lovable" runt of the raven litter. (In the original schema, Poe represented the animal spirit of linemen, Allan the skill position players, and Edgar the defensive backs and linebackers.) Edgar and Allan were unceremoniously mothballed after the 2008 season, leaving Poe as the team's sole costumed mascot. Two live ravens, **Rise and Conquer**, also represent the franchise at off-field events.

Pony Express

Controversial Denver Broncos cheerleading squad of the late 1970s known for its skimpy outfits, cowboy hats, and propensity for wild and sometimes lawless behavior. Two members of the Pony Express were fired from the squad in September of 1978 after they were caught on film stealing the

AP Images

wallet of an undercover policeman posing as a drunk outside a downtown Denver liquor store. That same year, several Pony Express members posed nude for a *Playboy* pictorial, sparking a furor that eventually resulted in the disbanding of the squad in 1980. Shortly before its demise, the troupe was featured in an episode of *Mork & Mindy* titled "Hold That Mork" during which Robin Williams donned a halter top and miniskirt and pranced along the sideline, much to the horror of the Mile High Stadium crowd. The Broncos went without a cheerleading squad until 1993, when the somewhat more demure Denver Broncos Cheerleaders succeeded the Pony Express.

Portis, Clinton

Pro Bowl running back of the 2000s best known for appearing at press conferences in character in a variety of outlandish disguises, a practice he attributed to boredom at traditional media Q&A sessions. Some of Portis'

The Clinton Administration

List of Clinton Portis' Press Conference Personae

The Mad Scientist	Eastern Motors Actor
Southeast Jerome	Bud Foxx
Dolemite Jenkins	Electra
Sheriff Gonna Getcha	Prime Minister Yah Mon
Inspector 2-2	Blondie
Reverend Gonna Change	Swine Flu
Dolla Bill	Jersey Number Contract Dispute Man
Coach Janky Spanky	
Dr. I Don't Know	Still Better Than Larry Johnson
Kid Bro Sweets	53 Men's Packages
Coconut Jones	Phillies Hat
Choo Choo	Hot Stuff
Dr. Do Itch Big	Psychic Bum-Bum
The Ghost of Southeast Jerome	Sir Lend-me-a-hand

more memorable creations include the Mad Scientist, a bespectacled Einstein-like figure on a quest to solve the mystery of getting into the end zone; Southeast Jerome, a masked pimp in a black robe and cape; Dr. I Don't Know, a blood-spattered surgeon; and Dolemite Jenkins, a bewigged nerd inspired by the independent film *Napoleon Dynamite*.

Pro Bowl

Annual NFL All-Star game played to general fan disinterest at the end of every season since 1939, with the exception of a seven-year stretch in the late 1940s. For many years, the game was played at the Los Angeles Memorial Coliseum. It was later staged at Aloha Stadium in Hawaii, where the allure of an exotic backdrop made the desultory contests somewhat palatable for television viewers. In general, Pro Bowls in the post-merger era have suffered from player apathy and an attendant unwillingness to tackle, run hard, or otherwise risk injury in a meaningless exhibition game. To try to gin up some interest in the fading All-Star spectacle, in 2010 the NFL moved the game to the week before, rather than the week after, the Super Bowl.

Professional Wrestling

Professional sports career pursued by numerous football stars before, during, and after their gridiron glory days. Notable pro football players turned pro wrestlers include Hall of Fame fullback **Bronko** Nagurski, **AFL**

Audibles

"In what other sport can you pick up a $14 pair of boots, 59-cent socks—spend maybe a total of $50—and convert it into $100,000 a year, if you are sharp and train?"

—Ernie "the Big Cat" Ladd, on the allure of professional wrestling for ex-NFL players

standouts **Wahoo McDaniel** and **Ernie "the Big Cat" Ladd**, and Chicago Bears defensive tackle Steve "Mongo" McMichael, among others.

Prothro, Tommy

Successful college and professional head coach of the 1950s, '60s, and '70s who was known for his hyperefficient, businessman's demeanor. Instantly recognizable for his fedora, black horn-rimmed glasses, and ever-present cigarette, Prothro was famous for carrying an attaché case on the sideline— the contents of which he never revealed.

Punt, Pass, and Kick

Popular youth football skills competition, sponsored by the NFL since 1961, whose winners are typically trotted out during national telecasts of divisional playoff games. (In the 1970s, it was customary for the finals themselves to be televised live.) Over the years, a number of PP&K alumni have gone on to play quarterback in the NFL—including **Brett Favre**, Drew Bledsoe, and Vinny Testaverde. Future Philadelphia Eagles head coach Andy Reid—then a hulking 13-year-old known as Andrew Reid—competed during halftime of a *Monday Night Football* contest in 1971. There have been embarrassing moments as well. In 2008, 14-year-old group winner Anna Grant was pitilessly booed by the crowd at a playoff game in Indianapolis for wearing a New England Patriots jersey during her introduction.

"Purple and Gold"

Dirge-like team **fight song** composed by Minneapolis-born pop star Prince in honor of the 2009 Minnesota Vikings. The faded funkmeister, a lifelong Vikings fan, was inspired to toss off the number after watching the Vikings defeat the Dallas Cowboys in an NFC playoff game from his skybox at the Hubert H. Humphrey Metrodome. "I saw the future," Prince declared to a local TV reporter after penning the funereal track. Indeed he had. Less than a week after the release of "Purple and Gold," the Vikings dropped dead in the final minutes of the NFC Championship Game, losing to the New Orleans Saints 31–28 in overtime.

Purple People Eaters

Colorful nickname bestowed on the defensive line of the Minnesota Vikings from the late 1960s through the mid-1970s and considered one of the most formidable front fours in NFL history. Carl Eller, **Jim Marshall**, Alan Page, and Gary Larsen made up the original Purple People Eaters (Larsen was eventually replaced by Doug Sutherland). They were so named for the Viking's bright purple uniforms, their proficiency at "eating" quarterbacks, and in homage to country singer Sheb Wooley's 1958 novelty hit "The Purple People Eater." The four linemen were also sometimes referred to as the Purple Gang.

Quick Kick

Seldom-used trick play—essentially a surprise punt—that is successfully executed about once in a generation in an NFL game. For some reason, quick kicks have traditionally been associated with the Philadelphia Eagles. Joe Muha, a two-way standout on the Eagles' 1948 championship team, was known as a master of the quick kick. His 82-yard boot against the New York Giants that season stood as the longest punt in franchise history until quarterback Randall Cunningham quick kicked a 91-yarder against the Giants in 1989. Cunningham's skill as a punter made him one of the last quick kick threats from the quarterback position. He successfully executed 20 quick kicks over the course of his 16-year career.

R

Ragnar

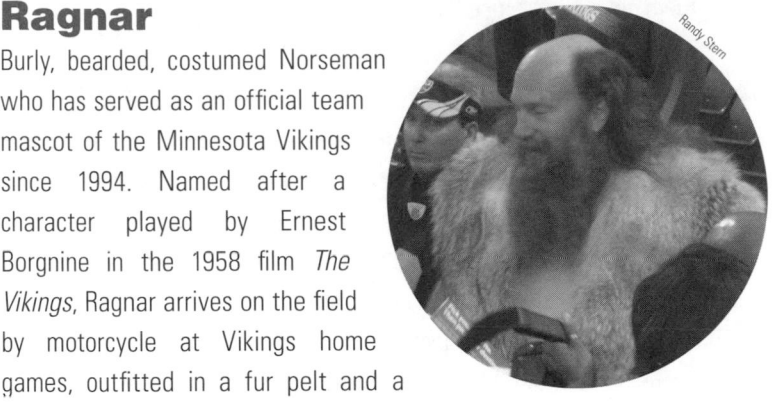

Randy Stern

Burly, bearded, costumed Norseman who has served as an official team mascot of the Minnesota Vikings since 1994. Named after a character played by Ernest Borgnine in the 1958 film *The Vikings*, Ragnar arrives on the field by motorcycle at Vikings home games, outfitted in a fur pelt and a horned helmet in the likeness of an old Norse warrior. He is the alter ego of Joseph Juranitch, a Minneapolis high school security guard and born-again Christian who tried out for the part at the suggestion of his wife during a series of open auditions held by the team in late 1993. To win the gig, Juranitch had to vanquish the son of original Viking **Hub Meeds**, who was also trying out for the role. At present, Ragnar is the NFL's only human mascot.

Raiderettes

Official name of the Oakland/Los Angeles Raiders cheerleading squad, known informally as "Football's Fabulous Females." The Raiderettes have entertained crowds at the team's home games since 1961. They are distinguished by their unique code of conduct. Raiderettes are forbidden to smoke or chew gum while in uniform, for instance.

Nicole Gottwald

However, they may date players—single ones, that is. For many years, the Raiderettes were supplied with a list specifying which Raiders were married and hence off-limits. Raiderettes are also barred from training camp, the locker room, and the practice field.

Rainbow Man

Bewigged born-again Christian whose public declarations of faith inspired the proliferation of **John 3:16** signs at NFL and college football games in the 1980s and '90s. Born the first time as Rollen Frederick Stewart (and also known by the secondary moniker Rock 'n' Rollen), Rainbow Man first started showing up at televised sporting events in the late 1970s. Dubbed Rainbow Man for his unexplained predilection for wearing a rainbow-colored afro hairpiece, he actually detests sports and hogs the camera solely as a means of alerting others about the imminent Second Coming of Jesus.

Rampage

Anthropomorphized bighorn sheep who has been the official mascot of the St. Louis Rams since 2010. Rampage was commissioned by the team in part to erase the memory of **Ramster**, the Rams' misbegotten mid-1990s hamster mascot. The new character "has the coating of a stuffed animal but the build of a superhero," in the words of a team executive. The name Rampage was selected from a list of more than 1,700 suggestions submitted by fans in an online "name the mascot" contest. The other four finalists were Archie, Ramsey, Rammer, and Rush.

Aaron Staebell

"I don't think it was something people missed when it went away."

–St. Louis Ram D'Marco Farr, on the demise of Ramster

Ramster

Short-lived hamster mascot of the 1995 St. Louis Rams. The fuzzy costumed rodent, whom some fans likened to a giant rat, lasted only one season on the Rams sideline before being mothballed forever. The team went without an official mascot until 2010, when **Rampage** made its debut.

Red Right 88

Playbook designation for the ill-fated pass play that ended the unlikely playoff run of the 1980 Cleveland Browns. The **Kardiac Kids** were in position for a winning field goal with less than a minute to go in the AFC playoff game against the Oakland Raiders at Municipal Stadium in Cleveland. Head coach Sam Rutigliano's decision to run a pass play on second down— in part due to his lack of confidence in placekicker Don Cockroft—resulted in an interception that sealed the win for the Raiders. The phrase "Red Right 88" immediately entered Cleveland football lore, where it would shortly be joined by **The Drive** and **The Fumble**.

Redskinettes

Official name of the Washington Redskins cheerleaders, the oldest such pep squad in the NFL. Originally called the Washington Redskins Cheerleaders and known informally by the sobriquet "the First Ladies of Football," the Redskinettes have been entertaining home crowds at Redskins games since 1962. In their early years, they wore stereotypical Native American

AP Images

costumes. In the late 1970s, complaints about the physical conditioning of some of the cheerleaders (one national publication derided them as "matronly") led the Redskinettes to adopt a sexier, more revealing look in the fashion of the wildly popular **Dallas Cowboys Cheerleaders**. The new outfits were cut high on the thigh, with a diamond-shaped cutout that showed off the cheerleaders' bare midriffs. Public outcry over the skimpy costumes soon compelled the team to abandon this approach, however, and the diamond-shaped navel port was covered up after only two Sundays.

Audibles

"I would forego navel exposure and bring back the good, old-fashioned cleavage."

–Washington Redskins fan Marilyn Fausnight, in a letter to the team's front office that ignited the **Redskinettes'** "Navelgate" controversy

Great Moments in Cheerleaders Scandal

In 2007, two **Redskinettes** were fired from their $75-a-week jobs after the team discovered they were both dating tight end Chris Cooley—a violation of franchise policy prohibiting fraternization with players. In response, outraged Redskinettes choreographed a routine in which they would turn their backs on Cooley during a home game.

Reggie's Prayer

Interminable 1996 movie melodrama starring NFL legend **Reggie White**. Made under the auspices of White's own production company and released straight to video, *Reggie's Prayer* combines turgid family melodrama, awkwardly staged action sequences, and evangelical Christian preaching to negligible cinematic effect. White plays Reggie Knox, a thinly veiled version of himself who abruptly retires from the gridiron to become an inner-city high school teacher in Portland, Oregon. His new life consists of whipping the school football team into shape and ministering to a troubled youth mixed up in the local narcotics trade. "Guiding the children—it ought to be your prayer. I guarantee you it's Reggie's prayer," White intones in one of the film's numerous solemn speeches. Professional wrestler Paul "the Big Show" Wight plays White's nemesis, a diabolical drug dealer who's

Audibles

"Finish the sweepin'. I gotta go change the urinal mints."

—Mike Holmgren to Brett Favre in a memorable scene from *Reggie's Prayer*

obsessed with toy trains. Pat Morita—Mr. Miyagi from *The Karate Kid*—dons an **Albert Einstein** wig to play Osaki, the school's wise principal. *Reggie's Prayer* also features cameo appearances from NFL greats Mel Renfro and **Roosevelt "Rosey" Grier** and Emilio "Luis from *Sesame Street*" Delgado. In one of many cringe-inducing scenes, **Brett Favre** and Mike Holmgren play a pair of dim-witted school janitors. MC Hammer plays a manic park ranger who helps Reggie bring the drug lord to justice. Boom mikes are visible in several scenes, a telltale sign of low production values.

Replacements, The

Tiresome 2000 comedy film loosely based on the 1987 NFL players' strike. Keanu Reeves stars as Shane "Footsteps" Falco, a washed-up former college quarterback who gets a second chance at NFL glory after the regular players walk out with three games left on the schedule. The frenetic crowd pleaser is rife with logic and continuity errors—such as the fact that games being played in Washington, D.C., in late December are depicted as taking place in broiling hot weather. Gene Hackman

phones in his performance as the head coach of the fictional Washington Sentinels. Announcers Pat Summerall and **John Madden** play themselves. This was veteran character actor Jack Warden's final film.

Revis Island

Metaphorical, Alcatraz-type land mass on which New York Jets All-Pro cornerback Darrelle Revis is said to isolate and contain opposing wide receivers.

Reynolds, Jillian

Willowy blonde weathercaster who rose to national prominence through her association with the FOX Sports NFL pregame show *FOX NFL Sunday*. Although she has no background in football (and, in fact, no background in meteorology), the Canadian native has ably reported the game-day weather conditions at various NFL sites since 2000—filling the pregame "babe" role pioneered by **Phyllis George** in the 1970s. She is the ex-wife of former Major League Baseball player Bret Barberie.

Riggins, John

Stalwart power running back of the 1970s and '80s best known for his MVP performance in Super Bowl XVII. "Riggo," or "the Diesel," as he was known to his New York Jets and Washington Redskins teammates, was considered something of a flake for the first decade of his career. He sat out the entire 1980 NFL season in a contract dispute, prompting Redskins coach Joe Gibbs to label him "a fruitcake." But his national profile was heightened during the 1982 playoffs, when he rushed for 610 yards and led the Redskins to their first Super Bowl victory. As a newly minted D.C. folk hero, the hard-living iconoclast occasionally ran into public relations trouble. His embarrassing behavior at a black-tie Salute to Congress banquet in 1985 is the stuff of legend. In short order, a drunken Riggins allegedly propositioned Supreme Court Justice **Sandra Day O'Connor**, passed a helium balloon to Virginia governor Chuck Robb, and passed out during a speech by Vice President George H.W. Bush. After retiring in 1985, Riggins pursued an acting and

"I'm bored, I'm broke, and I'm back."

–John Riggins, after returning to the game following his boycott of the 1980 season broadcasting career—highlighted by his portrayal of Bottom in an off-Broadway production of *A Midsummer Night's Dream* in 2004. "Former football great John Riggins is spectacularly good as Bottom," raved theater critic Martin Denton, "a swaggering innocent whose overblown ways can't quite infuriate for their naive simple-mindedness."

Rise and Conquer

Brother birds who have served as official avian ambassadors of the Baltimore Ravens since 2009. (Interestingly enough, they are not full-blooded ravens, but hybrids of a West African raven and a pied crow.) The names Rise and Conquer were chosen by fans in an online vote, narrowly beating out Blitz and Rush. The Ravens initially planned to have Rise and Conquer fly out of the team tunnel at home games, but were dissuaded from doing so by officials at the Maryland Zoo, where the birds reside.

Roary

Lauren Tolbert

Seven-foot-tall, blue-eyed, forlorn-looking costumed jungle cat who has been the official mascot of the Detroit Lions since 1983. Formerly known as Huddles, Roary has suffered more than his share of indignities through the decades as the Lions have struggled to regain respectability as a franchise. In his early years on the job, the mascot was routinely pelted with debris by angry Lions fans. A deranged man at an off-season function once tore the lion's tail off and ran away with it. And during a **Thanksgiving Day** rout at the hands of the Indianapolis Colts in 2004, Lions tight end Casey FitzSimmons took out his frustration by pegging Roary in the nose with a football.

Roberts, Mark

Liverpool-born professional streaker who ran semi-naked onto the field at Super Bowl XXXVIII in Houston, Texas. A past master of public nudity who had previously streaked his way onto center court at Wimbledon and the Tour de France bicycle race, among numerous other venues, the tubby English exhibitionist had long set his sights on America's premier sporting event. The second-half kickoff of the game between the New England Patriots and the Carolina Panthers was about to take place when Roberts charged the gridiron dressed as a referee, then immediately stripped down to a football-shaped G-string and started dancing on the 30-yard line. He was quickly subdued by a hit from New England linebacker Matt Chatham, hogtied, and carried off the field by police. Roberts' bum rush came just moments after singer **Janet Jackson** had scarred the retinas of America's youth with her infamous "wardrobe malfunction" during the halftime show. A Texas judge later fined him $1,000 for trespassing. Although he avoided jail time, Roberts is banned from reentering the United States.

Rome, Jim

Pugnacious Los Angeles–based sports radio talk show host who courted controversy in the mid-1990s with a sustained rhetorical assault on the manhood of Los Angeles Rams quarterback Jim Everett. Rome repeatedly belittled the contact-averse Everett as "Chris"—an apparent reference to female tennis great Chris Evert. The public humiliation campaign culminated in violence on the evening of April 6, 1994, when Rome repeated the taunt to Everett during a live television interview on ESPN2. An enraged Everett leapt up from his chair, overturned a table, and threw Rome to the floor. No charges were filed. Actor John C. McGinley played a thinly veiled version of Rome in the film *Any Given Sunday*.

Rowdy

Cartoonish costumed gunslinger who served as the official mascot of the Dallas Cowboys from 1996 to 2009. An Old West caricature with a rictus grin, six-shooter water pistols, and oversized 10-gallon hat, Rowdy was an extremely polarizing figure within the closed circle of the Cowboys fan community. Some rooters were charmed by his antics. Others were annoyed by them. Cowboys coach **Bill Parcells** once exiled the mascot from training camp and kicked him off the sideline in the middle of a game. An entire website, removerowdy.com, was devoted to lobbying for his ouster. The controversy finally came to a head in 2008, when Rowdy ran afoul of NFL brass for parking his pimped-out blue-and-silver four-wheel ATV in the end zone during receiving drills. Following a widely publicized *Monday Night Football* incident in which the overzealous mascot was caught on camera chest-bumping wideout **Terrell Owens** after a touchdown, Rowdy was banished from the sideline during games and largely relegated to T-shirt cannon duty. Despite maintaining a lucrative sideline of 300 personal appearances a year, charging as much as $500 an hour, the foam-headed desperado could not survive long without the added exposure of regular game-day appearances. In August of 2009, the Cowboys bowed to public pressure and fired Rowdy—although the club reserved the right to trot the character out for special events. His final appearance at Cowboys Stadium was for a Papa John's Pizza commercial. In the wake of his dismissal, Rowdy portrayer Ted Ovletrea threatened to write a tell-all book on his experiences as a Cowboys mascot.

Row Your Boat

Mocking **end zone dance** performed by Carolina Panthers wide receiver Steve Smith during a 38–13 rout of the Minnesota Vikings on October 30, 2005. After scoring a touchdown—part of an 11-catch, 201-yard performance—Smith sat down on the turf and pantomimed rowing a boat—an apparent reference to the Lake Minnetonka **Love Boat Scandal** that gripped the Vikings that season.

Russert, Tim

Respected TV newsman and longtime host of NBC's *Meet the Press* whose unabashed love for the Buffalo Bills made him a kind of unofficial NFL ambassador. Russert, who grew up in Buffalo, claimed to have attended the Woodstock music festival wearing a Bills jersey. During the NFL season, he often ended his *Meet the Press* broadcasts with the exhortation "Go Bills." He devoted an entire chapter of his best-selling memoir *Big Russ and Me* to his love of the team. Russert died suddenly of a massive heart attack in June of 2008. Shortly after his death, a stretch of Route 20A in Orchard Park, New York, near the Bills' home field at Ralph Wilson Stadium, was renamed the Timothy J. Russert Highway in his honor.

Ryan, Buddy

Colorful, combative NFL defensive coordinator/head coach who first came to national prominence as the architect of the legendarily stout "46" defense of the 1985 Chicago Bears. A notorious instigator, Ryan was beloved by his players but reviled by opponents and many of his coaching colleagues. As head man in Philadelphia in 1989, he famously placed a price on the head of kicker **Luis Zendejas** during the infamous **Bounty Bowl** game. In 1994, as defensive coordinator for the Houston Oilers, he punched offensive coordinator Kevin Gilbride in the jaw during a nationally televised game following a dispute over play-calling. Ryan is the subject of the 1988 Eagles team **music video "Buddy's Watching You."** His son is New York Jets head coach **Rex Ryan**.

Ryan, Rex

Vainglorious, dyslexic, obese son of legendary coach **Buddy Ryan**, famed for his bombastic public persona. In his first two years as head coach of the New York Jets, Ryan repeatedly courted controversy. He gave the finger to a group of boisterous Miami Dolphins fans at a mixed martial arts event in Florida; twice guaranteed (and failed to deliver) a Super Bowl title to the beleaguered New York franchise; and provoked the ire of soft-spoken coaching legend Tony Dungy with a series of profane tirades on the HBO reality series *Hard Knocks*. In December of 2010, the website Deadspin outed Ryan as a foot fetishist, calling attention to a series of YouTube videos purportedly showing the Jets' coach rhapsodizing about his wife's bodacious toes.

S

Sabol, Ed

Acclaimed documentary filmmaker and co-founder, with his son **Steve Sabol**, of **NFL Films**.

Sabol, Steve

Emmy Award–winning filmmaker who co-founded **NFL Films** with his father **Ed Sabol**. Among his many other accomplishments, Steve penned much of the portentous voice-over copy made famous by narrator/**"Voice of God" John Facenda**, including the legendary ode to the Oakland Raiders, "The Autumn Wind."

Sack Dance

Controversial celebratory routine popularized by New York Jets defensive end **Mark Gastineau** in the early 1980s, to the consternation of much of the NFL. The 6'5", 265-pound Gastineau—a charter member of the Jets' **New York Sack Exchange**—first began performing the Sack Dance in 1980. A spontaneous, spasmodic full-body freak-out precipitated by the lineman's every leveling of the quarterback, the dance infuriated opposing players, who felt they were being taunted, and offended anyone with an aesthetic sensibility. (*Sports Illustrated* remarked that Gastineau "looked less like a man dancing than someone who had just set fire to his clothes.") Many of Gastineau's own teammates were mortified by his antics, which succeeded in revving up home crowds but unnecessarily antagonized opponents. The league-wide fury over the Sack Dance finally came to a head during a game at Shea Stadium in September of 1983, when Los Angeles Rams offensive tackle Jackie Slater shoved Gastineau from behind in the middle of an especially exuberant post-sack celebration and set off a bench-clearing brawl. The incident cost Gastineau a $1,000 fine. That off-season, the NFL banned the Sack Dance forever.

Saintly Switch, A

Tepid 1999 made-for-TV movie about an over-the-hill NFL quarterback who switches bodies with his wife after their kids cast a voodoo spell on them. Fey comedian David Alan Grier is woefully miscast as Dan Anderson, a

VIVICA A. FOX   DAVID ALAN GRIER

Game Day for Sara.
Mother's Day for Dan.

trash-talking former Heisman Trophy winner who seeks one last chance at glory with the New Orleans Saints. His poor throwing form undermines the illusion that he's a rocket-armed passer, although he's more believable mincing about as Dan's stay-at-home spouse, Sara. A desperate Peter Bogdanovich (*The Last Picture Show*, **Paper Moon**) directed this shameless knockoff of *The Parent Trap*, *Freaky Friday*, and a thousand other better-executed body switch comedies.

Saintsations

Official name of the New Orleans Saints cheerleading squad, which has been enthralling home crowds at the Superdome since 1987. Established through the sponsorship of the New Orleans department store Maison Blanche, and so named by fans in a "name the cheerleaders" contest, the Saintsations are just the latest in a long line of Saints-rooting pep squads dating back to the team's 1967 inception. That list includes the **Lousiannes** (later known as the Saints Dancers), the Mademoiselles (later rechristened the **Mam'selles**), the **Bonnes Amies**, and the controversial, short-lived **New Orleans Saints Angels**. The Saintsations have been by far the best-loved and most visible of the squads, famous for their work with community charities and for annual USO trips to entertain American troops abroad. In 1992, the Saintsations were one of four NFL cheerleading squads to be featured in a collectible trading card set produced by Providence, Rhode Island–based Lime Rock International. (The others were the **Dallas Cowboys Cheerleaders**, the Los Angeles **Raiderettes**, and the Miami Dolphins Cheerleaders.) Since 1989, the Saintsations have also put out their own annual swimsuit calendar.

Sainz, Ines

Comely South of the Border television personality, the self-proclaimed "hottest sports reporter in Mexico," who emerged as a central figure in a sexual harassment scandal involving the New York Jets in September of 2010. Sainz was covering a team practice as a correspondent for Mexico's TV Azteca when she was allegedly subjected to salacious remarks and catcalls from several Jets players—including shouts of "I want to play with a Mexican," and "Eres muy guapa" (Spanish for "You are very beautiful"). The incident set off a media firestorm and prompted Jets owner Woody Johnson to issue a public apology.

Getty Images

"San Diego Super Chargers"

Catchy disco anthem that has been the official **fight song** of the San Diego Chargers since 1979. "San Diego Super Chargers" was co-written in a single day by Motown veterans Jerry Marcellino and David Sieff on a commission from Chargers owner Gene Klein and his son Michael, who wanted a fight song that would rev up the crowd at home games. A session band headed by R&B vocalist James Gaylen was brought in to lay down the track, using the fake band name Captain Q.B. and the Big Boys. Played incessantly over the San Diego Stadium loudspeakers during the team's glory years under Don Coryell, the bouncy dance tune quickly became a sing-along favorite and was released as a 45 RPM single. After being mothballed for a few years by new owner Alex Spanos, the song was brought back in a re-recorded version in 1989. The original recording has since been reinstated to the stadium playlist, while fans and San Diego–area musicians often post cover versions and remixes on YouTube. **Chris Berman** and Tom Jackson, the hosts of ESPN's *NFL Primetime*, often sing a portion of the song's chorus over Chargers highlights.

San Francisco Gold Rush

Name used by the San Francisco 49ers cheerleading squad since 1983. The 32-member Gold Rush succeeded the 49ers previous dance team, the **49er Nuggets**. Actress Teri Hatcher of TV's *Desperate Housewives* is an alumnus of the squad.

Wilhelm Yee

Santa Claus Incident

Notorious snowball pelting that took place at halftime of a game between the Philadelphia Eagles and the Minnesota Vikings at Franklin Field in Philadelphia on December 15, 1968. The last-place Eagles were playing out the string on a dismal 2–12 campaign that day, as a nasty, slushy snowstorm battered the City of Brotherly Love. Nevertheless, a spirited crowd of 54,535 showed up to cheer on the team—or, at the very least, to get some drinking done and voice their displeasure at team owner Jerry Wolman and coach/GM Joe Kuharich for their perceived mismanagement of the once-proud franchise. The scheduled halftime entertainment was a Christmas spectacular featuring the Sound of Brass band, the **Eaglettes** cheerleaders dressed in elf costumes, and an appearance by Santa Claus himself. When the official Santa failed to show, team officials entreated a 5'6", 19-year-old fan named **Frank Olivo**—who had shown up in the stands wearing a false beard and a corduroy Santa suit—to take his place. With his elaborate sleigh grounded by the inclement weather, Olivo was forced to take the field on foot, running at the head of a flying wedge of chesty Eaglettes to the accompaniment of "Here Comes Santa Claus" arranged for a 50-piece brass band. The liquored-up crowd almost immediately began booing and hurling snowballs at Olivo, who returned fire by wagging his finger at fans and informing them they would receive no presents on Christmas. In the end, hundreds of slushy projectiles were tossed. Several hit their mark. That night, **Howard Cosell** showed footage of the incident on his nationally televised sports highlight show, forever cementing Philadelphia's reputation as the home of the most depraved, obnoxious sports fans in the country.

Sas, Norman

Inventor of **Electric Football**.

Sea of Hands

Nickname for the memorable catch that climaxed an AFC playoff game between the Miami Dolphins and the Oakland Raiders at Oakland Coliseum on December 21, 1974. The Raiders were trailing with 24 seconds left in the game when quarterback Ken Stabler shot-putted a desperation pass under intense pressure in the general direction of the end zone. Injury-plagued running back Clarence Davis managed to corral the game-winning heave just as three Dolphins defenders collapsed on him, creating a "sea of hands" effect. The dramatic touchdown ended the game and with it the Dolphins' dream of a third straight Super Bowl championship.

"Seahawks Locker Room Rock, The"

Weirdly homoerotic team song and **music video** recorded by the 1985 Seattle Seahawks, often derided as one of the worst examples of the genre. Eschewing the rap stylings then prevalent in team videos, "The Seahawks

Locker Room Rock" is set to a grating, old-fashioned "Yakety Sax"–type ditty that recalls the background music to *TV's Bloopers & Practical Jokes*. Even more disturbing is the fact that the "action" takes place in and around the Seahawks locker room, where players lift weights and cavort in various stages of undress. At one point, a half-naked male saxophone player emerges from a foggy shower stall and grins lasciviously as he blows steam out of the bell of his horn. Future Minnesota Vikings coach Mike Tice is one of the players seen dancing, stripping, and pumping iron.

Seattle Sea Gals

Official Seattle Seahawks cheerleading squad, tasked with arousing fans at home games since the team's inception in 1976.

Second Effort

Legendary motivational sales training film starring Hall of Fame head coach Vince Lombardi. Produced by Dartnell Training Films in 1968 shortly after Lombardi's retirement as Green Bay Packers head coach, *Second Effort* has Lombardi schooling a timid salesman—played by character actor Ron Masak, best known as Sheriff Mort Metzger on the long-running TV mystery series *Murder, She Wrote*—in the finer points of closing a deal. Using football as a metaphor, Lombardi imparts some of the principles he developed on the gridiron in the form of aphorisms such as "Mental toughness is the essential key to success," "A man who is physically fit performs better at any job," and "Fatigue makes cowards of us all." The 30-minute film, shot in and around Lombardi's offices at Lambeau Field, features a cameo by Packers legend Jerry Kramer. According to Masak, Lombardi refused to wear makeup, declined to do retakes, and insisted on shooting the scenes in chronological order. He also kicked a Dartnell executive off the set for attempting to give him notes on his performance. In the years after its initial release, *Second Effort* became an international sensation, selling more than 50,000 copies and being incorporated into countless management and sales training seminars worldwide.

Second String

Anodyne 2002 TV movie chronicling an improbable Super Bowl run by the Buffalo Bills. Gil Bellows (Billy from TV's *Ally McBeal*) stars as Dan "Give 'Em Hell" Heller, a washed-up former quarterback who gives up his quiet life as an insurance salesman for a chance to play on the Bills' practice team. When the entire first-team offense is stricken with food poisoning on the eve of a playoff game, Heller and the rest of the taxi squad must take over for them. Academy Award winner Jon Voight, fresh off his bravura performance as **Howard Cosell** in Michael Mann's biopic *Ali*, plays the Bills' nut-cracking head coach. ESPN's **Chris Berman** and **Mike Ditka** have cameos. Quarterback **Doug Flutie** plays himself. The musical coordinator was Devo frontman Mark Mothersbaugh.

Semi-Tough

Football-themed 1977 film comedy loosely based on the novel of the same name by sportswriter Dan Jenkins. *Semi-Tough* stars Burt Reynolds and Kris Kristofferson as Billy Clyde Puckett and Marvin "Shake" Tiller, star halfback and wide receiver for the Miami Bucks, a fictitious professional team vying for its first Super Bowl title. Seventies fixture Jill Clayburgh plays Barbara Jane Bookman, the daughter of the team's owner, who harbors romantic feelings for both men. Numerous NFL stars of the era, including **Ed "Too Tall" Jones**, **John Matuszak**, and the ubiquitous **Joe Kapp** have cameo roles as players. **Carl Weathers**, the onetime journeyman linebacker turned Hollywood actor, portrays a mouthy pass rusher for the Bucks' Super Bowl opponent, the Chicago Marauders. Announcers Dick Schapp, Lindsey Nelson, and **Paul Hornung** also appear. While it's generously larded with guest stars, *Semi-Tough* ultimately has very little to do with football. About halfway through its running time, the film devolves into a broad satire of late-1970s self-improvement cults like EST. It climaxes with an inane fistfight at a wedding.

Sharpie Incident

Commonly used term for the October 14, 2002, stunt pulled by San Francisco 49ers wide receiver **Terrell Owens** in which he took a Sharpie brand marker out of his sock and signed the football after scoring a touchdown during a game against the Seattle Seahawks. The choreographed **end zone celebration** culminated in Owens' handing the autographed pigskin to his financial adviser, who was sitting in a nearby luxury suite. The NFL later fined Owens $5,000 for the prank and issued a ban on players bringing "foreign objects" onto the field. See also: **Cell Phone Incident**

Sheridan, Nicollette

Comely blonde television actress who generated a stir with her appearance alongside wide receiver **Terrell Owens** in a sexually suggestive opening skit on a ***Monday Night Football*** telecast in 2004. In the sketch, Sheridan, one of the stars of the popular ABC series *Desperate Housewives*, convinces Owens to forego playing in that night's game by leaping naked into his arms in the locker room.

Legends of the Fall

The pregame skit that caused so much controversy for **Nicollette Sheridan** was originally supposed to feature ***Monday Night Football*** commentator **John Madden**, not **Terrell Owens**.

Shockey, Jeremy

Grotesquely overrated tight end of the 2000s better known for his flowing blond locks, bald eagle tattoo, and controversial outbursts than his play on the field. Shockey famously called Hall of Fame head coach **Bill Parcells** a "homo" during an interview with *New York* magazine.

Audibles

"Once you've seen one huddle, you've seen them all... So you either look at the popcorn, the guys, or the ladies. The choice is clear for me."

–TV director **Andy Sidaris**, on the thinking behind the development of the cheerleader **honey shot**

Sidaris, Andy

Emmy Award–winning television director who pioneered the use of revealing close-ups of cheerleaders—also known as the **honey shot**—during NFL telecasts. A live sports veteran with hundreds of college and pro football, basketball, and Olympic broadcasts to his credit, Sidaris was perhaps best known as the first director of ABC's *Wide World of Sports*. His contribution to the sexing up of NFL telecasts earned him recognition from *Los Angeles* magazine as "the man who brings T&A from the gridiron to your home." After leaving network TV in the 1980s, Sidaris applied his unique talents to directing a series of "Bullets, Bombs, and Babes" B-movies starring former *Playboy* Playmates and *Penthouse* Pets.

"Silver and Black Attack"

Rock/rap **music video** recorded by the Los Angeles Raiders in advance of their 8–8 1986 campaign. "We wear the silver, we wear the black" goes the song's mind-numbingly repetitive chorus. "Don't get in our way." Leading the charge are such mid-1980s Raiders stars as Howie Long, Marcus Allen, Todd Christiansen, and a forlorn-looking Jim Plunkett. Each player takes turns rapping out a verse—or trying to—as does head coach Tom Flores, whose flow is surprisingly effective. By contrast, future Lions GM and NFL on Fox commentator Matt Millen seems especially tongue-tied spitting rhymes like "Matt Millen's my name, and I'm from Penn State/Those turkeys on offense are creatures I hate."

Simpson, Jessica

Pop music diva of the 2000s whose highly publicized relationship with the Dallas Cowboys' Tony Romo was widely credited with "ruining" the quarterback and sabotaging the team's playoff fortunes. At the height of the controversy in 2007, Cowboys detractors set up a website, ruinromo.com, where fans could download and print out demonic Jessica Simpson masks to wave at Romo during games.

Simpson, O.J.

Hall of Fame running back of the 1970s who attained worldwide infamy in the wake of his involvement in a sensational double murder in 1994. Known informally as "the Juice," the onetime Heisman Trophy winner was the first player chosen in the 1969 NFL-**AFL** Draft. As a member of the Buffalo Bills, he led the league in rushing four times and became the first man ever to run for 2,000 yards in a season. After retiring from the game in 1979, Simpson used his good looks and affable manner to forge a successful second career in entertainment and broadcasting. He spent two unremarkable seasons as an analyst in the **Monday Night Football** booth; appeared in films like *The Towering Inferno, Capricorn One*, and *The Naked Gun* trilogy; and starred in a series of TV commercials for Hertz Rental Cars in which he was seen racing through airports and leaping over luggage. His life of easy celebrity leisure might have gone on forever had he not become entangled in the brutal stabbing murders of his second wife Nicole Brown Simpson and her friend Ronald Goldman on June 12, 1994. Amid widespread speculation that a jealous Juice may have been responsible for the slayings, Simpson famously fled for the airport in a Ford Bronco with former teammate **Al "A.C." Cowlings**, $8,000 in cash, and a false goatee. The nationally televised low-speed chase captivated the world's attention, as did the ensuing arrest and trial of the gridiron great on murder charges. After a circus trial, Simpson was acquitted, but his genial public image suffered a mortal blow and Goldman's family members eventually prevailed in a $33.5 million wrongful death lawsuit. An increasingly pudgy Simpson retreated to his Florida redoubt, where he was permitted by law to live off his NFL pension and play as much golf as he wanted. Strapped for cash, he briefly tried to leverage his status as America's most celebrated unconvicted double murderer by writing a "fictionalized" confession titled *If I Did It*. Public outrage and legal threats from Goldman's family put the kibosh on that project. In 2007, the disgraced Hall of Famer ran afoul of the law again when authorities in Las Vegas busted him on armed robbery charges for attempting to steal his own sports memorabilia from a casino hotel room. This time, Simpson was convicted and sentenced to 33 years in prison.

Singletary, Mike

Legendary Chicago Bears linebacker who famously dropped his pants in an unsuccessful attempt to motivate his team at halftime of his first game as an NFL head coach on October 26, 2008. After two quarters, the 49ers were getting whipped at home 20–3 by the Seattle Seahawks when Singletary—who had recently taken over for the fired Mike Nolan—strode into the locker room, pulled down his trousers, and pointed to his bare buttocks to indicate what he thought of the team's first-half performance. "I used my pants to illustrate that we were getting our tails whipped on Sunday and how humiliating that should feel for all of us," he later explained in a blog post. "I needed to dramatize my point." The unusual take on the concept of a "teachable moment" clearly didn't work, as the Niners ended up losing the game 34–13.

Sir Purr

Six-foot-tall costumed catamount who has served as the official mascot of the Carolina Panthers since their inaugural season in 1995. Occasionally joined on the sideline by his diminutive sidekick (sometimes called his "son," "wife," or "baby sister") Mini Meow, Sir Purr is one of the more antic NFL **mascots**. He has ridden shotgun with NASCAR driver Jeff Gordon, flown in a helicopter, and schmoozed with Hollywood stars like Bruce Willis and Will Smith. On one memorable occasion, Sir Purr was rollerblading around the field when he collided into a wall, causing his headpiece to fly off. During a game between the Panthers and the Pittsburgh Steelers in December of 1996, Sir Purr created a stir when he fell on a live ball in the end zone following a Panthers punt. The play was ruled a touchback and did not impact the outcome of the game.

Sir Saint

Big-chinned goon who, with **Gumbo** the St. Bernard, was one of two original official **mascots** of the New Orleans Saints. The impish cartoon football player in the oversized helmet was designed for the team by an illustrator commissioned by Katsy Mecom, the wife of original Saints owner John Mecom. Although often featured

Erika Andresen

on Saints publications and merchandise during the franchise's early days, Sir Saint had all but disappeared from team paraphernalia by the time the Mecom family sold the team in 1985. In 2008, the Saints introduced a slightly redesigned Sir Saint—edgier, more muscular, and less comical in appearance. He joins forces with a slimmed-down costumed version of Gumbo who replaced the perpetually pooping live canine mascot in 1994.

"Skol, Vikings"

Official **fight song** of the Minnesota Vikings played at the team's home games since 1961. "Skol, Vikings, let's win this game," goes the chorus to the song, composed by the team's halftime music coordinator, James "Red" McLeod. "Skol, Vikings, honor your name." ("Skol" is a traditional Scandinavian toast.) The lyrics also inanely exhort the Vikings to "run out the score," proving that, whatever other virtues McLeod may have possessed, he didn't have a command of football terminology.

Sloth

Deformed goliath played by ex-NFL star **John Matuszak** in the 1985 fantasy adventure movie *The Goonies*.

Smart, Rod

See **He Hate Me**

Smith, Bubba

All-Pro defensive end of the 1970s who enjoyed a successful post-retirement acting career. Smith is perhaps best known for playing Moses Hightower, a gargantuan florist who longs to join the police force, in six *Police Academy* movies between 1984 and 1989. The 6'7" Texas native also worked regularly on television throughout the 1970s and '80s, appearing on *Wonder Woman*, *Charlie's Angels*, and as himself in a memorable episode of the TV sitcom

The Odd Couple. He was one of the original Lite Beer from Miller "**Lite All-Stars**," appearing in a series of TV commercials touting the low-calorie brew's "easy opening cans."

Smith, Jackie

Hall of Fame tight end of the 1960s and '70s whose long and distinguished career with the St. Louis Cardinals is overshadowed by his memorable dropped pass in Super Bowl XIII. Smith was playing out the string as a member of the Dallas Cowboys when he flubbed an easily catchable touchdown toss from Roger Staubach in the third quarter of a closely fought contest with the Pittsburgh Steelers. Smith's drop forced the Cowboys to settle for a field goal on a drive that otherwise would have tied the game. They ended up losing 35–31.

AP Images

Smith, Onterrio

Marginally talented NFL running back of the early 2000s who gained national notoriety in 2005 after he was stopped at the airport and confiscated of the drug-masking device known as **The Original Whizzinator**.

Smurfs

Nickname for three members of the Washington Redskins' 1980s receiving corps—Virgil Seay, **Alvin Garrett**, and Charlie Brown—none of whom was taller than 5'10". *The Smurfs* was a popular children's cartoon of the era, set in a land of diminutive, blue-skinned pixies. All the members of the Smurfs were also members of the **Fun Bunch**.

Snowplow Game

Infamous **bad weather game** played at Schaefer Stadium in Foxborough, Massachusetts, on December 12, 1982, which the New England Patriots won with the help of some timely snow removal by a member of their grounds crew. The game between the Patriots and the Miami Dolphins was a scoreless tie going into the final minutes of regulation, at which point New England placekicker John Smith lined up for what would become a 33-yard game-winning field goal. Making Smith's attempt that much easier was **Mark Henderson**, a convicted burglar on a prison work release, who appeared from out of the bowels of the stadium on a John Deere tractor outfitted with a spinning brush to plow a clear path between the kicker and his holder. Dolphins head coach Don Shula would later call Henderson's snow job "the most unfair act that had ever happened in a football game."

Audibles

"No one had the heart to get rid of it."

–New England Patriots stadium operations executive Jim Nolan, on why **Mark Henderson**'s snow-clearing tractor still hangs from the rafters at the team's current home, Gillette Stadium

Snyder, Jimmy "the Greek"

Professional name adopted by Dimetrios Georgios Synodinos, a Greek American oddsmaker and sports commentator who appeared weekly on CBS' **The NFL Today** pregame show from 1976 to 1988. A fixture on the Las Vegas gambling scene from the mid-1950s onward, the Steubenville, Ohio, native was hardly a football maven. Indeed, he first gained national attention for installing the Baltimore Colts as a 17-point favorite over the New York Jets in Super Bowl III. (**Joe Namath** and the Jets ended up winning 16–7.) But his flamboyant personal style—including a predilection for whiskey and loud check sportcoats—trumped his spotty record as a prognosticator and made him a natural fit for 1970s television. He joined Brent Musburger, **Phyllis George**, and Irv Cross on The NFL Today in September of 1976, completing a revamp of the program that would revolutionize pregame coverage of professional football and provide more than a decade of soaring ratings and gossip column headlines. In his most memorable segment, Snyder would feed his weekly picks to Musburger using an enormous analog toteboard on which he summarily checked off opposing teams' strengths and weaknesses. Off camera, the relationship between the two men was anything but friendly. They got into a celebrated fistfight in a New York City bar one night in October

Audibles

"The black is a better athlete to begin with because he's been bred to be that way, because of his high thighs and big thighs that goes up into his back, and they can jump higher and run faster because of their bigger thighs. This goes back all the way to the Civil War when during the slave trading, the owner, the slave owner would breed his big black to his big woman so that he could have a big black kid."

–Jimmy "the Greek" Snyder, offering the observations on African American athletic achievement that got him fired from **The NFL Today** in 1988

of 1980, reportedly over the allocation of air time. (They made light of the incident the following week by showing up on the set wearing boxing gloves.) George was another frequent target of Snyder's ire. He routinely demeaned the former beauty queen for her lack of football knowledge and for hogging his precious air time. This boorish backstage behavior did little to detract from Snyder's audience appeal, however. While his

performances grew more erratic as age, alcohol, and indifference began to take their toll, he remained both a Sunday afternoon staple and a sought-after celebrity spokesman deep into the 1980s. That all changed in January of 1988 when Snyder sparked a nationwide furor with remarks he made to a Washington, D.C., television reporter claiming that African Americans were superior athletes because of selective breeding during the days of slavery. The comments, which were aired as part of a news special that aired on Martin Luther King Jr. Day, received universal condemnation in the media and led to Snyder's firing by CBS. He spent the last eight years of his life as a virtual recluse before dying of a heart attack in 1996 at the age of 77.

Soccer-Style Kicking

Angled style of placekicking first introduced to the NFL by Hungarian native **Pete Gogolak** in the mid-1960s and popularized by Norwegian Jan Stenerud and others in the 1970s. Initially, soccer-style kickers—many of

---

Audibles

"Tighten immigration laws."

–Detroit Lions great **Alex Karras**, on what could be done to cut down on the number of field goals in the NFL

whom were born in Europe—were ridiculed for bringing a foreign influence to American football. By the late 1970s, however, traditional straight-ahead placekicking had all but disappeared from the sport. Washington Redskins great Mark Moseley was the last pure straight-ahead placekicker.

Something for Joey

Emmy Award–nominated 1977 made-for-TV movie dramatizing the relationship between 1973 Heisman Trophy winner John Cappelletti and his younger brother Joey, who was stricken with childhood leukemia. The tearjerking telefilm starred Canadian actor Marc Singer as Cappelletti, the Penn State running back who dedicated his Heisman to his brother in his acceptance speech and would go on to enjoy a nine-year NFL career. Joey, who succumbed to his illness in 1976 at the age of 14, was portrayed by child actor Jeffrey Lynas. The movie vied with 1971's *Brian's Song* for the heartstrings of a generation of Movie of the Week–watching 1970s football fans. It was based on a book of the same name by Richard E. Peck.

Soul Patrol

Collective nickname used by the hard-hitting Oakland Raiders defensive backfield of the 1970s. Each member of the Soul Patrol also had his own distinctive nickname: cornerbacks "Ol' Man" Willie Brown and Skip "Dr. Death" Thomas, and safeties George "the Hitman" Atkinson and **Jack "the Assassin" Tatum**.

Sourdough Sam

Costumed caricature of a 19th century gold prospector who has been the official mascot of the San Francisco 49ers since 1995. The original Sourdough Sam—the name reflects the popularity of sourdough bread in San Francisco—was a grizzled man with a scruffy brown beard and a moth-eaten 10-gallon hat, designed to evoke the prospector used on team logos

Caitlin Regan

since 1946. He would often emerge from the tunnel at Candlestick Park during pregame player introductions brandishing a gold mining pick that spewed sparklers. In 2006, the mascot was given a total body makeover, emerging as a younger, clean-shaven, less seedy-looking character with mad staring eyes and a rictus grin.

Spence, Sam

American expatriate film score composer best known to football fans for his work with **NFL Films**. A San Francisco native, accomplished jazz saxophonist, and former USC music teacher, Spence was living abroad in his adopted home city of Munich in 1966 when NFL Films scion **Steve Sabol** hired him to compose the background music for NFL highlight packages. "I wanted music that would speak to the passion of the game, and that would also be more contemporary," Sabol later said. Combining elements from jazz, British drinking songs, Irish ballads, and Israeli wedding music with lavish symphonic orchestrations, Spence concocted a series of bombastic musical cues that perfectly complemented the sonorous **"Voice of God"** of NFL Films narrator **John Facenda**. In all, he would spend more than 25 years as the company's principal composer. A number of his more memorable tracks—"Forearm Shiver," "West Side Rumble," and "Ramblin' Man From Grambling" among them—have been collected on CD and/or licensed for use in other media, including TV commercials and video games.

Spygate

Shorthand term for the scandal that enveloped the New England Patriots organization in 2007 after team officials were caught videotaping the defensive signals of the New York Jets—a violation of NFL rules. After an investigation by the league, head coach **Bill Belichick** was fined $500,000 for his role in the incident. The team was docked half that amount and ordered to forfeit a first-round draft choice. Similar allegations were leveled against since-fired Denver Broncos head coach Josh McDaniels—a former Belichick assistant—in 2010.

Staley Da Bear

Mike Shadle

Costumed bear who has served as the official mascot of the Chicago Bears since 2003. He is named after Augustus Eugene Staley, the Illinois food starch magnate who founded the franchise (originally known as the Decatur Staleys) in 1919. Staley Da Bear survived an inauspicious first month on the job (his costume head popped off when he was struck in the nose by a football during his second game as Bears mascot) to become an ursine pillar of the Chicagoland community. He makes regular appearances at area schools and teaches kids about nutrition as part of the a team-sponsored program called the First and Goal School Program: How to Score a Touchdown for a Healthy Life.

Audibles

"I pulled my football jersey over my head
and starting flopping around on the ground
like a fish out of water. All the while I'm screaming
'Get my head, get my head.'"

—Staley Da Bear, recalling his horrifying 2003 decapitation

Starbuck, Jo Jo

Alabama-born figure skating champion best known to football fans for her troubled eight-year marriage to Hall of Fame quarterback **Terry Bradshaw**. The celebrity union was beset by problems from the beginning, with Starbuck reportedly chafing at the demands of Bradshaw's NFL stardom and ill-suited for life on the couple's 440-acre Louisiana ranch. They divorced in 1983. "She didn't love me and she left me," Bradshaw later said.

Statue of Liberty Play

Seldom-used trick play in which the quarterback fakes a pass, then stands immobile with his arm reared back in a throwing motion, allowing a back to retrieve the ball and run with it. Popularized by legendary college coach Amos Alonzo Stagg, the play is rarely run in the pros. The Los Angeles Rams, Baltimore Colts, and Cincinnati Bengals all ran a version of the play in the 1970s. The last NFL team to run a conventional Statue of Liberty Play for a touchdown was the Tampa Bay Buccaneers in 1995.

Steagles

Nickname bestowed by fans on the 1943 Philadelphia-Pittsburgh Eagles, a temporary merger of the Philadelphia Eagles and the Pittsburgh Steelers necessitated by the departure of numerous players for military service during World War II. Comprised of players from both teams who had been deemed ineligible for the armed forces because of physical problems ranging from flat feet to ulcers, the Steagles wore the Eagles' colors and played the majority of their home games at Philadelphia's Shibe Park. The hybrid squad managed to go 5–4–1 before dissolving at the end of the season. In 1944, the Eagles returned to full strength, once again fielding their own team, while the Steelers teamed up with the Chicago Cardinals in the ill-starred "Card-Pitt" merger. After going 0–10, that team is not remembered nearly as fondly as the Steagles, which to this day still retain cult status in Pennsylvania.

Steel Curtain

Memorable nickname bestowed on the Pittsburgh Steelers defense of the 1970s by 14-year-old fan **Gregory Kronz**. Kronz submitted the name to radio station WTAE in 1971 as part of a radio contest to come up with the most distinctive moniker. His prize was a free trip to watch a Steelers-Dolphins game. Used interchangeably to refer to the defense as a whole and more specifically to the Steelers' venerable front four—**"Mean" Joe Greene**, L.C. Greenwood, Ernie Holmes, and Dwight White—Steel Curtain derives originally from the phrase "Iron Curtain," used by British prime minister Winston Churchill to describe the pall cast by Communism over Western Europe in his 1946 "Sinews of Peace" address at Westminster College.

Steelerettes

Pioneering NFL cheerleading squad, the first of its kind in the pro game, that urged on the Pittsburgh Steelers from 1961 to 1969. The black-and-gold-clad Steelerettes, who initially wore hard hats as part of their uniforms, were known for their famous pyramid. Members were all coeds from Pittsburgh's Robert Morris Junior College. Aspiring Steelerettes were selected for their clean-cut good looks and gymnastic ability and had to maintain a 2.0 grade-point average to stay on the squad. Long the object of disapproval from prudish Steelers owner Art Rooney, the cheerleaders were under strict orders to keep up a demure, "ladylike" appearance and eschew all sexually suggestive routines. When the team moved into its new home in Three Rivers Stadium in 1970, the Steelerettes were formally disbanded. Although

Audibles

"Our fans don't need other stimulation."

–Pittsburgh Steelers public relations director Joe Gordon, on the team's decision to break up the **Steelerettes** the Steelers have never replaced them, a commemorative website, steelerettes.com, keeps their flame alive for future generations.

Steely McBeam

Jessica Gelston

Cartoonish steelworker who has served as the official mascot of the Pittsburgh Steelers since 2007. An idealized representation of the industrial heritage of the city of Pittsburgh, Steely McBeam is instantly recognizable for his hard hat, black bib overalls, yellow plaid shirt, and jutting jaw. This last feature has led many fans to liken his appearance to that of legendary Steelers coach Bill Cowher, although the team has always denied that the resemblance was intentional. The mute mascot was rolled out in time for the franchise's 75th anniversary season in 2007, after his name was selected from a pool of more than 70,000 entries submitted by fans in a "name the mascot" contest. Diane Roles of Middlesex, Pennsylvania, came up with the winning moniker, in part to honor Jim Beam, her husband's alcoholic spirit of choice. (Oddly enough, one of Steely McBeam's portrayers, 24-year-old Mount Washington native Kenneth Hahey, was fired after cops caught him running a red light with a blood alcohol level of .166 in January of 2008.) Public reaction to the mascot—the first in the franchise's long history— was swift and negative. One prominent Steelers blogger offered "ten bucks to the brave soul who throttles Mr. McBeam with a **Terrible Towel**," while Canada's *National Post* likened the character to "a maniacal Muppet suffering from jaundice."

Sterger, Jenn

Onetime New York Jets "Gameday Host" who emerged as the central figure in the **Brett Favre** "sexting" scandal in 2010. The comely Florida State graduate became a YouTube sensation in 2005 after ABC cameras searching for a **honey shot** caught her cheering on her beloved Seminoles while wearing a cowboy hat and a low-cut top during an FSU-Miami college football telecast. Hired by the Jets in 2008 in a nebulous "hostess" role, she soon found her way onto Favre's cell phone contacts list. An exposé in October of 2010 published on the sports website Deadspin suggested that the then-39-year-old future Hall of Fame quarterback repeatedly sent her salacious text messages requesting after-hours rendezvous and, in at least one instance, a photo of his somewhat unimpressive penis.

Stewart, Rollen

See **Rainbow Man**

Stickum

Brand-name adhesive product used by All-Pro cornerback Lester Hayes to enhance his grip and facilitate interceptions. Hayes was introduced to Stickum by his Oakland Raiders teammate Fred Biletnikoff. The thick goop was banned by the NFL in 1981, a year after Hayes earned Defensive Player of the Year honors with 13 interceptions. The prohibition against Stickum is known informally as the Lester Hayes Rule in his honor.

Stram, Hank

Loquacious, toupéed head coach of the 1960s and '70s best known for leading the underdog Kansas City Chiefs to victory in Super Bowl IV while wearing a field microphone provided for him by **NFL Films**. While the practice of wiring NFL coaches for sound during games would become commonplace, Stram was the first to allow it. Due largely to Stram's colorful ejaculations—like "65 Toss Power Trap!" and "Just keep matriculatin' the ball down the field, boys!"—the Super Bowl IV highlight film is considered one of the most entertaining in the entire NFL Films canon. After retiring from the sideline in 1977, Stram became a successful TV color commentator. He was inducted into the Pro Football Hall of Fame in 2003.

Strode, Woody

Hulking linebacker turned actor who in 1946 became one of the first African Americans to play in the NFL. While his tenure with the Los Angeles Rams was short-lived, the former UCLA star went on to play professionally with the Calgary Stampeders of the Western Interprovincial Football Union. His acting career included parts in numerous westerns, war movies, and sword-and-sandal epics, where he often played glowering, shaven-headed exotics. Strode was nominated for a Golden Globe Award for his performance opposite Kirk Douglas in *Spartacus*. His other noteworthy credits include *The Ten Commandments*, *Sergeant Rutledge*, *The Man Who Shot Liberty Valance*, and *Once Upon a Time in the West*.

"Super Bowl Shuffle"

Endearingly amateurish rap song recorded by the 1985 world champion Chicago Bears that helped usher in the golden age of NFL team **music video**s. Appearing nearly a year after the San Francisco 49ers' pioneering **"We're the 49ers,"** "Super Bowl Shuffle" was not the first such recording by a Super Bowl team, but it was the first to gain nationwide attention.

Audibles

We are the Bears Shufflin' Crew.
Shufflin' on down, doin' it for you.
We're so bad we know we're good.
Blowin' your mind like we knew we would.
You know we're just struttin' for fun
Struttin' our stuff for everyone.
We're not here to start no trouble.
We're just here to do the Super Bowl Shuffle.

—lyrics to the "Super Bowl Shuffle"

Conceived and produced by Richard E. Meyer, the onetime chairman of the Jovan Perfume company and a rabid Bears fan, the song consisted of tongue-tied rapping from a "Shufflin' Crew" of Bears players, including Walter Payton, **Jim McMahon**, **Mike Singletary**, and **William "the Refrigerator" Perry**. The single and its accompanying video were released to radio and TV stations shortly before the Bears' appearance in Super Bowl XX. It would go on to sell more than 1 million copies and was nominated for a Grammy Award for Best R&B Vocal Performance by a Duo or Group.

Superfans
Collective name for obsessive, often costumed rooters who show up at their team's games to lead cheers, urge on rallies, or otherwise make a public spectacle of themselves in a noisy, clownish, or ritualized display of fervor.
See also: **Barrel Man**; **Chief Zee**; **Crazy Ray**; **Dolfan Denny**; **Hogettes**

Swami, The
Stereotypical Indian yogi persona adopted by burly ESPN personality **Chris Berman** whenever he prognosticates on the outcome of football games.

SwashBucklers

Original name of the Tampa Bay Buccaneers cheerleading squad, used from the team's 1976 inception until the radical redesign of the team's colors, logos, and attendant iconography in 1999. In their early years, the SwashBucklers wore feathered hats and boots and rocked a red, orange, and white color scheme consistent with the team's original "gay pirate" motif. See also: **Bucco Bruce**

Sweetness

Distinctive nickname bestowed by Jackson State University teammates on future Hall of Fame running back Walter Payton—either in recognition of his graceful running style or as an ironic commentary on his legendarily ferocious competitive nature.

Swoop

Anthropomorphized bird of prey who has been the official mascot of the Philadelphia Eagles since 1996. Swoop appears in costume at Eagles home games and personal appearances, and in cartoon form on the weekly *Eagles Kids Club* television series. He is known for leading the charge of Eagles players out of the end zone tunnel while waving an enormous team flag and for the occasional high-wire stunt like skydiving into the stadium.

Serge Berryman

Sym, Dennis
See **Dolfan Denny**

T

Tailgate Party

Traditional pregame social gathering, typically held in a stadium parking lot and marked by copious consumption of alcohol and grilled meat. Ad hoc avant kickoff gatherings are as old as football itself, with most historians dating the practice back to the very first college football game between Rutgers and Princeton at College Field in New Brunswick, New Jersey, in 1869. Before that contest, some 100 fans gathered in a mud-soaked field in horse-drawn carriages and cooked their food at the "tail end" of the horse. But the term "tailgating" in the sense of a car's rear end did not come into vogue until the advent of widespread automobile ownership in the 1950s. By the turn of the 21st century, as many as 50 million Americans were participating in tailgate events each year, according to the United States Tailgating Association.

Tank McNamara

Popular daily syndicated comic strip that chronicles the travails of the title character, a retired NFL defensive lineman turned TV sportscaster. A collaboration between writer Jeff Millar and cartoonist Bill Hinds, *Tank McNamara* has been syndicated through Universal Press Syndicate since 1974. The strip is known for its gentle social commentary, as exemplified by the annual "Sports Jerk of the Year" contest. In 2009, its creators courted controversy with a subplot in which former vice president Dick Cheney and NFL commissioner Roger Goodell discuss the feasibility of assassinating scandal-scarred quarterback **Michael Vick**.

Audibles

"My hits border on felonious assault."

—Jack "the Assassin" Tatum, writing in his autobiography *They Call Me Assassin*

Tatum, Jack "the Assassin"

Legendarily hard-hitting safety of the 1970s and a cornerstone of the Oakland Raiders' "**Soul Patrol**" secondary. He is best known for permanently paralyzing New England Patriots wide receiver Darryl Stingley during a preseason game in 1978. Tatum was widely criticized for the clean—if brutal—hit, which shattered Stingley's spinal cord. Much of the ire stemmed from the fact that Tatum refused to apologize for the incident, although Stingley himself ultimately forgave him. It was Tatum's collision with another opponent—Pittsburgh's John "Frenchy" Fuqua—that precipitated Franco Harris' famed **Immaculate Reception** in 1972.

Taylor, Lawrence

Hall of Fame linebacker of the 1980s and '90s whose penchant for cocaine-fueled debauchery was exhaustively chronicled in his tell-all 1987 memoir *LT: Living on the Edge*. In the early 2000s, the New York Giants legend figuratively drew a line under his previous indiscretions, suggesting that his acknowledged history of drug use and prostitute-wrangling be attributed to his youthful alter ego, "L.T." A 2010 indictment for statutory rape in a case involving a 16-year-old girl seemed to call that assertion into question.

T.D. (Browns mascot)

Jason Pero

Costumed German Shepherd dog who has comprised one-fourth of the Cleveland Browns' "Dawg Pound" of **mascots** since the franchise's NFL rebirth in 1999. T.D. runs with a pack that includes **C.B.** the bull mastiff, **Chomps** the Lab, and **Trapper** the Weimaraner.

T.D. (Dolphins mascot)

Seven-foot-tall costumed marine mammal who has been the official mascot of the Miami Dolphins since 1997. If you don't count the controversial **Flipper**, the turquoise dolphin is the first team-sanctioned mascot in the franchise's history. T.D.'s name was selected from a pool of 529 submitted by fans in a "name the mascot" contest that drew more than 13,000 entries from 50 states and 22 countries. In 2001, T.D. became the first NFL mascot to participate in the Hall of Fame Game in Canton, Ohio. In 2005, the peripatetic mascot traveled to Hong Kong at the behest of the Chinese government to take part in the Lunar New Year Parade.

"Team of the '80s"

Team **music video** recorded by members of the 1989 San Francisco 49ers, including Jerry Rice, Roger Craig, and Ronnie Lott. The tepid Bobby Brown—inspired rap ditty features the obligatory heavy metal guitar solo and wince-inducing lines like "We're more famous than Cosby and the Huxtables." The disarmingly low-budget video includes animated interstitials, shout-outs to absent teammates accompanied by player photographs, and numerous awkward cutaways to a dancing, mincing 49ers owner Eddie DeBartolo Jr.

Michelle DeMerse

Tecmo Super Bowl

Wildly popular 8-bit video game released for the Nintendo Entertainment System beginning in 1991. A vast improvement on its predecessor, *Tecmo Bowl*, *Tecmo Super Bowl* featured more realistic game play, detailed statistical tracking, and—perhaps most importantly—the combined licensing muscle of all 28 NFL teams and the players' union. Video game enthusiasts could—and, in tournaments held around the country, still do— play and replay the 1991 NFL season in its entirety from preseason to the **Pro Bowl**.

Terrible Towel

Traditional black-and-gold rally towel waved by Pittsburgh Steelers fans since 1975. The Terrible Towel was the brainchild of Steelers radio broadcaster Myron Cope, who was charged by WTAE station management with inventing a gimmick that would whip up fan enthusiasm for the team's 1975 playoff run. Cope believed that a conventional kitchen towel— lightweight, portable, and ubiquitous—would, if decked out in team colors, appeal to the franchise's blue-collar fan base. Fans could also wipe their seats with it, a not-insignificant consideration in snowy Pittsburgh. The

Terrible Towel made its debut on December 27, 1975, during a playoff game between the Steelers and the Indianapolis Colts. Some 30,000 showed up to twirl them, which soon became a Three Rivers Stadium postseason ritual. Over the ensuing decades, the towels have provided a convenient outlet for the disdain of Steelers opponents. Cincinnati Bengal T.J. Houshmandzadeh wiped his feet with a Terrible Towel in 2005. Phoenix mayor Phil Gordon blew his nose and mimed wiping his behind with one at a pep rally before Super Bowl XLIII in 2009.

Thanksgiving Day

Traditional American feasting holiday that for more than 70 years has served as a showcase for nationally broadcast NFL games. Although football games on Thanksgiving date back to the late 19th century, the NFL played its first Turkey Day game in 1920, when the Akron Pros defeated the Canton Bulldogs 7–0. Fourteen years later, the Detroit Lions played their first Thanksgiving game against the Chicago Bears. The Bears won 19–16. Since then the Lions have hosted an annual contest on the holiday to the consternation of many around the league, who cite the franchise's poor performance over the decades as a reason why the home teams should be rotated. The Dallas Cowboys began hosting a second annual game in 1966. Memorable Thanksgiving Day games include the 1974 Redskins-Cowboys game featuring a dramatic Dallas comeback engineered by backup quarterback **Clint Longley**; the fabled Eagles-Cowboys **Bounty Bowl** in 1989; the 1993 Dolphins-Cowboys tilt at a snowy Texas Stadium, in which Cowboys defensive tackle Leon Lett's bungled recovery of a blocked field goal facilitated a last-second Miami victory; and the 1998 Steelers-Lions fiasco at which official Phil Luckett botched the overtime coin toss, essentially handing the game to Detroit.

"Thanks to the 12th Man"

Team **music video** produced by the 1986 Washington Redskins as an expression of gratitude to their loyal fans. "You are about to witness something you have never witnessed before" begin the lyrics to the turgid pop/hip-hop number, which name-checks 50 years of Redskins stars from Sonny Jurgensen and Sam Huff to "Theismann and Riggins, just to name a few." The five-minute video features rapping and dancing from the likes of Doug Williams, Darrell Green, Dexter Manley, Joe Jacoby, and others, as well as footage of the high-fiving **Fun Bunch** and a blink-and-you-miss-it appearance by future Republican National Committee chairman Michael Steele. Proceeds from the video were donated to the National Challenge Committee on Disability.

That's Incredible!

Proto-reality show of the early 1980s that was co-hosted by Hall of Fame quarterback Fran Tarkenton. Like its NBC competitor *Real People*, ABC's *That's Incredible!* featured ordinary people performing amazing stunts like sword swallowing and fire walking. Entertainment personalities John Davidson and Cathy Lee Crosby were Tarkenton's co-hosts for the venture.

"They are who we thought they were!"

Keynote phrase in an infamous tirade delivered during a postgame press conference by Arizona Cardinals head coach Dennis Green following a crushing loss to the Chicago Bears in a *Monday Night Football* game on October 16, 2006. Green's Cardinals had utterly dominated the contest, forcing six Bears turnovers and taking a 20-point lead deep into the third quarter. But their intimate knowledge of Chicago's game plan and tendencies did not prove dispositive, as the Bears roared back to win 24–23. After the

Audibles

"The Bears are what we thought they were. They're what we thought they were. We played them in preseason—who the hell takes a third game of the preseason like it's bullshit? Bullshit! We played them in the third game—everybody played three quarters—the Bears are who we thought they were! That's why we took the damn field. Now if you want to crown them, then crown their ass! But they are who we thought they were! And we let 'em off the hook!"

—Dennis Green's "They are who we thought they were!" speech

game, Green attacked the assembled media for suggesting his team may have been taken by surprise. He later apologized for the outburst. The 42-second meltdown went viral on the Internet, however, and has since been incorporated into a popular series of Coors Light TV commercials.

Thing with Two Heads, The

Horror movie from 1972 starring Ray Milland as a terminally ill racist whose head is transplanted onto the body of a black death row inmate played by hulking Los Angeles Rams legend **Roosevelt "Rosey" Grier**. The low-budget sci-fi shocker, which has attained cult status, was Grier's feature film debut.

Thomas, Duane

Sullen, moody star running back of the 1970s, nicknamed "the Sphinx" for his tendency toward long, inscrutable silences. A prodigious rusher for the 1971 Super Bowl champion Dallas Cowboys, Thomas was renowned as much for his drug use, contract disputes, and outspoken criticism of team management. He famously labeled Cowboys head coach Tom Landry "Plastic Man...no man at all" and dismissed club president Tex Schramm as "sick, demented, and completely dishonest." Fed up with his aloof personality, the Cowboys traded him to the San Diego Chargers in 1972. In many ways, Thomas was a precursor to the similarly idiosyncratic tailback **Ricky Williams**.

Thompson, John "Big Dawg"

Computer accessory salesman and Cleveland Browns **superfan** who since the 1980s has served as the "canine-in-chief" of the team's boisterous end zone **Dawg Pound**. For four decades, the 385-pound Thompson—who legally changed his middle name to "Big Dawg" in 1999—has shown up at Browns home games in a tent-sized No. 98 Browns jersey, orange helmet, and rubber bulldog mask. With regular media exposure came opportunities for advocacy. In the mid-1990s he emerged as the unofficial spokesman for the fight to keep the Browns in Cleveland. In 1996, after the Browns had forsaken their longtime home city for Baltimore, Thompson testified before the House Judiciary Committee on the issue of franchise relocation. In the 2000s Thompson became bedeviled by numerous medical and legal challenges, including gastric bypass surgery, a lawsuit against video game maker EA Sports for the unlicensed use of his likeness, and a 2009 arrest for drunk driving.

Thor

Live bird of prey mascot employed by the Atlanta Falcons during their inaugural season in 1966. Trained to circle Atlanta Stadium three times before the Falcons players emerged from the tunnel for their first home game on September 11, 1966, Thor instead fled the stadium in terror. A succession of sequentially numbered Thor replacements proved equally maladroit at performing the trick on cue, so the mascot was quietly retired after a portion of one season. **Freddie Falcon**, a less unruly costumed bird, assumed official mascot duties in 1974.

Thunder

Majestic Arabian horse who has served as the official live animal mascot of the Denver Broncos since 1993. To date, there have actually been two Thunders. Thunder I, a stallion whose registered name was JB Kobast, retired in 2004 after the depredations of arthritis began to take their

Jeffrey Beall

toll. Thunder II, a gelding whose registered name is Winter Solstice, then took over. The original Thunder died in 2009 at the age of 27. Both horses were provided to the team by Denver socialite Sharon Magness Blake and trained and ridden by Ann Judge-Wegener. Thunder greets fans inside his corral at Invesco Field before Broncos home games. He gallops around the field after every Broncos touchdown to the delight of the crowds. Unfazed by the noise inside the stadium, the noble horse is apparently bothered only when the Wave sweeps through the stands. Thunder is currently the only live animal mascot in the NFL.

Toma, George

Groundskeeping legend, known informally as "the God of Sod," who rose from humble beginnings in a Pennsylvania coal-mining town to become the NFL's leading authority on all things turf-related. Based out of Kansas City, Toma is most closely associated with the Kansas City Chiefs, whose grounds he maintained from 1963 to 1991. His work attracted the attention of owners around the league and of NFL commissioner Pete Rozelle, who put Toma in charge of tilling the soil at the annual Super Bowl game in 1967. Toma's favorite sod was Dakota Peat. Honored by the Pro Football Hall of Fame in 2001, Toma published his autobiography, *Nitty Gritty Dirt Man*, in 2004.

Spin Martin

Tooz

See **Matuszak, John**

TopCats

Name used by the Carolina Panthers cheerleading squad since the team's 1993 NFL inception.

Great Moments in Cheerleaders Scandal

In 2005, two members of the **TopCats** were arrested following an altercation with police at a Banana Joe's nightclub in Tampa, Florida, where the Carolina Panthers were visiting for a game against the Buccaneers. According to police reports, the cheerleaders were engaged in a protracted cunnilingus session in a ladies' room toilet stall. When other patrons complained, a brawl ensued. The Panthers later fired the pair.

Torbert, Michael "Mikey T."

Founder of the **Hogettes**. Also known as "Boss Hogette."

Toro

Six-foot-tall costumed bull who has been the official mascot of the Houston Texans since 2001. Toro actually started working for the team before the Texans even took the field for the first time. He was introduced to the fans of Houston in April of 2001, a full 17 months before the Texans' inaugural season, when he was whisked by private helicopter to a popular Houston restaurant, accompanied by four Secret Service agents. When he isn't tooling around Reliant Stadium on a motorcycle or a Segway, Toro can often be found in school cafeterias teaching children about the value of good nutrition as part of his "Toro's Training Table" program.

Audibles

"I was told never to aim a T-shirt gun at the president again."

–Houston Texans mascot coordinator Jonathan Frost, recounting one of his early mishaps portraying **Toro**

T-Rac

Drag racing, Greek helmet–wearing costumed raccoon who has served as the official mascot of the Tennessee Titans since 1999. T-Rac stands for "Titans Raccoon." Although the connection between a raccoon and the

Audibles

"I get paid hundreds to do this, I make hundreds, hundreds. In fact, I'm a hundredaire. Tell that to all the ladies. I'm a hundredaire, and if you're a female raccoon, come see me. I'm a hundredaire, and I have my own minivan."

—**T-Rac**, the Titans raccoon, on the basis of his appeal

Titans of ancient Greek mythology remains unclear, the state of Tennessee has designated the raccoon as its official state wild animal since 1971. Although T-Rac spends most of his time tooling harmlessly around the field in a variety of pimped-out all-terrain vehicles and shooting prizes into the stands, he has not steered entirely clear of controversy. At halftime of a preseason game in August of 2006, the mascot careened his golf cart into New Orleans Saints backup quarterback Adrian McPherson, severely bruising McPherson's knee and ending his NFL career. McPherson later filed a $20 million lawsuit against the Titans, citing T-Rac's "reckless disregard for the safety of players of the opposite team."

Trapper

Woody Myers

Costumed dog—a Weimaraner to be exact—who has been a pack member of the Cleveland Browns' "Dawg Pound" of official **mascots** since 1999. Trapper is positioned in team literature as the most active and sporty of the team's mascots, a group that also includes **C.B.** the bull mastiff, **Chomps** the Labrador, and **T.D.** the German Shepherd.

Trick Plays

See **Flea Flicker**; **Fumblerooski**; **Hook and Lateral**; **Quick Kick**; **Statue of Liberty Play**

Triplets

Nickname for the Hall of Fame trio of quarterback Troy Aikman, running back Emmitt Smith, and wide receiver Michael Irvin that spearheaded the Dallas Cowboys' revival in the 1990s.

Trump, Donald J.

Orange-haired moneybags who famously ran the **USFL** into the ground in the 1980s. The son of a prominent New York City real estate developer, Trump used part of his vast inheritance to buy the USFL's New Jersey Generals in 1984. Styling himself a backroom impresario in the mold of legendary NFL *machers* like Lamar Hunt and Wellington Mara, Trump agitated behind the scenes for a more direct competitive assault on the NFL in the form of a fall schedule and an antitrust lawsuit—most likely intended to blackmail the older league into a merger. The plan proved catastrophic when the fledgling league's pyrrhic victory in the lawsuit (the court awarded it $3.76 in damages) resulted in its dissolution before teams could play a single autumn game.

Tuck Rule, The

Informal name for Rule 3, Section 21, Article 2, Note 2 of the official NFL rules, which clarifies the difference between an incomplete pass and a fumble by the quarterback. Citation of the obscure rule by announcers became exponentially more prevalent after the 2001 AFC playoff game between the New England Patriots and the Oakland Raiders. In the waning moments of that contest, what appeared to be a game-clinching fumble recovery by the Raiders was ruled an incomplete pass after officials deemed

Audibles

"When a player is holding the ball to pass it forward, any intentional forward movement of his hand starts a forward pass, even if the player loses possession of the ball as he is attempting to tuck it back toward his body. Also, if the player has tucked the ball into his body and then loses possession, it is a fumble."

—**The Tuck Rule**, as stated in the *Official Rules of the NFL*

that Patriots quarterback Tom Brady was in the act of "tucking" when he lost possession of the football. The Patriots went on to win the game 16–13.

Tuna

Nickname bestowed on legendary NFL head coach Bill Parcells during his tenure as linebackers coach of the New England Patriots in 1980. Sometimes rendered as "the Big Tuna," the name is a reference to Charlie the Tuna, cartoon mascot of the StarKist tuna fish company. Charlie is routinely thwarted in his efforts to get himself netted, ground up, and canned by the seafood purveyor. According to Parcells, his players were attempting to gull him into doing something when the words "You must think I'm Charlie the Tuna" blurted from his lips—and a nickname was born. Showdowns between Parcells-coached teams and teams he used to coach are often hyped in the press as "Tuna Bowl" games.

Turducken

Monstrous poultry dish popularized by football analyst **John Madden** during **Thanksgiving Day** telecasts for CBS and Fox in the 1980s and '90s. Essentially a deboned chicken stuffed inside of a deboned duck stuffed inside of a deboned turkey, turducken was a culinary oddity rarely consumed outside of Louisiana (where, legend has it, it was created by celebrity chef Paul Prudhomme). Madden was introduced to the dish while visiting the Big Easy for a CBS telecast in the 1970s. "The P.R. guy for the Saints brought me one," he later told *The New York Times*. "It smelled and looked so good. I didn't have any plates or silverware or anything, and I just started eating it with my hands." He loved it so much, in fact, that he began buying three turduckens a year to feed himself and his broadcast crew during the annual Thanksgiving Day game. On the air, he effusively extolled the virtues of the so-called six-legged bird, appearing on camera at one point to personally carve one with his bare hands. After moving on to Fox, Madden began awarding turduckens to the Most Valuable Players in the Turkey Day contest.

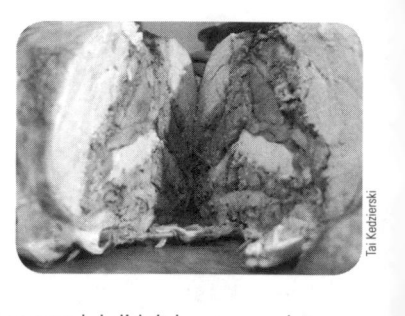

"Twelve Days of a Cleveland Browns Christmas"

Yuletide novelty song recorded by the Houston-based pop trio Elliott, Walter & Bennett to honor the 1980 **Kardiac Kids** Cleveland Browns. Released at the height of the team's unlikely playoff drive, the song name-checks quarterback Brian Sipe, tight end Ozzie Newsome, and coach Sam Rutigliano, among others, in its list of things owner **Art Modell** gave to the city of Cleveland for Christmas.

Two-Minute Warning

Blockbuster football-themed 1976 disaster movie about a crazed sniper on the loose at a Super Bowl–like championship game. (Unlike 1977's ***Black Sunday***, producers of *Two-Minute Warning* failed to secure the rights to use the official Super Bowl name and NFL team logos.) Charlton Heston heads an all-star cast that also includes Martin Balsam, Jack Klugman, and John Cassavetes (as the absurdly named SWAT team commander Sgt. Button). Heston, playing a stolid police captain, is forced to keep a straight face while delivering lines like "He butt-stroked a maintenance man off a 60-foot ladder." Stock footage of a USC-Stanford college football game is used to represent the game action. *Monday Night Football* stars **Frank Gifford** and **Howard Cosell** play themselves, while former Minnesota Vikings quarterback **Joe Kapp** appears briefly as the starting quarterback for one of the teams.

"U Can't Touch Us"

Rewritten rendition of the MC Hammer hit "U Can't Touch This" that was recorded and released as a team **music video** by members of the 1990 Miami Dolphins. "Give us the ball. We'll score. Makin' 'em sweat, that's why they're sore," goes one of the deathless lines in the keytar-driven pop rap song, which is officially credited to "Cory and the Fins." The video also incorporates lyrics from LL Cool J's "Mama Said Knock You Out" and features scantily clad Hooters girls, stock footage of porpoises, and the obligatory break preceded by "Stop! Dolphin time!" All the players wear Dolphins uniform tops and the then-fashionable striped Zubaz pants.

University of Mars

Fictitious institute of higher learning cited by *Monday Night Football* analyst **Alex Karras** as the alma mater of Oakland Raiders defensive lineman Otis Sistrunk. The citation occurred during a *Monday Night* telecast on September 16, 1974, and may have resulted from Karras' deliberate misreading of a reference to Sistrunk's service in the U.S. Marine Corps in the Raiders media guide.

Days of Infamy | September 27, 1981

Otis Sistrunk and his **professional wrestling** partner Michael Hayes defeat Jimmy "Superfly" Snuka and Terry Gordy to capture the Georgia Championship Wrestling tag team championship

Up with People

Insufferably peppy music and dance troupe that performed in four Super Bowl **half-time shows** between 1976 and 1986. Founded in 1965 by philanthropist J. Blanton Belk, Up with People was nominally a nonprofit organization devoted to social service, volunteering, and providing a "positive voice for young people." But most television viewers of the 1970s and '80s remember it for its entertainment auxiliary—a group of well-groomed, perpetually smiling teenagers swaying their hips to pallid pop tunes promoting the cause of world peace and intercultural harmony. "Up, up with people," went one of the troupe's signature numbers. "You meet 'em wherever you go." Always on the lookout for nonthreatening entertainers to enliven his Super Bowl halftime extravaganzas, NFL commissioner Pete Rozelle first hired Up with People to perform a Bicentennially themed routine at Super Bowl X in 1976 (footage of which was later used in the 1977 "exploding terrorist blimp" feature **Black Sunday**). It was a decision he would later come to regret. Up with People returned for Super Bowls XIV, XVI, and XX—each time with a more elaborate and bizarre production. The group reached its nadir at Super Bowl XX in 1986, performing "Beat of the Future," a 10-minute-long science fiction mind trip that incorporated a medley of Bruce Springsteen's "Born in the USA," Huey Lewis and the News' "The Power of Love," and Stevie

Audibles

**"Three words I never want to hear ever again:
Up with People."**

—NFL commissioner Pete Rozelle, following the performance troupe's
fourth and final Super Bowl halftime show appearance in 1986

Wonder's "I Just Called to Say I Love You." At the climax of the spectacle, a giant inflatable "city of tomorrow" was suspended from the ceiling of the Louisiana Superdome, in what NBC play-by-play man Dick Enberg weirdly called "a fitting tribute to the memory of Dr. Martin Luther King Jr."

USFL

Acronym for the United States Football League, an upstart professional league that competed with the NFL in the 1980s. Founded in 1982 by former New Orleans Saints executive David Dixon, the new circuit began play in the spring of 1983. The quality of play was superior to that of previous challengers to NFL hegemony, like the **WFL**, in part because the 12-team league was able to poach a number of high-quality draftees from the big-time college ranks. Heisman Trophy winner Herschel Walker, Jim Kelly, and Steve Young were just a few of the college stars who got their start in the USFL. A number of television-friendly innovations ushered in by USFL commissioner Chet Simmons (a former ESPN executive) helped generate fan interest as well. These included the two-point conversion and the use of instant replay to overturn bad calls. Initial public response was positive. Crowds of 20,000 or more were common at springtime games, while telecasts on ABC and ESPN notched respectable ratings. Eventually, however, overexpansion and dissension within the ranks of ownership began to take a toll. New Jersey Generals owner **Donald J. Trump**'s insistence on moving games to the fall to compete more directly with the NFL proved a disastrous gambit. Attendance plummeted and several major-market teams folded. In the final year of its existence, the fledgling league was reduced to filing a kamikaze antitrust lawsuit against the NFL in hopes of forcing a merger. The USFL won the suit, but was awarded only $3.76 in damages. When it folded in 1986, it was more than $160 million in debt.

Vertical-Striped Socks

Questionable sartorial innovation introduced to professional football by the 1960 Denver Broncos. The socks featured alternating stripes of yellow and brown that roughly coordinated with the team's drab mustard yellow uniforms. The idea for the aesthetically egregious hosiery came from general manager Dean Griffing, a notorious tightwad who purchased them used from a college football All-Star game in Tucson, Arizona. While Griffing contended that the outlandish stripes made the players look taller, most Broncos thought they just made them look ridiculous. Safety Goose Gonsoulin likened the overall effect to that of a sailor fitted with a peg leg. By 1961, many players simply refused to wear the socks, preferring to bring their own from home. In 1962, new owner Cal Kunz fired Griffing and ordered the remaining stock of socks destroyed in a ritual bonfire before the team's first preseason game. One by one, members of the Broncos filed up to the large Olympic-style torch and dumped their socks into the cleansing flame. The cathartic ceremony, which also featured men costumed as Roman centurions, was witnessed by a cheering crowd of 8,377.

Audibles

"I have two weapons—my legs,
my arm, and my brains."

—Michael Vick

Vick, Michael

Controversial scrambling quarterback of the 2000s widely loathed for his involvement in an interstate dogfighting ring. In August of 2007, Vick—then a member of the Atlanta Falcons—plead guilty to a federal felony charge after he was exposed as the kingpin of **Bad Newz Kennels**, a thriving dogfighting concern headquartered on the grounds of his Virginia estate. He was sentenced to 23 months in federal prison and indefinitely suspended by NFL commissioner Roger Goodell. After completing his prison sentence, Vick was conditionally reinstated and cleared to play six games into the 2009 season. Now a member of the Philadelphia Eagles, he reclaimed a starting job in 2010 and regained his **Pro Bowl** form.

Vikadontis Rex

Purple foam dinosaur who served as an official mascot of the Minnesota Vikings during the 1990s. The short-lived mascot, inspired by the Barney the Dinosaur craze, was the brainchild of Minneapolis costume shop proprietor Henry Gomez, who donned the costume at Vikings home games and personal appearances until the character was mothballed in 2000.

Viking, The

Fur-wearing, broadsword-wielding Norse warrior who served as an official mascot of the Minnesota Vikings from 1970 to 1990. Portraying the character for all those years was Hub Meeds, a truck driver from White Bear Lake,

Minnesota, who donned his first rented Viking costume at Super Bowl IV in 1970. His cheerleading proved so popular with fans that the team granted Meeds official mascot status and field access, although he received no compensation for his capering. The Viking's act included spelling out the team's name in shields along the sideline before each home game. Meeds relinquished his sword in 1990. The team's current human Viking mascot, **Ragnar**, succeeded him in 1994.

Viktor the Viking

Karen Hartmann

Mustachioed branded Viking character who has served as an official mascot of the Minnesota Vikings since 2007. Viktor was created as a secondary mascot to **Ragnar**, the team's human Viking portrayer, in part to provide a family friendly (and team-owned) alternative to the sometimes uncontrollable bushy-bearded, Harley-riding Norse wild man. Designed to the franchise's specifications by the marketing agency Creative Consumer Concepts—best known for their work creating Happy Meal–style "Wacky Packs" for the Sonic fast food chain—the musclebound Viktor sports an oversized Viking helmet, a purple jersey, and a blond walrus mustache that reminds many fans of professional wrestler Hulk Hogan. He made his debut at the Vikings' 2007 preseason home opener.

Audibles

"Ragnar did a great job. But ownership wanted to elevate their brand in the community."

–Creative Consumer Concepts CEO Bob Cutler,
on the impetus behind the creation of Viktor the Viking

Violent World of Sam Huff, The

Eye-opening CBS News special, narrated by Walter Cronkite, which gave viewers an unprecedented up-close-and-personal look at life in the trenches of the NFL. Aired on Halloween night of 1960 as an installment of the network's Sunday evening documentary series *The Twentieth Century*, *The Violent World of Sam Huff* chronicled the on-field exploits of brutish New York Giants linebacker Sam Huff. Huff was wired for sound during an exhibition game and shown wheezing, cursing, exhorting his teammates, and taunting his opponents. The documentary, which featured numerous bone-crunching close-ups of enormous men slamming into each other, helped to revolutionize the depiction of football on television. See also: ***Mayhem on a Sunday Afternoon***

"Voice of God"

Commonly used nickname for legendary **NFL Films** narrator **John Facenda**.

"Waiting All Day for Sunday Night"

Inane rewritten version of the Joan Jett 1988 hit "I Hate Myself for Loving You" that has served as the opening theme to NBC's *Sunday Night Football* telecasts since 2006. Like **Hank Williams Jr.**'s ***Monday Night Football*** theme **"All My Rowdy Friends Are Here for Monday Night,"** "Waiting All Day for Sunday Night" features custom-crafted football-themed lyrics so wincingly puerile they could have been scribbled onto a cocktail napkin by a network executive on his way to the production meeting. "Hey Jack, it's a fact, the best show in town," goes one representative couplet. "*Sunday Night Football*, we ain't messin' around." Hired to sing the theme for *SNF*'s inaugural season was pop star Pink. After just one year, however, the "Get

Audibles

"This song sums up what *Sunday Night Football* is all about: the big game."

—NBC *Sunday Night Football* producer Fred Gaudelli,
attempting to explain the thinking behind **"Waiting All Day for Sunday Night"**

the Party Started" singer was deemed "too urban" and replaced by the more Nashville-friendly Faith Hill, who has been butchering Jett's tune ever since.

Wardrobe Malfunction

See **Jackson, Janet**

Warpaint

Live paint horse mascot of the Kansas City Chiefs who entertained crowds at the team's home games from 1963 to 1989. Riding bareback on Warpaint (or Warpaints, to be precise, for there were five different horses in all) for each of those 17 years was **Bob Johnson**, an erstwhile rodeo performer and mule wrangler for Kansas City A's owner Charles O. Finley. Dressed in a full Sioux Indian war bonnet, Johnson would lead the gelding at a furious gallop around the Chiefs home field at Municipal (and later

AP Images

Arrowhead) Stadium before every game, and again each time the Chiefs scored a touchdown. Johnson and Warpaint were regular targets for Native American advocacy groups, who staged protests and filed lawsuits against the team for what they considered the demeaning representation of traditional Native American religious practices. To the relief of some and the consternation of many, Johnson finally hung up his spurs in 1989, taking the last pinto to bear the name Warpaint with him. But in 2009, as part of a ceremony marking the 50th anniversary of the American Football League, the Chiefs unleashed a new Warpaint on the world. This time the rider was Susie Derouchey, a chesty Chiefs cheerleader who eschewed the offending headdress and thus managed to elude all controversy.

Waverly Wonders, The

Short-lived 1977 TV sitcom starring recently retired NFL great **Joe Namath**. A painfully unfunny knockoff of the then-popular *Welcome Back, Kotter* (and a precursor to the similarly themed but vastly superior *White Shadow*), *The Waverly Wonders* starred Namath as Joe Casey, a has-been professional basketball star who becomes the coach of a rag-tag high school hoops team. Former *I Dream of Jeannie* star Larry Hagman reportedly turned down the role of Casey in favor of the more promising part of J.R. Ewing on *Dallas*. Good call. *The Waverly Wonders* lasted only nine episodes. Along with the big-screen bomb ***C.C. and Company***, it is one of the low points of Namath's abortive acting career.

"We Are the 49ers"

Team **music video** recorded by Dwight Clark, Ronnie Lott, and 12 other members of the 1984 San Francisco 49ers, one of the first such songs recorded by a Super Bowl team. "We will rock you till we win the fight," go the simplistic lyrics of the R&B ditty. "We're the 49ers! We're dynamite." (The song's co-writer and producer had better luck later in the decade, collaborating on numerous chart-topping singles, including "How Will I Know" by Whitney Houston and "Freeway of Love" by Aretha Franklin.) While "We Are the 49ers" did not catch fire nationally, it did pave the way for more successful team songs to come, like the Chicago Bears' **"Super Bowl Shuffle."**

Weathers, Carl

Marginally talented linebacker of the early 1970s, far better known for his acting career than his short-lived stints in the American and Canadian professional football leagues. A native of New Orleans, Weathers spent parts of two seasons with the Oakland Raiders and another three with the **CFL**'s BC Lions. But acting was always his true passion. "I'm more than just an animal," he once remarked. "I want to be thought of as a human being introduced to other things, like the arts." After retiring from the game, he got his start playing bit parts in blaxploitation movies before securing what would be his signature role as Apollo Creed in 1976's *Rocky*. He reprised that portrayal in three sequels over the course of the 1980s and went on to appear in **Semi-Tough,** *Predator*, *Action Jackson*, and *Happy Gilmore*, among a slew of other TV and movie gigs. In 2004, Weathers mocked his own public persona by playing an antic, stew-obsessed version of himself on the cult classic TV sitcom *Arrested Development*.

Webster

Popular 1980s TV sitcom about a pint-sized African American orphan who is adopted by an affluent white couple. Onetime NFL defensive tackle **Alex Karras** starred as George Papadapolis, a retired pro football star living in a well-appointed Chicago high rise with his socialite wife Katherine (played by Karras' real-life wife Susan Clark). Dwarf actor Emmanuel Lewis played the titular adoptee, Webster Lewis, the son of one of Papadapolis' former teammates who had recently been killed in a tragic car crash. Although shamelessly derivative of the similarly themed NBC sitcom *Diff'rent Strokes*, ABC's *Webster* would outlast that series by eight months, wrapping up its six-year run in September of 1987. To date, it remains Karras' last major recurring television role.

"We Fly High"

Jim Jones hip-hop anthem that became the unofficial **fight song** of the 2006 New York Giants. The song's repeated shouts of "Ballin'!" sparked a nationwide jump-shot dance craze that migrated onto the gridiron in the form of choreographed sack dance celebrations by Giants defensive players. Widespread, overindulgent jump-shooting eventually prompted the NFL to clarify its policy on excessive celebrations in order to forbid the practice.

WFL

Acronym for the World Football League, a short-lived professional league of the mid-1970s. Founded in 1973 by attorney and American Basketball Association mastermind Gary Davidson with the aim of providing global competition for the NFL, the WFL made a huge initial splash through the signing of numerous NFL stars to high-salary contracts. Miami Dolphins stalwarts Larry Csonka, Jim Kiick, and Paul Warfield were all poached off the 1973 Super Bowl champions, giving the fledgling league the jolt of publicity and competitive credibility it needed to get off the ground. But while attendance was robust at the beginning, teams quickly found themselves beset with financial problems and riven by constant ownership changes. (Soul legends Isaac Hayes and Marvin Gaye were among the league's early big-name investors.) In the end, the WFL would fold midway through its second season after incurring some $30 million in aggregate losses. The enterprise was not a total catastrophe, however. John McVay, Marty Schottenheimer, and Jim Fassel were among the future NFL head coaches who got their start in the WFL. The rock group Pink Floyd used

footage from a WFL game in their music video "Money." And like all rogue leagues, the WFL introduced a menu of intriguing organizational and rules changes designed to differentiate its brand of football from that of the NFL. Seasons started in midsummer, fair catches were outlawed, and extra-point kicks were abolished (touchdowns were worth seven points, with additional "action points" tacked on via run or pass). In the most absurd innovation, uniform pants were color-coded by position.

Worldwide Pants

Color scheme for WFL uniform pants, devised by management consultant Bill Finneran

Quarterbacks and kickers: White
Offensive linemen: Purple
Running backs: Green
Receivers: Orange
Defensive linemen: Blue
Linebackers: Red
Defensive backs: Yellow

"Whasssuuuup?"

Inane catchphrase of the early 2000s that made its national debut in a Budweiser commercial that aired during the December 20, 1999, **Monday Night Football** game between the Minnesota Vikings and the Green Bay Packers. The beer ad, which was derived from a short film titled *True* created by director Charles Stone III, centered on a group of African American friends who converse by telephone while drinking Budweiser and mindlessly repeating the "Whasssuuuup?" greeting. The attendant ad campaign caught fire with a fin de siècle public and briefly made stars of the actors involved.

"What It Was, Was Football"

Immensely popular football-themed monologue recorded in 1953 by cornpone comedian Andy Griffith. Released on 45, the five-minute-long routine chronicles the observations of a befuddled hayseed who stumbles upon his first-ever college football game. The record sold nearly 1 million copies in its first year of release and helped make Griffith a star.

White, Byron "Whizzer"

Collegiate All-American turned successful NFL halfback who parlayed his gridiron prowess into a successful legal career and a seat on the United States Supreme Court. A speedy mainstay of the Colorado Buffaloes' 1937 Cotton Bowl team, White was given the moniker "Whizzer" by Leonard Cahn, a sportswriter for the *Rocky Mountain News*. He would grow to hate the nickname. His other distinguishing characteristic was the enormity of his hands, which the *Brooklyn Eagle* once likened to "the business end of a brace of steam shovels." The big-pawed Rhodes Scholar schmoozed with the Kennedy family at Oxford, and when football was in season he carried the pigskin for the Pittsburgh Pirates and later for the Detroit Lions. He led the National Football League in rushing in 1938 and 1940. His college pal John F. Kennedy appointed him to serve on the Supreme Court in 1962, a post White held until 1993. At 6'2" and 190 pounds, White was one of the most impressive physical specimens ever to sit on the high court.

Beyond Sports

Whizzer White

White House, The

Infamous party pad maintained by the mid-1990s Dallas Cowboys as a discreet base of operations for their sex-and-drug-fueled bacchanalia. The hard-living Cowboys started renting the two-story brick home, which was located on a sleepy suburban cul-de-sac near the team's Valley Ranch practice facility, in 1994 after players grew tired of fending off autograph seekers and paparazzi when they partied at area strip clubs. Dubbed "the

Audibles

"We've got a little place over here
where we're running some whores in and
out, trying to be responsible."

–Dallas Cowboys offensive lineman Nate Newton, on **the White House**

White House," the abode became a special haven for married Cowboys looking to indulge in a little after-hours recreation away from the prying eyes of their wives. According to some accounts, prostitution and drug use were rampant. Media reports of the debauchery on display at the White House eventually prompted the Cowboys front office to deny all knowledge of its existence.

White, Reggie

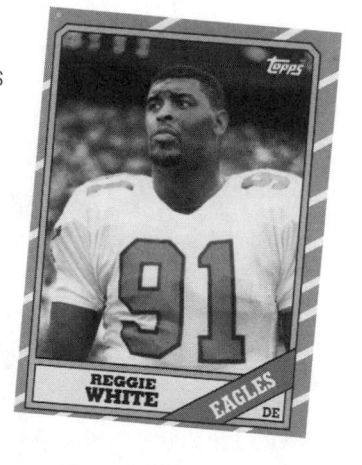

Hall of Fame defensive end of the 1990s whose gentle mien often provided cover for his faith-based bigotry. An ordained Evangelical reverend nicknamed "the Minister of Defense," White channeled much of his religious fervor into his 1996 film ***Reggie's Prayer***. After retiring from the game, the 13-time **Pro Bowl** selection gravitated more and more toward an especially strident strain of Messianic Judaism. An unapologetic homophobe, White saw his promising career as a pregame analyst go up in smoke after he made anti-gay comments on the ABC news magazine *20/20* in 1998. He suffered a fatal heart attack in 2004.

Audibles

> "Homosexuality is a decision. It's not a race. People from all different ethnic backgrounds live in this lifestyle. But people from all different ethnic backgrounds also are liars and cheaters and malicious and back-stabbing."
>
> —Reggie White, on gays

Whizzinator

See **Original Whizzinator, The**

Who Dat

Longtime rallying cry of the New Orleans Saints that first gained widespread circulation in the early 1980s. While the phrase "Who Dat" had been a fixture of minstrel show stage patter dating back to the late 19th century, its association with New Orleans football originated during the 1983 season. That's when fans at the Louisiana Superdome first started chanting "Who dat? Who dat? Who dat say dey gonna beat dem Saints?" The phrase was publicized on local media and incorporated into a novelty recording of "When the Saints Go Marching In" by Big Easy jazz legend Aaron Neville. The terms "Who Dats" and "Who Dat Nation" have since come to refer to the Saints' fan base as a whole.

Who Dey

Longtime rallying cry of the Cincinnati Bengals whose origin predates that of the New Orleans Saints' "Who Dat" by several years. Bengals fans began bellowing "Who dey! Who dey! Who dey think gonna beat dem Bengals? Nooooooobody!" during the team's unexpected Super Bowl run in 1981, and a local craze for the phrase was born. A 45 RPM record of the cheer was distributed in the Cincinnati area. The Hudepohl Brewing Company produced a special edition beer called Hu-Dey. The chant gained national exposure during the team's 1988 AFC championship season and again in the mid-2000s when the franchise regained some measure of respectability. According to legend, model Carmen Electra has the words "Who Dey" tattooed on her ankle. In January of 2006, Pittsburgh Steelers head coach Bill Cowher enraged Bengals fans when he led his team in a mocking "Who Dey?" chant in the locker room after a 31–17 playoff win at Cincinnati's Paul Brown Stadium. Who Dey is also the name of the team's official mascot, a grinning 6'5" bengal tiger outfitted in traditional black-and-orange apparel.

"Who Dey Rap"

Team **music video** recorded in 1989 by the Cincinnati Bengals, in a riff on the team's "**Who Dey**" catchphrase. Mike Martin, **Ickey** Woods, and other members of the defending AFC champions spew their rhymes over an oppressive drum machine beat, which is embellished by one of the most cacophonous cowbell tracks ever recorded.

Williams Jr., Hank

Country music superstar, also known as Bocephus, who adapted his 1984 hit song "All My Rowdy Friends Are Coming Over Tonight" into the opening theme of **Monday Night Football** in 1989. See also: **"All My Rowdy Friends Are Here for Monday Night"**

Williams, Ricky

Notoriously idiosyncratic running back of the 2000s, famed as much for his single-minded devotion to marijuana use as his accomplishments on the gridiron. Williams, the 1998 Heisman Trophy winner, was the fifth man chosen in the 1999 NFL Draft, but he never lived up to his advance billing in the pros. After signing a highly unconventional incentive-laden contract with the New Orleans Saints, he provoked widespread derision by posing for the cover of *ESPN the Magazine* in a bridal gown alongside head coach **Mike Ditka**. Traded to the Miami Dolphins in 2002, Williams at last began to play up to his potential—and amped up his odd behavior even further. He shaved off his trademark dreadlocks, insisted on keeping his helmet on during media interviews, and revealed that he suffered from social anxiety disorder, which he claimed to be "treating" by smoking pot. Suspended by the NFL in 2004 for violating its substance abuse policy, Williams abruptly retired from football, converted to Hinduism, and devoted himself to the study of ayurveda, a 5,000-year-old holistic science developed in India. He later rejoined the professional ranks, first in the **CFL** and then back with the

AP Images

Dolphins, where his continued consumption of "herbs" as part of a yogic healing regimen led to a second drug suspension in 2006. He has remained an intermittently productive member of the Miami backfield ever since.

Williams, Zema

See **Chief Zee**

Williamson, Fred "the Hammer"

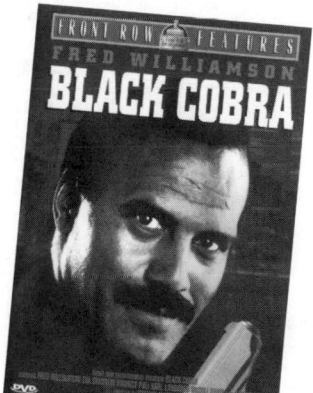

Hard-hitting **AFL** defensive back best known for his on-field braggadocio and his fitfully successful post-retirement career as an actor and media commentator. Williamson first attracted national attention in the run-up to Super Bowl I in 1967, when, as a member of the Kansas City Chiefs, he boasted that he would knock Green Bay Packers receivers Carroll Dale and Boyd Dowler out of the game by applying his trademark "hammer" (a kind of perpendicular karate chop delivered to the crown of an opponent's helmet). Instead, ironically, it was Williamson who ended up carted off the field after getting trampled by running back Donny Anderson in the fourth quarter of a Green Bay rout. After retiring from the game the following season, Williamson turned to acting, appearing mostly in low-budget blaxploitation films like *Hell Up in Harlem*, *Black Caesar*, and *The Legend of Nigger Charley*. In 1974, he was selected to replace **Don Meredith** as an analyst on **Monday Night Football**. Unfortunately, it was to be a short-lived gig. Declaring that he had a mandate to "bring some color to the booth," Williamson seemed to delight in alienating MNF's mainstream white audience. (At his first meeting with the show's executive producer,

Roone Arledge, Williamson showed up with two eye-catching pendants around his neck: a black power salute and a penis.) On the air, he dressed like a pimp, refusing to wear a tie because it would cover his jewelry. His "analysis" amounted to little more than a repetition of jock clichés. And he infuriated the show's star, **Howard Cosell**, with intemperate and provocative insults. "Even an old cripple like you could have made yardage through that hole, Howard!" the Hammer thundered during one telecast. Ultimately, Williamson proved so incompetent that he lasted only three preseason games. He was fired prior to the start of the 1974 regular season and replaced with former Detroit Lions defensive tackle **Alex Karras**. Returning to a movie career that continues to this day, Williamson added a slew of new feature films to his oeuvre, including 1975's charmingly titled *Boss Nigger*, the original *Inglorious Bastards*, and the epic trilogy of *Black Cobra 1*, *2*, and *3*.

Winemaking

Unlikely avocation pursued with increasing frequency by a growing number of NFL players, as well as retired coaches like **Mike Ditka** and Dick Vermeil. Kicker Morten Andersen, linebacker London Fletcher, offensive linemen Chris Samuels and Nick Mangold, and defensive backs Shawn Springs and Terry Hoage (who markets his own football-themed wines, including one named "The 46" in homage to Eagles head coach **Buddy Ryan**) are among the many avid oenophiles in the ranks of current or former NFL players. Indianapolis Colts legend Chris Hinton even went the extra mile, opening and operating his own gourmet wine shop in Alpharetta, Georgia. Many in the gridiron wine brigade can trace their passion for the grape back to Vermeil, a longtime wine enthusiast who corked his first vintage of Jean Louis Vermeil Cabernet Sauvignon shortly before his St. Louis Rams won Super Bowl XXXIV. When he was coach of the Philadelphia Eagles, Vermeil would routinely leave cases of wine in the opposing locker room for Pittsburgh Steelers coach Chuck Noll.

Grape Nuts

NFL Greats on Wine

"I've really enjoyed teaching kids how to drink wine."—retired head coach Dick Vermeil

"The explosive richness of a well-made Napa cabernet unleashed something within me."—former Seattle Seahawks quarterback Rick Mirer

"Being able to tell a wine's story—that's romantic."—retired offensive tackle Chris Hinton

"I'm a cabernet guy. I've enjoyed blends. When you start mixing different things, like when you get a cab sav and then a cab franc together with a little merlot, it's excellent."—New York Jets All-Pro center Nick Mangold

"If you don't have an ego, you're a wino."—**Conrad Dobler**

Wonderlic Test

Personnel exam administered by NFL teams in an attempt to assess the cognitive abilities and problem-solving skills of professional football players. Named for its developer, Depression-era psychologist Eldon F. Wonderlic, the Wonderlic Test consists of 50 questions that must be answered in 12 minutes. The higher a player scores, the better equipped he is to handle complex job assignments, at least according to common wisdom. A typical NFL quarterback scores somewhere in the mid-20s. Those who score under 10 are considered subliterate.

Football by the Numbers | 6

Score achieved by quarterback Vince Young on the **Wonderlic Test** in 2006

Audibles

**"Wanting to do a dance is an inducement
and a motivation to train harder and focus."**

—Elmo Wright, on the rationale behind the end zone dance

Wright, Elmo

Middling wide receiver of the 1970s best known for being the father of the
end zone dance. Though he caught only six touchdown passes in a five-
year NFL career cut short by injuries, Wright
managed to change the game forever on the
night of October 18, 1971. That night, as a
member of the Kansas City Chiefs, Wright
celebrated a score in a 38–16 victory over the
Pittsburgh Steelers by high-stepping his way
through the end zone—a move he had first
perfected in college. For the record, Wright
also claims to have invented the spike, although
most historians credit that innovation to New
York Giant **Homer Jones**.

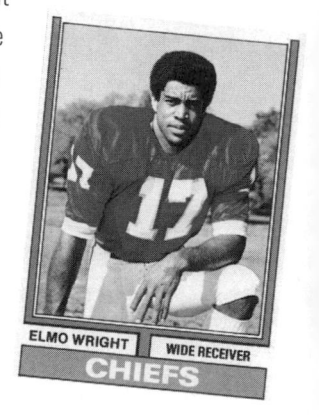

ELMO WRIGHT   WIDE RECEIVER
CHIEFS

XFL

Short-lived "extreme" professional football league founded by the NBC
television network and World Wrestling Entertainment impresario **Vince
McMahon** in 2000. Created on the premise that NFL football had grown
tame and stale due to overly restrictive rules regulating violent contact and
excessive celebration, the XFL was defined by a raucous, no-holds-barred

style of play and show business production values inspired by the world of **professional wrestling**. (Ex-WWE stars Jesse "the Body" Ventura and Jerry "the King" Lawler were enlisted as TV color commentators.) Trash-talking was encouraged, the pregame coin flip was replaced by a rugby-type scrum, and scantily clad cheerleaders cavorted like exotic dancers on the sidelines. League play kicked off in February of 2001, with teams comprised

of NFL cast-offs and flamboyant wannabes like Rod **"He Hate Me"** Smart. While initial TV ratings were encouraging, the combination of poor play and negative publicity quickly began to take a toll. In May of 2001, McMahon and NBC announced plans to disband the XFL after just one season, at a loss of some $70 million.

Yepremian, Garo

Doll-sized Armenian American placekicker of the 1960s and '70s who helped usher in the golden era of the eccentric foreign-born **soccer-style kicking** field-goal specialist. Prematurely bald and tipping the scales at just 148 pounds, Yepremian charmed fans in four cities with his self-deprecating manner and penchant for speaking in broken English ("I keek a touchdown" became his catchphrase

GARO YEPREMIAN
PLACE KICKER
DOLPHINS-A.F.C.

Days of Infamy | December 10, 1972

Several members of the Los Angeles Rams and the St. Louis Cardinals are severely burned when Busch Stadium groundskeepers mistakenly melt the snow with calcium chloride, a caustic chemical used in wastewater treatment.

and the title of his autobiography.) A regular object of mockery on *The Tonight Show Starring Johnny Carson*, Yepremian joined in the fun by playing a thinly veiled version of himself on an episode of ***The Odd Couple*** in 1974. He is perhaps best remembered as a linchpin of the undefeated 1972 Miami Dolphins and for trying to throw an ill-considered pass in the aftermath of a botched field-goal attempt in the waning moments of Super Bowl VII. Footage of Yepremian frantically fumbling and batting the ball up in the air—which resulted in the only touchdown of the day for the Washington Redskins—has been a staple of NFL blooper reels ever since.

Z

Zendejas, Luis

Diminutive Dallas Cowboys placekicker who alleged that Philadelphia Eagles head coach **Buddy Ryan** put a $200 bounty on his head during the infamous **Bounty Bowl** game in 1989.

Bibliography

Allen, George. *Strategies for Winning: A Top Coach's Game Plan for Victory in Football and in Life*. New York: McGraw-Hill, 1990.

Attner, Paul. *The Complete Handbook of Pro Football*. New York: New American Library, 1982.

Bass, Jack and Marilyn W. Thompson. *Ol' Strom: An Unauthorized Biography of Strom Thurmond*. Columbia, SC: The University of South Carolina Press, 2003.

Bayless, Skip. *The Boys*. New York: Simon & Schuster, 1993.

Bosworth, Brian and Rick Reilly. *The Boz: Confessions of a Modern Anti-Hero*. New York: Doubleday, 1988.

Byrne, Jim. *The $1 League: The Rise and Fall of the USFL*. New York: Prentice Hall, 1986.

Daly, Dan and Bob O'Donnell. *The Pro Football Chronicle: The Complete (Well, Almost) Record of the Best Players, the Greatest Photos, the Hardest Hits, the Biggest Scandals, and the Funniest Stories in Pro Football*. New York: Collier Books, 1990.

Donovan, Jim, Ken Sins, and Frank Coffey. *The Dallas Cowboys Encyclopedia: The Ultimate Guide to America's Team*. Secaucus, NJ: Citadel Press, 1996.

Eskenazi, Gerald. *Gang Green: An Irreverent Look Behind the Scenes at Thirty-Eight (Well, Thirty-Seven) Seasons of New York Jets Football Futility*. New York: Simon & Schuster, 1998.

Forrest, Brett. *Long Bomb: How the XFL Became TV's Biggest Fiasco*. New York: Crown, 2002.

Gallagher, Robert C. *The Express: The Ernie Davis Story*. New York: Ballantine, 2008.

Harris, David. *The Genius: How Bill Walsh Reinvented Football and Created an NFL Dynasty*. New York: Random House, 2008.

Heston, Charlton. *In the Arena: An Autobiography*. New York: Simon & Schuster, 1995.

Hoffmann, Frank and Beulah B. Ramirez. *Sports and Recreation Fads*. New York: Routledge, 1991.

Kun, Michael and Adam Hoff. *The Football Uncyclopedia: A Highly Opinionated, Myth-Busting Guide to America's Most Popular Game*. Cincinnati, OH: Clerisy Press, 2008.

Macambridge, Michael. *America's Game: The Epic Story of How Pro Football Captured a Nation*. New York: Anchor Books, 2005.

Maraniss, David. *When Pride Still Mattered: A Life of Vince Lombardi*. New York: Simon & Schuster, 1999.

Martirano, Ron. *Book of Football Stuff: Great Records, Weird Happenings, Odd Facts, Amazing Moments & Cool Things.* Morganville, NJ: Imagine Publishing, 2010.

Matuszak, John (with Steve Delson). *Cruisin' with the Tooz.* New York: Charter Books, 1988.

Miller, Jeff. *Going Long: The Wild 10-Year Saga of the Renegade American Football League in the Words of Those Who Lived It.* New York: McGraw-Hill, 2004.

Morris, Frank. *Ask Your Uncle Football Trivia.* Boston, MA: Ghost to the Post Books, 2009.

Nash, Bruce and Allan Zullo. *The Football Hall of Shame.* New York: Pocket Books, 1986.

Nash, Bruce and Allan Zullo. *The Football Hall of Shame 2.* New York: Pocket Books, 1990.

Pearlman, Jeff. *Boys Will Be Boys. The Glory Days and Party Nights of the Dallas Cowboys Dynasty.* New York: HarperCollins, 2008.

Rand, Jonathan. *300 Pounds of Attitude: The Wildest Stories and Craziest Characters the NFL Has Ever Seen.* Guilford, CT: The Lyons Press, 2006.

Rielly, Edward J. *Football: An Encyclopedia of Popular Culture.* Lincoln, NE: University of Nebraska Press, 2009.

Rovell, Darren. *First in Thirst: How Gatorade Turned The Science of Sweat Into A Cultural Phenomenon.* New York: AMACOM, 2005.

Sharpton, Al and Anthony Walton. *Go and Tell Pharaoh: The Autobiography of the Reverend Al Sharpton.* New York: Doubleday, 1996.

Simpson, Alan K. *Right in the Old Gazoo: A Lifetime of Scrapping with the Press.* New York: William Morrow & Company, 1997.

Acknowledgments

Thanks to Tom Bast, Adam Motin, Paul Petrowksy, and the entire team at Triumph Books. Thanks to Gary Teubner and Frank Morris of Ask Your Uncle Trivia for their research help. Thanks to Vince Ferragamo, James Harris, John Cappelletti, and the rest of the mighty Los Angeles Rams for making me a football fan. Finally, thanks to all the fans who generously contributed their photos to this project.

About the Author

Robert Schnakenberg is a member of the Professional Football Researchers Association and the author of numerous books of irreverent nonfiction, including *Distory: A Treasury of Historical Insults*, *Christopher Walken A-to-Z*, and *The Underground Baseball Encyclopedia*. He lives in Brooklyn and can be found online at www.robertschnakenberg.com.